Political Thought from

PLATO to NATO

Political Thought from

PLATO
to
NATO

Introduced by
Brian Redhead
By arrangement with BBC Books,
a division of BBC Enterprises Ltd.

1988

Brooks/Cole Publishing Company
Pacific Grove, California

The Publishers wish to thank Brian Redhead, Iain Hampsher-Monk and
Sarah Hamilton-Fairley for their assistance in the preparation of this book.
Thanks are also due to Maggi Fielder who typed the manuscript and held
the project together.

Picture Credits

BBC HULTON PICTURE LIBRARY pp. 21, 87, 99, 138, and 161;

THE MANSELL COLLECTION pp. 32, 47, 63, 75, 111, 125, and 151.

First published in 1984 by BBC Enterprises Ltd.
Paperback edition published in 1988 by
The Dorsey Press

ISBN 0-534-10801-6
former ISBN 0-256-06461-X
Library of Congress Catalog Card No. 87–72104

Printed in the United States of America

10 9 8 7 6 5 4 3 2

Contents

Introduction
Brian Redhead

The history of political thought is the history of the attempts over the centuries to answer the question: 'Why should I obey the State?' The question has remained unchanged and is still asked. The answers have ranged from

the pragmatic – *'Because if I don't they will cut my head off'*
to the theological – *'Because it is God's will'*
from the contractual – *'Because the State and I have done a deal'*
to the metaphysical – *'Because the State is the actuality of the ethical idea'.*

No one answer existed in isolation, though some held sway in certain centuries. Few have been discarded for all time, and most still linger somewhere carrying a greater or lesser authority.

For most of recorded history the greatest minds have been directed to this question. This book of essays plumps for a dozen of the great thinkers of the past, plus half a dozen in our century. Readers in the know will undoubtedly boggle at the omissions, and some may jib at the title. But *'Plato to NATO'* is student slang at every institute of learning in the land where such a course is on offer, and it is infectious. The choice of thinkers, or rather the number it was possible to discuss, was determined by the constraints of a series of half-hour programmes on BBC Radio 4. The commission was to make six with two thinkers in each, plus a seventh on the twentieth century. Plato and Aristotle, Augustine and Aquinas, and Hobbes and Locke chose themselves. It would, or so it seemed to me, have been unthinkable to omit any one of those six and folly not to pair them. Modern scholars may prefer to pit Filmer against Locke, and even Harrington against Hobbes, but anyone new to the subject had best start with the giants. By that criterion, Machiavelli (though no great philosopher), Rousseau, and Marx chose themselves. Calvin was to be preferred to Luther. Mill is a must in any choice aimed at English readers. And on the argument that every dog has his day, Adam Smith seemed worth a walk round the park.

But I cannot deny that there are serious omissions. One contributor squealed with rage at the prospect of no discussion of Cicero and the fundamental republican tradition in the West. Not only was Cicero enormously important in his own time and certainly for Augustine, but he was the major influence on seventeenth and eighteenth century republicanism in Britain and America, to say nothing of his central role in the Renaissance. The whole Natural Law tradition stems from Cicero as does the theory of the State as fundamentally a guardian of private property.

Even more to be regretted, I think, is the omission of Hegel. But imagine trying to explain him in half of a half an hour programme. The basis of the State, says Hegel, is the power of reason actualising itself as will. Men will the State in accordance with reason. The State is reason. It is mind on earth consciously realising itself there. It is the actuality of the ethical Idea. Actuality is the unity both of essence and of existence. Only when mind is present in consciousness, when it knows itself as a really existent object, is it the State.

Are you with me?

The State is the end of the dialectical process of history, the realisation of moral principles and concrete freedom. The development of the State is the development of absolute self-consciousness, the progressive realisation of freedom. The State is 'the march of God in the world'. The State is the whole of which the individual is part. Dissociated from the State, the individual has no meaning. Because the State is mind objectified, it is only as one of its members that the individual himself has objectivity, real individuality, and an ethical life. Because it is reason, the State bestows on man whatever value he has. The State is not an accumulation of separate individuals artificially united by a conscious agreement, but a divine rationality by which and for which its members exist.

After that Marx is easy meat. It was once fashionable to argue, as Dick Crossman did, that Hegel would have had little importance in the history of political ideas had not Marx been his pupil. Indeed, it is a popular examination question at universities – popular with those who set the papers if not with those who attempt them. It is a question worth asking and answering because the whole intention of Marx's political thought is to abolish the State. The State is no more than a weapon in the class war. The unremitting march of history which is bound to lead to a classless society, says Marx, will also lead to the abolition of the State. But if the revolution is confined to one country, or even to a number of countries, then the first stage of the revolution, in which the leaders of the proletariat make use of the State, will have to be prolonged. The State will be needed not only to crush the bourgeoisie within the country of revolution but also to defend the country against foreign aggression. Marx thought that the Socialist State would be the briefest and last phase of government, whereas it promises to be another extended phase in the history of government. It is a new form of the nation-state, another step in the dialectical process of history beyond the liberal national state. And in this Socialist State, the relationship between the individual and the State can be defined just as Hegel defined it. It is an end in itself and the individual is a means to that end.

But I digress. Omissions there may be, but this collection of essays adds up to a very good book. The essays complement each other very well, lead on neatly from one to the other, and are both consistent and helpful. Even the title, though flippant, is surprisingly apt. The whole is an exercise to be commended because it is a capital investment. Everyone who makes a serious study of the history of political thought becomes aware that he has acquired a treasure and not simply of knowledge which will be dissipated. Long after he has forgotten the ten reasons for executing Charles I, he will recall Hobbes's theory of natural law. I say he: I include she. Because women were long denied a say in politics, the history of political thought has been written in terms of Man and men. Throughout this book for Man and men, read mankind. Or, if you prefer, the people.

The purpose of the radio programmes is to awaken interest. The purpose of these essays is to point the way. This is an evangelical exercise to lead you to the scriptures, to the words of the thinkers themselves, to the greatest thoughts of the greatest minds. In the days when I attempted to teach the history of political thought, with what can fairly be described as varying degrees of success, I used to argue that students should read the texts and nothing else. That was a trifle arrogant. Most of us need a word or two of introduction. Not because we shall not understand the thinkers at a first attempt but because we *fear* we might not. It takes not so much brains as courage, especially if you are called upon to say out loud what it is that Plato says.

Plato distinguishes two worlds, one of essential Ideas, timeless and unchanging, the other of mere appearances, transitory and various reflections of the Ideas. The visible and tangible appearances, commonly called real, can be apprehended by opinion; the Ideas, which are the true reality, can be apprehended only by intelligence and reason. For Plato, knowledge is the apprehension of the real world of Ideas. Most men are content to live in the world of appearances, the world of imagining and belief, but by education, those whose souls are so ordered that they are controlled by reason and intelligence, and not by ambition nor material appetite, can enter the world of Ideas, the world of real knowledge and understanding. These are the philosophers, seeking the knowledge of the whole of truth and reality, seeking an understanding not only of man's end or good, but also of the Good itself, the final cause of all that is good in the universe and of its very existence. They are to be the kings, for without having had a vision of this Good, which is sovereign in the intangible world and the parent of intelligence and truth, 'no one' says Plato, 'can act with wisdom either in his own life or in matters of state'.

Aristotle is unable to accept Plato's doctrine of timeless and unchanging Ideas existing separately from appearances, the ephemeral and approximate reflections of those Ideas. On the contrary, he believes that Ideas do not exist separately from visible and tangible things, but rather that the essential nature of anything is the Idea in it. This Idea, or Form, tries constantly to realise itself in the growth and development of the thing, and is realised when that growth is complete. The essential nature of anything is its end, or final cause, which completes and fulfils its nature. Logically the end exists prior to the thing, for it is the presupposition of its true and full life. But Aristotle cannot contemplate the supreme end without reference to the means by which it will be realised. He cannot escape the visible and tangible world because he cannot separate means from ends. Indeed they are inseparable because the one determines the other. And when he looked at the way in which people actually go about things, Aristotle was happy to settle for the best possible rather than the ideal. To that extent I believe that he, rather than Plato, is the father of political thought. Plato is a poet; Aristotle a political scientist. Plato is a good guide to religion; Aristotle a better guide to politics.

Augustine had to do without Aristotle. The philosopher's works had been mislaid, lodged with the Arabic world, and the bishop turned to Plato and to Christ for guidance. Augustine distinguishes two cities, the city of God and the earthly city. The former is not exclusively celestial, in as much as some of its residents enjoy temporary residence on earth, nor is the latter exclusively terrestrial because some of its citizens are fallen angels. The city of God is the city of the righteous, of the just. For Augustine, as for Plato, justice is moral not legal. Both conceive of justice as a right order of relations, of each individual performing the function or service for which he is rightly suited. But whereas Plato is concerned with right order between men, Augustine is concerned with right order between man and God. The true and just end for man is to serve God. It is as just for God to be in authority over men, as for the soul to be in authority over the body. The city of God therefore is the society and communion of the just in right order, and it unites God, His angels, and His saints in heaven with the just who are in temporary residence on earth. But it does not embrace the entire Universe because it does not include the legions of the unjust – the fallen angels, the souls of the unjust, and the unjust living on earth. They are the citizens of the earthly city, which cannot be identified with any actual organised society on earth. It is something more in that it includes fallen angels as well as men; and something less, in that it does not include the just who are living on earth. Like the city of God, it is ideal. It is not identical with the State, which is mortal not immortal. The citizens of the city of God must regard themselves as pilgrims or aliens during their residence on earth. They must make the best of a bad job and keep their thoughts on the next world. They must obey the State because it fulfils a useful function, the maintenance of earthly peace, but it is no substitute for the city of God, which is the goal of creation, the one and only final society.

With Aquinas we are back with Aristotle, or rather, he with us, returned with thanks by the Arabs. Aquinas was set the task of reconciling the teachings of the Church with the philosophy of Aristotle. Although, like Augustine, Aquinas believes that the ultimate end of man is only to be achieved in the next world, he does not, as Augustine does, conceive of this world as necessarily the result of man's sin, a place through which the faithful must pass as pilgrims. He shares Aristotle's belief in temporal felicity as man's end in this world, and accepts this as an end in itself, but as an end in time, an end which is subordinate to the ultimate end of man, the eternal blessedness only attainable in the next world. The temporal end is not only subordinate to the eternal end, but itself must be directed towards that superior end. Politics determine the means by which man attains his temporal end, and they must always be directed towards man's ultimate end. The State has a position within the divine order. It must obey Natural Law if it is to be obeyed.

Natural Law, or the Law of Nature, preceded Christianity. It is the idea of universal order, conceived and shaped by reason. Early philosophers, in their speculations about the regularity they had observed in the working of physical forces and the uniform growth they had perceived in living organisms, concluded that some force must be controlling the movements and processes of the material universe. This force they chose to call Nature. Similarly, in their speculation upon man as a rational being, they discovered general rules of his moral and physical constitution, and assumed that these were directed by a force with an intelligent purpose. This force they chose to call the rational will. Having recognised reason as the harmonising principle in man, they conceived of Nature as an intelligent force moulding phenomena on regular lines towards definite ends. Consequently when the Greek philosophers began to speculate about human society and observed that certain rules and customs were to be found among all tribes and races, they concluded that these rules and customs must be Natural, that they must be the result of Reason, the intelligent principle guiding man. They shaped their speculations on human society in theories about laws. Certain laws they found were common to all communities; others only to particular communities. And following the same line of reasoning as before, they concluded that the laws which were common to all communities must be Natural, because they apparently issued out of the mental and moral constitution of man, as man. These laws, which belonged to the human race as a whole, they conceived to be essentially anterior in thought and date to the laws which each particular community made for itself. These laws they believed to be imposed on the world by Nature, the ruling force, and they called the law which Nature sets upon mankind, the Law of Nature, or Natural Law.

For Aquinas, Natural Law is the part of God's law which man by his reason can perceive. He distinguishes four types of law. First, Eternal Law, which is the one prior to all the others and is the divine wisdom known in its entirety only to God. Then comes Natural Law, which is that proportion of Eternal Law which human beings can perceive by their reason. The third is Human Law, which is deduced from Natural Law to be binding within the State. This positive law of the State is therefore in accord with Natural Law and ultimately with Eternal Law, and if it is not in accord with Natural Law, then it is not, for Aquinas, law at all. And if it is not law at all, it need not be obeyed. It is not seditious, he says, to overthrow a tyranny. In fact he goes further than that. His fourth category of law is Divine Law which God reveals to man to direct him to the ultimate end of eternal blessedness. This is the Law which man is incapable of perceiving by reason alone. 'Not all that a man has or is, is subject to political obligation,' said Aquinas. 'But all that a man is, and all that he has or can be, must bear a certain relationship to God.' And that is revolutionary talk.

It took Machiavelli to break the stranglehold of Natural Law. He concentrates on what men actually do. He has no conception of legitimate power bestowed by God, but believes that power belongs to those who have the skill to seize it. A ruler must answer for his actions on the spot and the only sin is failure. The Prince, he says, must never be afraid to act immorally if that is the only way to succeed, but it is also necessary for him to have the appearance of virtue, for that is another requisite for success. It is better to rule by goodwill than by force, not *morally* better, but better in the sense of being more likely to succeed. No government can be safe without the goodwill of the governed. But although Machiavelli appears to be very pragmatic, he was both superstitious and pagan. He had a touching faith in the virtues of Republican Rome not based wholly on the evidence, and where a man's choice is determined by circumstances beyond his control, when in fact events determine his choice, Machiavelli ascribes the cause of these events to Fortune. Fortune, to Machiavelli, is a capricious deity, which seems to be not merely the figurative expression of the incalculable element in life, but a being with human passions and attributes. And Fortune is a woman. As the song has it, 'Luck be a Lady tonight.'

Calvin toyed with no such fancy, nor Hobbes, nor Locke. They went back to Natural Law. But whereas medieval exponents of Natural Law began with God, law, and obligation, Hobbes began with man, freedom, and right. He starts introspectively with man's senses and emotions to find the source of will. This will is absolute because it is neither conditioned by rules nor directed towards some end. It is free both from law and from obligation. This freedom from obligation is man's natural right, his liberty to use his own power as he wills himself for the preservation of his own life. It derives directly from the character of individual will and not from some higher Law or from Reason. Neither Law nor Reason can create Right. Man strives to attain what he has willed but the success of each individual is thwarted by the willed actions of every other individual. All men are competitors in their efforts to achieve what they have willed. Man's natural right, however, includes not only the liberty to act upon his will but also to formulate general truths by reasoning about the pursuit of what he wills. And reasoning leads man to formulate a general rule to forbid himself doing that which is self-destructive. This rule is the fundamental Law of Nature, which is that man should seek peace as the only sure method of self-preservation. From this follows a second law that to avoid war a man must lay down his natural rights and retain only the liberty against other men which he would allow them against him. In other words man must will not to will and transfer his rights to a beneficiary. This beneficiary must be the representative of each man possessing the authority to will in place of the will of each separate man. He must be not a common will but a single representative will. This transfer of rights creates a civil society in which freedom is replaced by law; right by obligation. And it is artificial, not natural. It is the product of will. It is man-made, not the gift of God. And what man has put together, man can put asunder, if he wills to will again.

Rousseau will accept neither Hobbes's transference of will, of willing not to will, nor Locke's giving of it on trust. He wishes to compromise neither the freedom of the individual nor the authority of the State. He postulates instead the 'general will'. Starting from the assumption that all nature is a harmony, he argues that because of this harmony all men have a real will which is identical in all men. In their heart of hearts, if they are really true to themselves, they all want the same. This will which is common to all men is the general will. It is by definition good, and men are free only in conforming to it. Men should obey the State in Rousseau's ideal State because the Sovereign is a moral person expressing the general will. The people are both the subjects and the sovereign, and therefore in obeying the sovereign the individual is obeying his real self. The only just social contract is the agreement to obey the general will, the agreement of people to obey their real selves, not to obey someone they appoint. But in practice the people are not always aware of their real will and must commission a wise legislator to interpret the general will for them. The wise legislator is a declarer of the law, not a maker of the law, and therefore cannot be above the law. He cannot be an instrument for anything but the good because he alone knows what men really want. He forces them to be free. He forces them to live in a rational manner. To discard their chains.

'An inner burning lunatic vision, wrapped in a strait jacket of Calvinist logic.' I can hear the words now, delivered on BBC Radio thirty years ago by Isaiah Berlin. He was talking about Rousseau. I have never forgotten either what he said or the vehemence with which he said it. Rousseau came face to face with the paradox of two absolutes that he had constructed – liberty and authority. Liberty he saw as a religious concept, identical with human personality. A man is free. If he is not free he is not a man. Freedom cannot be bartered for security. There can be no compromise between freedom and authority. But men live in society. Society must have rules, and these rules are graven on the heart of nature. They are inherent laws. Secular Calvinism this, said Berlin. Laws seen not as conventions but as sacred absolute truths. How then can these two absolutes, liberty and authority, be reconciled? Like a maniac, said Berlin, Rousseau suddenly saw the light, the one and only answer, which he alone had discovered. It was possible to obtain personal freedom which was the same as complete authority. 'Each man giving himself to all, gives himself to nobody.' Only those are free who know what they want. And as nature is a harmony (Rousseau's basic dubious premise), all rational men will want the same. Corrupt men, irrational men, seek ends which conflict. Natural, good, rational men seek the same end. This end is equally good for all other natural men. Men must recapture the innocent good. Rousseau denounces not only the rich and the powerful, but also the arts, the sciences, and sophistication. He is the first of the militant philistines, the ancestor of the *petit bourgeois* revolutionaries. His is a violent vision expressed in apparent deductive reason. His concept of the General Will is mystical. The State is religious. It is myself yet it is greater than myself. Men who know what they truly want, want the same. It is the argument used by all dictators who say they alone know what men truly want. The evil Rousseau did, said Berlin, was to invent the mythology of the real self. He claimed to be one of the most ardent lovers of freedom ever, whereas in fact he was one of the most sinister and most formidable enemies of liberty.

To study the history of political thought is to engage in the great arguments of history, arguments that still rage. To seek to understand them is to seek great satisfaction for there is nothing to match the satisfaction of understanding.

Socrates said that, so it must be true.

Plato:
the search for
an ideal form of state

Christopher Rowe

Plato was born in Athens in the early 420s BC and died in 347.
Because of the lack of a reliable ancient biographical tradition,
very little is known about his life. He apparently took no part in
public affairs; his sole excursion into practical politics came when
he was invited to Syracuse to exert an improving philosophical
influence on its young ruler, Dionysius II (the adventure ended in
failure). His major achievements were a large collection of
dialogues, many of which are works of literature as well as major
works of philosophy; and the foundation in the 380s BC of the
Academy, which provided a base for succeeding generations of
Platonists until the Emperor Justinian prohibited pagan
philosophers from teaching in AD 529.

Plato was the first ancient thinker to write systematically on the
subject of politics. He was an Athenian, living and working in
Athens, which at the time of his birth was still the most powerful
and wealthy of the Greek city-states. It was also noted for its
culture, and attracted to it intellectuals from all over the Greek
world, from southern Italy in the west to the coast of Asia Minor
in the east. Literature, the visual arts, philosophy – all flourished
in Athens to a degree which seems quite out of proportion to its
size (some 30,000 male citizens, occupying an area of some 1,000
square miles); and they continued to do so even despite the
political and economic decline which the city began to experience towards the end of the fifth century BC. Athens' ascendancy
as a centre of philosophical activity was particularly marked, as is
shown by the fact that the city-state played host to all the four
major Greek philosophical schools which were founded in the
course of the fourth century – Plato's Academy, Aristotle's
Lyceum, and the Epicurean and Stoic schools. True, only a few
of the philosophers themselves were native-born Athenians. Yet
these included two of the three who were on any account the
most outstanding, Plato, and the pivotal figure of Socrates.
(Aristotle, the third member of the triad, came to Athens from

Stagira, a city in northern Greece.)

It was Socrates who, in Cicero's words, 'called down philosophy from the skies'. With few exceptions, previous thinkers had directed their attention chiefly to questions about the origin and structure of the cosmos; Socrates' concern, by contrast, was exclusively with things human. The ultimate aim of his incessant conversations (though they tended to turn into cross-examinations) appears to have been to achieve moral certainty, to discover a set of final answers to what he saw as the most important question of all, how a man should conduct his life. This change of direction was of fundamental importance for the subsequent development of Greek philosophy. His skill in argument and his passionate commitment to the ideals of truth and clear thinking also provided a paradigm for philosophical thought which remains as valid now as it was then. But Socrates wrote nothing. He owes his prominence in the history of philosophy in large part to his pupil Plato, and to the subtlety with which Plato builds on his Socratic inheritance.

Plato was born into a family which was rich and distinguished on both sides. Until his mid-twenties, Athens was involved almost continuously in long and disastrous wars with Sparta, its rival for supremacy among the Greek states. In 404 BC came the final defeat. Democracy was replaced by a particularly vicious oligarchy in the shape of the so-called 'Thirty Tyrants' – only to be restored in the following year. Four years later Socrates was tried and executed, an event which, according to the seventh of a series of letters which survive as part of the Platonic corpus, was the main factor in Plato's final decision not to take the kind of active role in politics which might have been expected of someone of his wealth and status. It is still disputed whether the letter was written by Plato himself, but in this respect its information is likely to be accurate enough. The letter says that he had had high hopes of the oligarchy of the Thirty, since they included some of his friends and relations, but that those hopes were destroyed by their actual behaviour. One particular occasion is picked out, when they attempted, unsuccessfully, to implicate Socrates – introduced, by a singular understatement, as 'an older friend of mine' – in the judicial murder of one of their democratic opponents. Yet it was the 501 members of a democratic court who finally voted by a large majority for Socrates' execution when he was brought before them by a private individual on a charge of impiety. Plato's conclusion, we are told, was that no one could take part in political life and retain his integrity under existing conditions; that only philosophical reflection (by implication, perhaps, of the type to which Socrates devoted himself) could enable one to see what was right and just in both public and private life; and that the only cure for the ills of contemporary society was the establishment of philosophical rule: that either philosophers should become rulers, or that existing rulers should become philosophers.

This proposal is argued for at length in Plato's *Republic*. Like nearly all Plato's writings, the *Republic* has the form of a dialogue; Socrates is chief speaker. Plato never casts himself as a character, preferring to put forward his ideas and arguments through the mouths of others, and especially, we may presume, through that of Socrates. We must not assume, of course, that Socrates, or indeed any other historical figure, would have agreed with everything that Plato makes him say. Aristotle, for one, states quite explicitly that Socrates did not, for example, hold the set of ideas, advanced in the *Republic* and elsewhere, which traditionally goes under the heading of 'the theory of forms' (of which I shall say more later); that is strictly a Platonic development. Although in many cases, if not always, Plato uses the character of Socrates for his own purposes, this is justified by the fact that even when his ideas go beyond those of the historical Socrates, they are usually firmly rooted in genuinely Socratic ground. So with the demand for the union of political power and philosophy.

Socrates belonged to no political grouping, either oligarchic or democratic, simply playing to the full the role of the democratic citizen: for example, he took part in several military campaigns as a hoplite, or heavy-armed infantryman, and served his time as member of the council of 500 which organised the meetings of the assembly. However, his loyalty as a citizen evidently did not prevent his raising questions about current political practice. In particular, he thought it odd that while on some issues, say on those involving ship-building, or the construction of public works, the assembly would defer as a matter of course to the relevant experts, they would allow anyone and everyone a hearing when it came to the more important issues. (For 'anyone and everyone' here read 'any and every adult male citizen'. Even at its most generous, Athenian democracy was extremely restricted in extent, excluding women, slaves and other groups which together must have accounted for three-quarters of the adult population.) The more important issues for Socrates will have been those involving questions of right and wrong, rather than,

Plato (*c.* 427–347 BC)

say, strictly economic issues; and the oddity – if oddity it is – to which he was pointing was the implied assumption that either there was no such thing as moral knowledge, in so far as no experts in it were recognised, or if there were, everyone had an equal claim to it, which would make it unlike any other kind of expert knowledge. He seems to have believed that moral knowledge was indeed possible, and that moreover it was a necessary (and sufficient) condition of our acting rightly; while his experience in talking to people confirmed, if confirmation were needed, that it was not widely distributed. Many people laid claim to moral certainty, but in response to Socrates' questioning, none – on Plato's account – could give an adequate account of himself. It was left to Plato, however, to draw out the positive consequences of Socrates' position for practical politics.

It is, of course, implicit in that position that moral rightness is the most important consideration for those in power. But that is no more than a particular application of a more general principle: that right action, virtue, is that which matters most for each and every individual, and on which his happiness depends. That principle, added to the premisses that the moral knowledge which ensures right behaviour is accessible to reason, and that the function of government is to advance the good of the governed, constitutes the core of Plato's political thinking, both in the *Republic* and in other dialogues. Paradoxically, the apolitical Socrates becomes in Plato the paradigm of true statesmanship: the true statesman will be the one who possesses the requisite expert knowledge (though the real Socrates regularly *disclaimed* knowledge), and works single-mindedly for the moral improvement of his fellow citizens.

None of the recognised political goals – wealth, freedom, the avoidance of *stasis*, or political unrest – is to be regarded as an end in itself; although the second and third would be by-products of the creation of a virtuous community, it is this last which is the only true end of politics. Increase of personal wealth is the supposed aim of the oligarch; freedom the catchword of the democrat: Plato thus implicitly rejects the two main rival ideologies. In dismissing the removal of unrest as an end in itself, he also rejects the kind of political solution which would later attract Aristotle, and with which we are most familiar – the attempt to achieve a balance between the interests of competing groups in society. Plato is not interested in the reform of existing patterns of political life, but rather in the substitution for them of a completely new order which is consistent with his revolutionary view of the proper aim of society – namely, to provide the conditions for the achievement by its members of virtue, and so of happiness, to whatever degree they are capable of it.

The chief formal purpose of the *Republic* is to mount a rational case for preferring justice to injustice. A first task is clearly to define the two terms; and it is in the course of the attempt to define them that Plato begins the construction of his imaginary ideal state. What we want to identify is the nature of justice in the individual, since the case is that justice is what is best for each person; but Socrates (that is, the character Socrates in the dialogue) proposes to look first at justice in the context of the state, on the grounds that it will be easier to identify it there. He gradually builds up his picture of the perfectly just state: one in which each member will perform that function, and only that function, for which he is destined by nature. There emerges an arrangement of three classes or groups: the philosopher-guardians, who will rule by virtue of their superior rational endowment, which gives them access to the relevant knowledge; a military class; and a third class which will provide for the economic needs of the citizen-body as a whole. It is clear, however, that the most important division is between the highest function, that of ruling, and the other two. The crucial point is that power is to remain exclusively in the hands of those properly capable of wielding it.

Justice in the individual is then identified in analogous terms. The individual soul is also found to have three parts, or aspects, corresponding to the three parts of the state; and it will be just, Socrates suggests, when each of the three parts performs its own proper function. The three parts are the rational, which entitles us to be called rational beings, the 'spirited', responsible for our 'higher' emotions such as anger, and the 'appetitive', which is responsible for our lower desires. But a just soul will also be wise, courageous and self-controlled (or 'temperate'): wise, because the rational part is in the right condition; courageous, because the 'spirited' part is so; and self-controlled because both the two lower parts 'agree' to be ruled by the highest. Similarly, the just state will be wise by virtue of the excellence of its rulers, courageous because of the quality of its soldiers, and self-controlled in so far as the members of the highest class set a limit to the desires of the two lower classes. The two lower classes will not dissent from this because, if they did dissent, they would be disputing the right of the highest class to govern, and therefore exceeding their allotted role.

Many other proposals are made, for the production of citizens of the right sort and for the maintenance and effective running of the whole system: tight control of education, the restriction of the arts to the representation of characters and actions of the right sort, and the institution of mating festivals. Women and children are to be held in common (although Plato allows that the guardians may include women, if any appear with suitable qualities), and private property is to be abolished, at least for the two higher classes.

Plato's ideal state in the *Republic* has often been compared with modern totalitarian states; but it differs from them in a number of respects, not least that tighter restrictions are placed on the governors than on the governed, about whom little is said. It is true that Plato appears to put the interests of the state or community above those of the individual, to the point where individual identity might almost be supposed to disappear. Yet we must not forget that the members of Callipolis, 'the beautiful city', will in fact be happy, according to Plato's understanding of happiness, since even those who belong to the lowest class will possess that part of virtue which is appropriate to them – namely, self-control. (It is hardly *self*-control; but the problem is less obvious with the original Greek term.) The essential requirement is that our souls and our actions should be governed by reason, since reason alone is capable of determining what is truly good for us; if we are incapable of reasoning properly for ourselves, then others must do it for us. If the course of our lives is determined by our irrational impulses, the result can only be misery. The wisdom of the philosophical ruler, Plato claims, will be precisely parallel to the expert knowledge of the doctor: just as the doctor is able to prescribe for our physical well-being, so the wise ruler will prescribe for our moral well-being, on which our possession of the good depends.

The knowledge which the philosopher-ruler will supposedly possess, and which is his qualification for power, will include both knowledge of justice and the other virtues, and the knowledge that these constitute the good for man. It is at this point that we need to introduce the so-called 'theory of forms'. Socrates had apparently spent his time in an exercise which we might describe as looking for general definitions of moral terms – courage, say, or justice – as a means of establishing practical rules for conduct. We may put this, as Plato does, by saying that he was looking for the 'form' of courage, or of justice; by which is meant that characteristic or set of characteristics which is common to all courageous or just actions, by virtue of which they are called courageous or just. The distinctive step which Plato has taken by the time of the *Republic* is to suggest that these 'forms', which are the objects of definition, are entities in themselves, subsisting outside time and space, in which particular things come to 'share', or which they 'imitate'. Thus to say, for example, that a man or an action is just will be to say that he or it 'shares in', or 'imitates' justice. These curious entities are arranged in a kind of hierarchy; at its apex is the 'form of the good', by grasping which the philosopher will finally achieve full understanding of all the rest. In the case of justice and the other virtues, this will amount to a complete understanding of their nature as goods, and so of the desirability for us of becoming virtuous.

There is obviously much more that needs to be said about the philosophical basis of the theory, but for present purposes the sketch just given must suffice. The important points are, first, that the answers both to moral questions and to the more general question about how we should live become objectively discoverable, like, say, the truths of mathematics; and secondly, that the forms, and so the knowledge which a grasp of them provides, are accessible only to a few: they can be 'seen' by the mind alone, and only by minds which have undergone a long period of training and reflection. Government thus becomes a true skill or craft, the domain of the qualified expert.

There seems to be a crucial difference, however, between Plato's true ruler and the experts in other spheres. In all other cases (in medicine, for example, which is Plato's favourite example, or in navigation), the expert is concerned with working towards ends which are previously agreed; whereas the philosopher-ruler will apparently be dictating the end as well as the means to it. Granted that we all, or most of us, want to be happy, it hardly seems to be a matter for philosophical reflection to decide what happiness, or the good for us, consists in. It is more than likely that a high proportion of our actual desires and aims would be frustrated in the kind of state which Plato outlines: if so, we would hardly agree that it had provided the good life for us – since how will it be *good* if it fails to satisfy our desires?

Plato's reply to this obvious point is that the virtuous life is the one which answers to our 'real' desires, in the sense that if we lived it, we would in fact find it more satisfying than any other. This is not in itself a wholly implausible proposition, at least to the extent that most of us would include the observation of certain moral standards as a necessary component of a satisfactory life. We might agree, even, that moral considerations are in principle more important than considerations of any other kind. But we are unlikely to agree that virtue is the only thing valuable in itself, or that, as Plato begins to suggest, especially towards the end of his life, a proper concern for virtue rules out the pursuit of any other goal, for either individual or community. It is the hospitality of democracy to a variety of different ends that constitutes one of the main charges in Plato's eloquent condemnation of democracy in the *Republic* – though he is almost equally scathing about the oligarch's obsession with wealth and property. His fundamental objection to a pluralistic society is perhaps that it leaves open the possibility that we will make the wrong choices; but the objection is hardly compelling, unless he can show, as he cannot, that virtue is a sufficient condition, and not merely a necessary condition, of happiness. Indeed, it might well be argued that we display our real moral qualities just when our interests, as we perceive them, appear to conflict with our principles; if so, then Plato may be in danger of throwing the baby out with the bath-water, since in Callipolis, where our interests will largely have been identified with virtue, such conflicts will not arise. There is certainly a case for moral education, and for the kind of rational argument about moral issues which abounds in the *Republic* itself, but there is none – and Plato comes nowhere near to providing one – for the kind of large-scale social engineering which he proposes. (In his imaginary state, of course, the knowledge of the philosopher-rulers renders all moral debate at best unnecessary and at worst dangerous – a strange conclusion, from someone as devoted to argument as Plato.)

Plato's thought rarely stands still. The *Republic* belongs to the dialogues of his middle period. Two later dialogues, the *Statesman* and the *Laws*, reveal his maturer political thinking. One of the central questions raised in the *Statesman* is whether ultimate authority in the state should lie with an individual – one who embodies the art of ruling – or with the law. Laws, Plato argues, are inevitably imperfect: they are too general to be capable of dealing properly with the complexities of actual life; and because they are static, they are unable to cope with changing conditions. It would be, he thinks, far better for rule to be in the hands of the expert individual, who can prescribe for each case as it arises. Plato still probably thinks of the ideal statesman as having privileged access to eternal truths (although it is wrong to assume that all the ideas about 'forms' developed in the *Republic* and other dialogues of his middle period had survived unscathed, especially when the *Parmenides*, another late dialogue, subjects them to sharp criticism). The emphasis, however, is now rather on the skill which would be necessary for the practical application of those truths – which would themselves, presumably, take the form of general principles – to the problems of actual life. Plato here perhaps implies a more plausible account of the nature of moral knowledge than the one suggested in the *Republic*. Another difference is that he is more realistic about the possibilities of achieving the ideal form of government. The fact is that outstanding individuals of the type required are likely to be rare indeed. In their absence, men are forced to rely on laws, under one of the existing forms of constitution, which Plato now accepts, grudgingly, as offering some kind of framework for living: established laws, he suggests, will at least be 'imitations of the truth'. Monarchy will be best, then oligarchy, then democracy – provided, that is, that they continue to be based on law; if not, the order of preference is reversed. In the first case, the principle seems to be that the better men will always be fewer in number; in the second, it is that the more widely power is distributed, the less capable it will be of being misused.

In the *Laws*, his last and longest work, Plato constructs a second Utopia. This time it is to be a new foundation or colony (the Greeks were inveterate colonisers); and he selects an actual site for it (in Crete), well enough provided with natural resources to avoid the need to trade – which would bring in corrupting external influences – and far enough from the sea to avoid the temptation to do so. This neatly sums up Plato's attitude towards international relations: in general, he is against them. (In the *Republic*, he refers to only two kinds of relationship between states: either they are at war, or they are not. There are, however, to be special rules for the conduct of war between Greek states.)

Another, more important, reason for placing the new city of Magnesia inland is to prevent it from having a navy. Rowers count as arms-bearers and therefore as citizens. They would swell the citizen population unnecessarily, and diminish its quality. (There is an implicit reference here to Athens, which had the largest navy of any Greek state.) There are to be 5,040 citizens, of roughly equal capacities, who, though possessing land, will devote themselves exclusively to administering the state, and living the life of virtue.

The tripartite arrangement of the state in the *Republic*, which was based on the analogy of the tripartite division of the soul, has disappeared; all production is to be in the hands of slaves or aliens. The constitution will in effect be a compromise between the ideal kingship discussed in the *Statesman*, and the three existing forms of constitution; legally based, but with allowance for moderate revision of the laws, if experience shows this to be desirable; and avoiding the polarisation implicit in monarchy, oligarchy and democracy in their unmixed forms. The last traces of the old ideal of the philosophical ruler are to be found in the institution of a 'nocturnal council', whose members are to be charged with keeping the laws under review, and with preserving a reasoned understanding of the purposes of the state. Since the state is founded on law, it will be no more than a second-best; but it will come closer than any actual state to 'the truest constitution', in so far as it gives recognition to virtue as the true goal of the political community. Among actual states, only Sparta and the Cretan cities pay any systematic attention to the requirements of virtue; and they make the mistake of emphasising one virtue, courage, at the expense of the rest.

The bulk of the *Laws*, as its title suggests, is concerned with laying out in precise detail the laws and institutions by which Magnesia will be governed, with special emphasis on those concerned with education. Some have thought that the *Laws* was intended as a kind of handbook for aspiring politicians, perhaps for use in the Academy; and this is quite possible, although the training of statesmen would not have been the only function of the Academy, and probably not even its most important.

In some respects Plato's political thinking is alien to us: he was writing within a different political context, that of the small, independent, warring city-state; he also wrote in a different cultural and linguistic context (a point which I have deliberately underplayed in my account). But the main questions which he raises, particularly about the nature and purpose of government, and about the basis of political authority, are entirely general in type, as indeed he intended them to be. Although he wrote at Athens, he was not writing exclusively for Athens: he frequently refers, implicitly or explicitly, to Athens, but only as an example, both of the way in which a city will decline into lawlessness if it is not governed in accordance with true principle, and of the consequences of such a decline. (This verdict on the Athens of his day is, incidentally, singularly unfair.) He offers his panaceas to all states without distinction. It should not be surprising that his ideas had little or no visible impact on actual political practice, whether at Athens or in the cities whose young men came to learn from him. But they had a profound influence on sub-sequent political theory, especially through Aristotle, who him-self came to Athens to work in the Academy, and later through Cicero; both men based their own Utopian essays closely on the Platonic model. Plato's significance, however, does not lie merely in the degree of his influence on later thinkers; he can justly be called the founder of political theory itself.

Aristotle:
ideals and realities

Peter Nicholson

Aristotle (384–322 BC) was born in northern Greece, and as a young man went to Athens to study under Plato. After many years of travelling and scholarly research, he returned to Athens in 336 BC and set up his college, the Lyceum. He wrote extensively on philosophy, science, literature and politics, but much of his work has been lost. His *Politics* is an acute and terse analysis of fundamental theoretical issues, which not only reflects both the ideals and the shortcomings of ancient Greek political life, but also contains valuable ideas for today.

'Man', said Aristotle, 'is by nature a political animal.' But he did not mean quite what the modern reader would expect. Aristotle's view of humanity, nature and politics was rooted in the social life of ancient Greece, and that was very different from our own. My aims in this survey are on the one hand to indicate the alien features in Aristotle's political thought, many of which must strike us as outmoded and repugnant; and on the other to argue that, none the less, his discussions are still important. They deal with fundamental and permanent issues in politics, and they include ideals which, adapted to the changed conditions of our world, are still valuable.

Aristotle was born in 384 BC in Stagira (the modern Stavro), within the sphere of influence of Macedonia. This northern Greek kingdom had previously been on the fringe of the Greek world, but came to dominate it during Aristotle's lifetime. His father was a doctor and royal physician, and this medical background may have started Aristotle's interest in science. Both Aristotle's parents died while he was a boy. When he was seventeen he went to Athens to study at Plato's Academy. Aristotle must have got to know Plato and his ideas well during the twenty years he spent there, first as pupil, then as teacher and colleague, even though Plato was away in Sicily for several years. Plato called Aristotle 'the reader' and 'the brain'.

When Plato died in 347 BC, Aristotle left Athens; perhaps because he disagreed with those then running the Academy, or perhaps because Athens was beginning to see Macedonia as a dangerous enemy. Aristotle joined a small group of Platonists in Assos on the eastern coast of the Aegean. They were under the protection of Hermias of Atarneus who was, in Greek terms, a 'tyrant', having acquired supreme political power by force. He took a serious interest in philosophy: he may have visited the Academy, and he certainly gave his patronage to several of Plato's old pupils. They are said to have persuaded him to moderate his rule. He was later to meet an ugly death at Persian hands, betrayed while plotting to transfer his support from Persia to Macedonia, which led the Greeks, including Aristotle, to celebrate him as a martyr. After two or three years, Aristotle moved to the nearby island of Lesbos. During the period away from Athens he conducted extensive scientific research, especially in marine biology.

In 343 BC Aristotle accepted an invitation, offered perhaps through his father's connections or Hermias's influence, to become tutor to the son of Philip II, King of Macedonia. This is one of the most famous educational encounters in history: the tutor was to be recognised as one of the world's greatest philosophers, and the pupil was to become Alexander the Great, conqueror of much of the known world. Aristotle does not appear, however, to have influenced Alexander's ideas significantly; indeed, many of Alexander's later actions were out of tune with Aristotle's political views. In 340 BC Alexander, aged sixteen, governed Macedonia as regent during his father's absence, and Aristotle returned to Stagira. Some five years later he went back to Athens and opened the Lyceum, a school for further education similar to Plato's Academy. Here Aristotle provided both popular and more advanced teaching, directed research in all branches of learning, and built up a museum and library. He had been studying and writing for years, but his published works have not survived. The writings we have belong to his time at the Lyceum, though they draw upon his earlier work, and appear to be principally material for teaching and research.

Athens had been finally defeated by Philip in 338 BC and was now, with the rest of Greece, controlled by a Macedonian governor, Antipater. Antipater was Aristotle's friend, and sent his son to the Lyceum. Alexander had succeeded to the throne of Macedonia in 336 BC, when his father was assassinated, and was conducting the campaigns which took him as far south as Egypt

Aristotle (384–322 BC)

and as far east as the Indus. Then, in 323 BC, disaster struck: Alexander fell ill and died. Athens declared war on Macedonia and Aristotle, a Macedonian and personal friend of Alexander and Antipater, was in an exposed position. When his enemies lodged a charge of impiety against him, Aristotle left, allegedly saying that he did not wish Athens to sin against philosophy twice – a reference to its execution of Socrates. A year later Aristotle died. He had been married, and had two children.

Like every political philosopher, Aristotle was deeply influenced by the political institutions and ideas of his own day. His political thought is a critical analysis of the Greek *polis* (plural, *poleis*; usually translated as 'state', though that can mislead). Ancient 'Greece' was not a single political unit, but consisted of several hundred *poleis*, each independent, self-governing and a complete society and economy in itself. *Poleis* were small. Athens, the largest, was exceptional in having a population of perhaps a quarter of a million; most were far smaller, and some had only a few thousand inhabitants. The way in which they organised their government varied considerably. One key feature, however, was always the same: women, slaves and those of foreign origin could not participate in politics, so that citizenship was a prerogative of a minority. The precise distribution of power varied from *polis* to *polis*, ranging from its concentration in the hands of a few wealthy men, to its more or less equal division among all members of the citizen-minority. Thus even the widest distribution of political rights, which the Greeks called *dēmokratia*, was far from democratic in our sense because so many people were not citizens. On the other hand, *dēmokratia* was more democratic in that political power was exercised directly by the citizens themselves. Laws were made by an assembly of the citizens, not by a body of full-time representatives; policies were executed by citizen committees with rotating membership, not by bureaucrats; and civil disputes, criminal cases and political trials were all decided by panels of citizens, not by professional judges. Though citizenship was possessed by fewer people than in a modern democracy, being a citizen meant far more. It is perhaps unsurprising that there were frequent power struggles between the various groups within the citizen minority, particularly between the rich and the poor. Although sometimes a single man took advantage of this factiousness to make himself 'tyrant', or dictator, that was regarded as an aberration.

Aristotle was also deeply influenced by Plato. The *Politics* inherits many of his questions and some of his answers, especially from the *Laws*, on which Plato was working when Aristotle knew him. Yet Aristotle was no mere disciple, but a powerful and original thinker. He dissented from some of Plato's answers, and he dismissed some of Plato's questions. Aristotle reached crucially different conclusions about what philosophy is and can do, and this affected his political thought. His main disagreement concerned Plato's 'forms'. Plato had been trying to answer Socrates' questions, such as 'What is beauty?' and 'What is justice?', which Socrates had left unresolved. Plato did not think that answers could be found in the beautiful objects we see and the just actions we witness, because they are so numerous, diverse, and variable according to changing circumstances, that there is no common feature which can be 'beauty' or 'justice'. He claimed that beautiful objects and just actions should be understood as particular and differing instances of true beauty and true justice, which appear partially and imperfectly in each object and action. Beauty and justice themselves – and all similar ideas – are forms, and exist whole, pure and perfect in another world, a heaven. In our world of the senses – the 'real' world, as we mistakenly call it – forms can appear only imperfectly, as particular instances. The central political argument of the *Republic* was that properly educated philosophers have the exclusive title to rule because they alone know the forms in the other, eternal world of 'truth'. Philosopher-rulers, therefore, are able to create in our world the closest possible approximations to goodness, justice and happiness, both in societies and in individuals.

The forms, especially as developed into mathematical abstractions by Plato's successors, were rejected by Aristotle as idle talk and poetic metaphor. He pointed out difficulties which meant that the forms failed to solve the problem raised by Socrates' questions. He also provided an alternative solution to the problem. Aristotle agreed that we must distinguish the particular instances of, say, justice on the one hand, and on the other a quality which is common or universal to them all. It is a very different matter, though, and in Aristotle's contention redundant and misleading, to think that the universal quality has a separate existence in another world. Plato had thought that in order to reach truth and reality, we had to move from actual instances to the other-worldly forms. Aristotle, on the contrary, believed that *this* is the real world, and that any answer about universals and any general truths, and, above all, any explanation of change, of growth and decay, can be discovered only by studying the actual instances themselves. Actual instances, individual beautiful objects and just actions, embody universals; the individual cases are where universals exist, and are the only existence they can have.

For Aristotle, then, reality is in this world, in its objects, events and actions. His starting point was the observed facts: the structure of a dissected animal, ordinary opinions about justice, the history of the constitution of some *polis*. From studying such facts, we can build up knowledge. Aristotle assumed that our world is intelligible: the philosopher's task was to formulate the general principles which make sense of it. This philosophical position has major consequences for Aristotle's political thought. The philosopher lost the claim to rule which Plato had given him, and Aristotle is led to extend the study of politics further than Plato.

Aristotle offered an analogy to help explain his idea of the scope of the study of politics. What, he asked, are the proper concerns of a professional trainer in gymnastics? He should, Aristotle suggested, have an expert knowledge in four areas: (1) He will know the ideal training for the ideal physique, and be able to prescribe the best exercises for the person with the best possible natural endowment. (2) Most people lack the ideal physique, and many also lack the time to devote to the ideal training. So the expert will also know special exercises suitable for these people's particular requirements, to get them as fit as their circumstances allow. (3) Further, the trainer will know what kind of exercises can be generally recommended. This is the average course of exercises, not tailored to any particular type of individual, from which most people could benefit. (4) Finally, the expert will be faced with those who are not interested in being as fit as they can be, but simply in making themselves somewhat less unfit.

Correspondingly, the student of politics should seek knowledge in four areas: (1) He should know the ideal constitution, suitable for a *polis* whose members possess ideal characters, and which is ideally situated. (2) Since actual *poleis* do not meet the ideal conditions, he should also know which constitution is the best possible for any particular *polis* in its circumstances. (3) Further, he should know the average kind of constitution which would suit most *poleis*, and which they could achieve with profit. (4) Finally, he should know what to say to a *polis* which is not interested in having as good a constitution as it is capable of, which could not cope with the average constitution, and which wants simply to make the most of its defective constitution and avoid further decline.

In Aristotle's hands, political science became far wider in scope: Plato had limited himself to the first two areas. Aristotle agreed that the ideal *polis* had to be considered, both as a goal and as a standard for judging the defects of actual constitutions. He thought, however, as we have seen, that knowledge of the ideal can be obtained solely through investigation of actual *poleis*. This was one reason why he conducted extensive empirical and historical research into Greek constitutions. Furthermore, like many Greek thinkers, he believed that political science should be useful, and improve political practice: hence his concern with solving the problems of ordinary *poleis*, the flabby and unfit, so to speak. Here too a close knowledge of the workings of actual *poleis* was essential. Aristotle is said to have organised his assistants and associates to compile studies of 158 *poleis*. A single monograph has survived, on Athens, probably by Aristotle himself.

In order to analyse a complex whole, Aristotle thought, we must break it down into its components. In the case of the *polis*, he began with the pair, man and woman. Their union is natural, that is, necessary if they are to have children. It is also natural that the man should rule the woman, who has less reason than he, as husband (that is, rule her as one who is otherwise his equal), and as father should rule their children, whose reason is undeveloped (rule them absolutely, but in their interests and temporarily). From this biological unit, Aristotle proceeded to the household, an organisation for satisfying daily needs, such as food. The household consists of the biological family plus its possessions, including slaves ('living tools'). Aristotle criticised the contemporary practice of slavery for sometimes enslaving people who should be free. He argued, however, that there are some human beings (certain non-Greeks) who are intended by nature to be slaves. They possess physical strength for work, but low intelligence. Other human beings, less strong but fully rational, are intended by nature to be masters. Slavery, in its natural form, is thus mutually beneficial. Master and slave form an effective team, the master getting his work done and the slave gaining a share of the produce and protection (exactly as a domesticated animal is more secure than one in the wild). The household's property is a collection of tools for living, and so there is a limit on how much it should possess: more than what is needed to live a plain, simple, moral and civilised life is unnatural excess, and to be avoided. Aristotle rejected, on moral grounds, the accumulation of property for its own sake, and especially the pursuit of profit (hence his condemnation of usury as unnatural). From the household, Aristotle moved to the village, a collection of households able to satisfy more than merely daily needs; and thence to the *polis*, an association of villages able to provide economic self-sufficiency. Though the *polis* originates in the search for the satisfaction of physical needs, its justification becomes its ability to satisfy moral needs, the needs of the soul, by enabling its members to live 'well'. It is at this point that Aristotle said that the *polis* is natural and that man is intended by nature to live in the *polis*.

In Aristotle's view, however, human beings do not have a uniform nature. He divided them into groups, principally male and female, and free and slave, differing in capability. Accordingly, what could be expected of each kind of human being differed, and so did their special 'virtue': for example, a free woman's function is to help run the household, and it is a virtue to be silent in public, while a free man's function is to share the running of the *polis*, and it is a virtue to speak in public. In the same way, different kinds of human beings are capable of different forms and degrees of happiness. All human beings, whatever their kind, can be most virtuous, and therefore happiest, in the *polis*, each in his or her own way.

The key words in this analysis are 'nature' and 'natural'. Aristotle believed that all living things, including human beings, are to be understood in terms of their natures. The nature of a thing, what it really is, is what it becomes when its growth is completed. An acorn's nature, for example, is to become an oak tree; and an acorn is really, and should be understood as, a potential oak tree. Human beings too are to be seen in terms of the potential they can develop, the end towards which they are moving. Man's end is life in the *polis*, because that life is the best conceivable for human beings. It follows that the household, the village, the *polis*, language, morality, law and justice – everything necessary for, and part of, that life – are natural. It follows too that the political scientist is not a mechanic creating political organisation, as some Greeks and some moderns have argued; he is like a gardener. Exactly as an acorn needs a fertile soil, water, sunlight, air, and so on in order to flourish, so certain economic, social and political conditions must be met if the members of a human community are to achieve their potential as rational and moral beings. One of the political scientist's tasks is to discover those conditions, and base the ideal constitution upon them. At a general level, many think this argument has some appeal (versions of it can be found, for instance, in Rousseau, in Marx and in J S Mill). None the less, there are obvious problems about finding out what is natural, and Aristotle's discussion highlights them. As he himself said, we should always observe specimens in their natural, peak condition, rather than degenerate or defective ones. Yet the comparison between trees (or any natural organism) and men breaks down at this vital point. We can see mature and healthy oak trees, and use them to judge the defects of others which are stunted, damaged or decaying. But what society will serve as the exemplar for the fully developed and perfected human life? Aristotle admitted that all the actual Greek *poleis* were less than ideal. He also claimed, we saw, that our knowledge must come from actual instances. The likely consequence of these two positions in combination did in fact occur: all too often Aristotle commended as natural practices and ideas which were simply those accepted in his own day. His endorsement of the conventional Greek view of women, and of much of the Greek view of slavery, are but two leading examples.

So far, Aristotle has looked at the free man in relation to other kinds of human beings, considering him as husband, father and master. The analysis proceeded next to the culminating human association, the *polis*. Here he dealt solely with free men, the heads of households, and asked how they should be associated. They are all men who, because of their natural superiority, rule other human beings: on what terms should they organise their own common affairs? Aristotle laid down the principle of justice that equals must be treated equally. In the present case, those are equal who contribute to the *polis* by being free, by possessing sufficient property for the needs of his household and the public needs of the *polis*, and by practising social virtues such as valour, self-restraint, justice and good sense in decision-making. In Aristotle's eyes, this meant that the virtuous should be the citizens. Free birth and adequate means may not seem to us to have anything to do with virtue, but Aristotle valued them as conditions enabling a man to act virtuously. Only free men have the capacity to reason and be virtuous in the full sense. Only the propertied can afford to devote enough time to acquiring and practising these virtues and have the means to do so, important considerations when virtuous activity includes, for instance, equipping and training oneself to fight courageously in the citizen army, or being generous to one's friends.

Aristotle considered the theoretical possibility that one man might be so much more virtuous than everyone else that his virtue exceeded all of theirs added together. According to his principle of justice, he recognised, such a man has the best claim to rule, and the ideal constitution would be kingship, where one man rules absolutely over everyone else, in the interests of all. Aristotle also considered the possibility that a few might between them be more virtuous than all the rest, in which case they should rule and the ideal constitution would be aristocracy, where the best men rule equally over one another and absolutely over everyone else, in the interests of all. He did not think either possibility at all probable, and concentrated on the third form of the ideal constitution, where all the heads of households are citizens (his name for this constitution is not clear). Since all citizens are equal, they must rule over one another equally. Since everyone cannot govern, or hold administrative or judicial office at the same time, they must take turn and turn about. The younger, stronger men will serve in the army, the older, experienced men will belong to the assembly which makes laws and elects the officials of the *polis* (taking turns at filling the offices), and the aged will retire from citizenship into priesthoods. Citizens will devote their time and energy to the public affairs of the *polis*, thereby living 'well'. Hence farming, which is time-consuming, and manual work and commerce, which are demeaning, are incompatible with citizenship (an attitude common among richer Greeks). Those functions are of course necessary, so they must be performed by slaves or by imported labour.

All the provisions of the constitution, such as the powers and duties of officials and scrutiny of their performance, are laid down formally, and the citizens always act through law, which is impersonal. Aristotle was a keen advocate of what we call constitutionalism, or the rule of law. Aristotle also recommended, among other things, the best possible kind of territory, the size and social structure of the population, and the site and layout of the capital. Finally, he explained the form of public education best suited to producing citizens fit for the ideal *polis*, a matter which, like Plato, he thought fundamental. His account is unfortunately incomplete, but its main thrust is clear. The right habits must be formed in youth and reinforced throughout adult life.

In his discussion of the ideal constitution it is noticeable that Aristotle sticks to what is strictly practicable: this is not a *polis* which could occur only by some miracle, as Plato said of his ideal, but one which could actually be founded. Yet ultimately the ideal *poleis* of Plato and of Aristotle are not far apart. It is true that whereas Plato had thought that the sole title to rule is the philosopher's knowledge, Aristotle rejected the very possibility of such knowledge. He proposed instead that those men should rule who have a range of virtues, one of which is the kind of practical knowledge which comes from advancing years and experience (which to Plato would have seemed not knowledge but opinion). None the less, when one compares the kind of people who would be the philosophers and their helpers in Plato's Callipolis with the citizens of Aristotle's ideal *polis*, they look very similar (except that Plato includes women). Furthermore, those whom they exclude from politics are identical (women again excepted). This is not surprising of course, if it is true that political philosophers tend to reflect their own times, as well as to reflect on them.

Aristotle judged all existing constitutions imperfect. Their principal defect was that their rulers, whether one man (*tyrannis*), a few men (*oligarchia*) or many men (*dēmokratia*), aimed at their own interests rather than at the interests of all. Oligarchs, for instance, promoted their own interests, the interests of the rich, at the expense of the poor. Democrats promoted their own interests, the interests of the poor, at the expense of the rich. Notice that Aristotle defined 'democracy' as simply the opposite of 'oligarchy', and saw it as rule by the *dēmos*, the people, in the sense of rule by the mass of the people, namely, the poor. It is interesting how explicit he is here. He saw that the two criteria of *dēmokratia*, rule by the many and rule by the poor, would conflict if there were a *polis* where the poor were few and were the rulers (this could occur if 'rich' and 'poor' are defined in terms of fixed amounts of property, rather than relatively to one another). He expressly stated that such a *polis* would be a *dēmokratia*, showing that his real criterion was economic, not numerical.

Aristotle tried to work out how to stabilise and preserve each kind of constitution, and how to construct the 'average' best. His discussion is rich in actual cases, drawn from the Lyceum's research archive. His main theme was the mixing of elements from different constitutions, elaborating and refining some of Plato's later ideas. Any constitution which is a pure example of its type is weak. Thus an oligarchy which reserves power exclusively for the rich is more likely to be overthrown than one which concedes a carefully limited amount of power to the poor – for instance, by allowing them to participate in the election of officials but not to stand for office. Likewise, a democracy which thinks only of the poor and disregards the rich is more likely to suffer a revolution than one which gives the rich some role in public life – for instance, filling honourable but expensive posts such as ambassadorships. Aristotle's analysis turned on a moral factor, the sense of justice of those involved. Stability depends on enough people supporting the constitution, and this ceases when people are discontented because they think they are being unfairly treated. Aristotle's solution, then, was to mix some democratic elements into *oligarchia*, and some oligarchic elements into *dēmokratia*, in order to make each more stable. Similarly, his prescription for the average constitution was a well balanced mixture of *oligarchia* and *dēmokratia* which he called 'polity'. For it to receive the support it needs, there has to be a good proportion of citizens with a middling amount of wealth.

The worst constitution, of course, is tyranny. Once more, Aristotle investigated actual instances, and drew conclusions about how tyranny can be preserved. For example, he repeated the story of one successful tyrant's advice to another:

> . . . to Thrasybulus' messenger, Periander returned no answer; but while walking in a field, reduced all the stalks to one level by lopping off the tallest. The messenger did not understand the motive for this action, but ´reported the action to Thrasybulus, who perceived that he ought to remove the outstanding men.

At this point some readers feel that Aristotle must have taken a radically wrong turning. Political science is supposed to be about justice, and improving politics, yet here is Aristotle telling a tyrant how to retain his power by eliminating potential rivals. Aristotle seems frequently to have met the complaint that philosophy is useless: hence his relish in telling how Thales made a lot of money by securing a monopoly in olive oil presses one year. But in making political science useful to tyrants, has not Aristotle gone too far?

This is a misunderstanding. His aim was less to preserve what is bad than to prevent something worse. He tried to show, for instance, how to stop a moderate *dēmokratia* from changing into an extreme one which in turn is liable to collapse into a tyranny. Even a tyranny is worth keeping if the alternative is outright civil war. Moreover, Aristotle thought that the process is reversible.

Political science can show a tyrant how it is in his own interest to improve his regime; and that paves the way for a proper constitution when his rule ends, as it must. Similarly, political science can show an *oligarchia* or *dēmokratia* how to maintain itself; and carrying out that advice, which is to mix in an element of the opposite constitution, is also a step towards a better constitution, the polity. Beyond the polity, which is a compromise between *oligarchia* and *dēmokratia*, and still a deviant constitution, stands the ideal constitution, which Aristotle may have thought was then within reach, since it is a kind of improved polity. The ideal constitution too is a mixture of elements, free birth from *dēmokratia* and wealth from *oligarchia*, but both subordinated to virtue. The social composition of the ideal *polis* has, moreover, eliminated both the poor and the rich with all their faults of moral character, since every citizen has property sufficient for his needs but no more. Finally, as a result, the ideal citizens rule in the interests of all, not because they are forced to by checks and balances, as in the polity, but because they see that it is right to do so.

Considered in this light, Aristotle was a gradualist. His emphasis was upon the obstacles to sudden or large change. First, a *polis* can sustain a constitution only as good as its conditions permit. For example, if it is poor, and most of its potential citizens have to labour at menial tasks to gain a living, some form of *dēmokratia* will be appropriate, and nothing better. A *polis* must not overreach itself, any more than someone trying to get fit should take on exercises which are too demanding. Aristotle does not seem to have envisaged ways in which economic development could be promoted and a *polis* made wealthier, but put prosperity down to fortune. Overcoming the second obstacle to change, on the other hand, is very much in human hands and within the scope of political science. *Poleis* frequently have defective constitutions because their citizens hold wrong ideas. Oligarchs, for instance, mistakenly think that money is the most important thing in life, and this biases their constitution when in other respects they might be capable of moving first towards polity and then nearer the ideal.

Education is obviously the method which the Aristotelian political scientist would recommend here. Correct education can bring reform, but only in the long run: education is itself a gradualist approach. Aristotle thought that education is as important for defective constitutions as for the ideal. The most difficult problem is the bad *polis* whose citizens do not want to be reformed but to carry on as they are, much as the man with pleasurable though unhealthy habits does not want to relinquish them but simply to stave off death for as long as possible. In both cases improvement is impossible except through persuasion, although this is likely to take considerable time because those who have built up bad habits are least amenable to reason.

I hope I have now explained how the statement that 'man is by nature a political animal' should be understood. Human beings are innately different, but for all of them the best life is 'political' (that is, life in the *polis*), either as members or as contributing parts. Aristotle's major achievement was to use these ideas as a framework for the ordered analysis of politics as it was in addition to politics as it might be. Although Plato has the stronger claim to be the founder of political theory, Aristotle is the founder of political science, the composite study of philosophy and politics.

Aristotle's influence has often been considerable. His ideas are an important component of Aquinas's thought, for example. Because Aristotle's political thought has many sides to it, he has appealed to subsequent writers in different ways. Machiavelli, for instance, appreciated his realism. Locke shared some of his views on the family. Probably Hegel is the philosopher most deeply affected by Aristotle; he set out to revise and reapply the best of Aristotle. Marx, who called Aristotle 'a giant thinker', took some ideas from him directly, and others indirectly via Hegel. In the past, much of Aristotle's attractiveness has undoubtedly been that his political ideas favoured the social class which was politically dominant and to which his admirers generally belonged. By the nineteenth century this was no longer true, and his influence waned. J S Mill thought him a 'moderate aristocratical politician', and his *Politics* 'a philosophical consecration of existing facts'.

Most people today would accept this verdict. Only exceptionally does one find a thinker, such as Hannah Arendt, who expressly incorporates Aristotle's ideas into his or her own work. This is unfortunate, because Aristotle still has much to offer. In the first place, most modern states and the international system of states suffer from much the same stresses from conflicts of interests which Aristotle sought to prevent. We face similar questions about how people *can* live together, and his discussions are still relevant in some respects. In the second place, Aristotle's principles of 'political' association state an ideal about the good life that people *should* live together. That ideal, it is true, has defects: but that is a reason for improving it, not abandoning it. Indeed, one might see much of the subsequent history of political thought as attempting to extend and deepen Aristotle's ideal and to apply it more widely, eventually, to all human beings. Furthermore, history has shown that we should not think of our knowledge of human nature as complete but as open to development, as human beings create new kinds of political life. In these respects, Aristotle's limitations stand as a warning of what to avoid. Perhaps he also provides an example to follow. It is, at the very least, worth enquiring whether our own 'observed facts', the greatly changed economic and social conditions of our world, have not made the life of Aristotle's ideal citizen possible for everyone.

St Augustine:
Christian political thought at the end of the Roman empire

Janet Coleman

Augustine was born in AD 354 at Thagaste, now in Algeria. He trained in classical Latin rhetoric in North Africa and in AD 383 sailed to Rome, becoming Professor of Rhetoric the following year in Milan, where he met Ambrose, Bishop of Milan. He experienced an emotional conversion to Christianity, after having previously been a Manichee, and went on to read numerous works of the Platonists. He returned to North Africa where he founded a monastery and was ordained priest. There he deepened his knowledge of the Bible and asked Jerome to send him Latin translations of Greek commentaries on the Bible. He was involved in the Donatist schism in the Church, preached widely at Carthage, Hippo and elsewhere, and preached against the Pelagians. In AD 410 Rome was sacked by the barbarian Alaric, and Augustine began his work on *The City of God* in AD 413, in part to answer pagan attacks on the Church. He thereafter developed his influential doctrines on grace, and continued writing *The City of God* in instalments until AD 425. By AD 429 the barbarian Vandals had reached the North African coast and Augustine died in AD 430, as the Vandals ravaged the Roman cities and countryside of Africa.

The first Christians in the Roman world were Jews who differed from the Old Testament tradition in having faith in Jesus as the realisation of the Jewish Messiah. They appeared as one of many sects within an already diverse Judaism. The early Church undertook a mission to the Gentiles, criticising Judaism for its exclusiveness and drawing recruits from all groups and classes in Roman imperial society. Theirs was seen as a reconciling role for all mankind, Jew and Gentile alike, religious and irreligious. During the first centuries of its existence the Church was viewed as a revolutionary religious movement whose apparent indifference to worldly power identified it as a movement without a political ideology. But soon there were those who realised that

Christian quietism had the power to capture and transform all strata of society, and the social and political order of the Roman empire was seen to be threatened.

Many of the educated and powerful in the Roman empire were trained in rhetoric and oratory, and adhered to an imperial polytheism as well as to the moral principles of ancient Greece. In contrast, during the early centuries of Christianity the agents of its diffusion were neither highly educated nor trained in oratory, and they attracted the down-trodden, the impotent, women and slaves, with extraordinary skill and speed. By the fourth century all that was needed – and it came – was the conversion of the Roman emperor himself. Christian apologists saw this as the successful establishment of the *Pax Romana* (Roman peace) brought to its conclusion, the providential divine preparation of Rome for a universally realised gospel. The divine will was now established in the very heart of governmental decision-making just as it had previously conquered the common people through four centuries of missionary work. The spread of Christianity had been hindered by phases of persecution and indifference that were now accepted as a part of divine providence. The gospel was to achieve its historical fulfilment through Rome the eternal.

When Constantine was proclaimed Emperor in AD 305 he worshipped the sun, but at a major military crisis in his career by which he sought to gain sole power in the west, he invoked the Christian God with success. Subsequently, religious toleration of Christian and pagan alike was proclaimed. During the third century, Christianity had been outlawed because augurs and oracles had indicated that the Roman gods were displeased with having been replaced by the false god of the Christians. Now this repression was essentially at an end, but the legacy of persecution continued a debate within the Church itself. During the persecution of Christians for reasons of state, Christians had been required to hand over sacred scripture and some bishops succumbed to civil threats. With the coming of toleration there was a deep schism among Christians as they argued over the extent and degree to which Christians were to give unto Caesar what was decreed to be his. At what point was resistance to the state to be absolute if the state demanded what was perceived to be sinful? Radical Christians known as Donatists argued that those bishops who had traded in holy writ on state orders were not to be received back into the Church. Those who had lost the Spirit by apostasy or schism, even during persecution, should

St Augustine (354–430)

not, thereafter, confer the gifts of the Spirit through the sacraments. Donatists became increasingly fanatical, and were determined to keep the Church pure and uncompromising. The schism between Catholics and Donatists was to dominate the Church, especially in North Africa, for the whole fourth century and beyond.

The personal conversion of the Emperor Constantine can now be seen as a watershed in the history of the Church and of Europe. Not only was persecution at an end but the civil power was henceforth thrown behind the development of the institutional Church, and consequently the Church became increasingly implicated in legal and political decisions. Christianity was not yet made the official state religion; that would come at the end of the fourth century. But Constantine's charitable benefactions to the Church, his building programme, his presidency over the first ecumenical Church council at Nicaea, throw light on the developing power organisation of the Church and the increasing tendency for Church policy to be matters of imperial pronouncement.

Paganism was still the religion of the majority and remained so until well into the fourth century. The high-ranked and highly educated upheld the old religion as a form of patriotism and adherence to traditions that had made Rome great. But under the emperorships of Constantine's sons, paganism, especially mystery cults, were moved against decisively. By the end of the fourth century the church had virtually captured the whole of society and the time was right for the emergence of an independent Latin theology to replace a Christian theology that had been dominated by the Greek Fathers. Jerome was producing the Latin (Vulgate) Bible, translating the Greek and Hebrew into a legalistic Latin that would create the distinctive language of Latin Christianity of the west, and Augustine was to evolve its distinctive theology.

Augustine was born in AD 354 in what is now a small town in Algeria. His father was a pagan but was converted to Christianity just before his death; his mother, Monica, was a devout believer, and ambitious for her intelligent son. Augustine's education was partly financed by a wealthy benefactor, and he completed his studies of Latin literature, Virgil, Cicero and public oratory at Carthage. This was the normal route for success in the Roman legal profession or the civil service, and Augustine secured the professorships of rhetoric at Carthage, then Rome, then Milan where he sought a provincial governorship.

At the age of thirty-two he experienced an emotional and decisive conversion to Christianity, having previously travelled the way of what he later condemned as a misguided and sensual youth. He described his conversion in one of the most moving documents of all literature, an extended autobiographical prayer entitled *The Confessions*, written in AD 399, thirteen years after his conversion. He says he was moved by a personal quest for truth after reading a standard tract of the school curriculum, Cicero's *Hortensius*. Because he found the literary style of the Bible inferior to that of the Latin classics, and because he could see the Old Testament only as a collection of 'old wives' tales', he became convinced that his mother's Church lacked any cultural distinction. He joined the dualist sect known as the Manichees who rejected the Old Testament, and he stayed with them, converting others, for nine years.

His career ambitions took him to Milan in AD 384, and there he heard and met Ambrose, the Bishop of Milan, who was skilled in combining classical oratory and philosophy with Christian theology. Augustine was overwhelmed by Ambrose's erudition, his Christian devotion combined with Neoplatonism. He began to read Neoplatonists like Porphyry and Plotinus, who stressed how the inward mind of man was a correlate of God, and went away on retreat with philosophically-minded friends. In a famous passage in *The Confessions* he describes how, sitting one day in a garden, he heard the voice of a child playing from a house not far off, repeating, 'Take up and read, take up and read.' He picked up the Bible as instructed and experienced his conversion, reading: 'Not in rioting and drunkenness, not in chambering and wantonness, not in strife and envying, but put ye on the Lord Christ and make no provision for the flesh and its concupiscences.' His conversion, under the influence of Ambrose, was to Neoplatonism and Christianity, so nearly simultaneously that it would take years before he could become seriously critical of Platonist metaphysics as being insufficient. It is thought that the Platonic element in his conversion was the most serious influence that led him to decide to live a life of celibacy after having lived for years with a concubine who had borne him a son.

With the death of Monica, his mother, he returned to Africa and set up an ascetic community in his native town. But a visit to Hippo by such a man of extraordinary talents inspired the populace to press him to be ordained as presbyter, and thereafter he became ordained Bishop of Hippo. His ordination marked a momentous change in his attitude. Whereas he had previously been writing a kind of Christian philosophy and a polemic against the Manichees in favour of Catholicism, his ordination led him to serious Biblical exegesis and a focus on St Paul's letters. He deepened his grasp of theology and developed his unique doctrines of grace and predestination as theological responses to political and theological crises within the Church he came to rule in North Africa.

He experienced the Catholic–Donatist schism at first hand, each community claiming to be the one mystical body of Christ

and the sole haven of salvation. Augustine rejected the exclusiveness and puritanical moralism of the Donatists, arguing that the
visible church militant has within it the pure and impure, the
clean and the unclean alike. Only the Last Judgement would
separate the wheat from the chaff. Furthermore, he argued that
the efficacy of the sacrament does not depend on the standing of
the minister. The sacraments belong to Christ, and their validity
rests in the act, not in the state of the minister's soul. A priest's
ordination is independent of his moral and spiritual condition;
upon his character is imprinted at the moment of ordination an
awareness that sacramental actions which he administers are, in
effect, the whole Church acting. Augustine had entered an
eighty-five-year-old schism and helped to achieve its resolution
by arguing in favour of imperial edicts against paganism and
heresy, whereby coercion was justified as a rebuke of religious
dissent and seen as a kind of paternal correction. As in many of
his decisions, Augustine expressed a theoretical justification of
imperial policy, rejecting crude physical force on schismatics,
but accepting a scale of fines and confiscation of dissenters'
property. The Donatist problem was only one example of the
Augustinian mind seeking intellectual justification for events as
they are, explaining what was being done as an often inscrutable
mode of divine providence.

The Donatist schism was, at least temporarily, pushed to one
side, and Augustine was faced with a much larger issue when, in
410, the barbarian Alaric and his Goths sacked Rome and
refugees poured into North Africa. Alaric had lived most of his
life within Roman frontiers and had threatened authorities with
the destructiveness of his tribe to gain a post in the high command of the Roman state. And then he struck. The question of
understanding divine providence in history was raised especially
when many of the fleeing Roman aristocrats interpreted the
catastrophe as due to the abandonment of traditional Roman
gods in favour of the Christian god and the Christian teaching
that the state was not the means to human fulfilment. Rome had
symbolised the security of a long-established civilised life.
Jerome wrote, 'If Rome can perish, what can be safe?'

On the suggestion of the Spanish priest Orosius, Augustine
set to writing a defence of Christianity to answer pagan historio-
graphy. From 413 to 427 he wrote his gigantic work, *The City of
God*, to defend Christianity on all fronts. These twenty-two
books, wide-ranging and diffuse, present Augustine's social and
political theory, a response to Roman imperialism, an evaluation

of government and society, in a vast *summa* which discusses the consequences of believing that man's true end lies not in political honour and involvement but beyond this life. He argues that no earthly state can ensure security from internal and external attack, but that government is none the less ordained by God; that history is no more than a catalogue of wars attempting to secure a shaky peace; and that man without God must always be a victim of ignorance, fear, irrational self-love and lack of social and self-control. He argues that a proper concern for justice in any state must include God, although governments do indeed exist without justice and are consequently no more than large-scale robber bands. He is not arguing for the establishment of a theocracy as such in the world, but he is formulating a doctrine of human nature, corrupted beyond any hopes of self-amelioration as a result of inherited sin from Adam's first disobedience and fall. His theology of grace, of man's fallen nature, his analysis of the meaning of history as inscrutably more than a mere flux of outward events, a hidden drama of sin and redemption that can only be resolved after history, is seen to unfold. *The City of God* is the one work into which feed all the streams of Augustine's personal experiences, of the mind and in the world. It is an encyclopaedia of Christian interpretation of the late fourth and early fifth century Christian imperial Rome.

Although one of the overriding subjects of *The City of God* is the relation of Church and state, this treatise is not specifically about politics. It is first and foremost an apologetic defence of Christianity, a *livre de circonstance*, a controversial pamphlet written under the pressure of immediate events and necessity in the trained language of rhetoric which, none the less, is always personal. The practical needs of his world enabled him to write in such a way as to universalise his own inner life and its responses to contemporary reality. Did the calamity of Alaric's sack of Rome occur because pagan Rome had forgotten its ancient ways? This is the first issue to which Augustine addresses himself, and he shows himself to be a meeting place of two worlds, Roman and Christian. He wrote for learned men of leisure and cited the great names of Latin literature to appeal to a generation of antiquarians. But he speaks of 'your' Virgil and 'our' scriptures. Books I–V are meant as a reply to those who say that pagan gods are to be worshipped for the sake of civil security and peace. Books VI–X reply to the contention of the philosophers that worship of the old Roman gods leads to the real good and the eternal life for men. Books XI–XIV allow

Augustine to begin to construct his theory of society and history, and he tells of the origin of the two cities, that of God and that of men. In Books XV–XVIII he traces the course of the two cities in time and history; and then in Books XIX–XXII he relates the consummation of the two cities in eternity.

Throughout, Augustine contrasts the values of the temporal world with eternal motives and intentions, both of individuals and of nations. He believes that social life for man is divinely ordained and natural. But he sets up a distinct kind of social life against the values of Roman social life where worldly honour and self-assertive patriotism seem, to him, to exalt the love of self over all else. Alaric's sack of Rome is not a supreme crisis: the true crises in the history of man were Eden and Calvary. But considering the natural social condition of humanity we find that kings must exist and they ought to serve God as kings, thus admitting a distinctive sacred character in the sovereign power of state which would be made much of in the Middle Ages. He denies that Christianity is a civic peril; nor does it condemn all wars. The doctrine of Christ is the salvation of every common-wealth rather than being incompatible with the well-being of the state. Some form of state is needed, and even the worst tyranny has some justification. He condemns imperialism and the tyranny of strong nations over the weak, especially when the ruling passion is merely a lust for domination. It is the limitations of man's reason and his inability to know himself truly and com-pletely, to say nothing of knowing his neighbour, that lies at the heart of the divine ordination of civil power, the state. It is a con-sequence of Adam's sin which mankind inherits, that man requires government, private property, coercive laws, all to keep the peace that man so dearly seeks but cannot achieve on his own.

The good at which all imperfectly just societies throughout history aim is peace and security; this good can be momentarily secured and thus governments of whatever kind must be used as imperfect means of keeping the peace. The civil authority can never be destroyed; it is divinely ordained for men *in via*, on their way to a hoped-for salvation after all states and all history. In effect, peace and security are of such high value, according to Augustine, that no amount of civil tyranny can ever justify sedition and insurrection. Civil society throughout history has often been perverted by evil wills, by the will to dominate others out of self-interest, and yet in the actual world of fallen man even these states are to be preferred to none. Augustine argues that Christianity, in teaching the love of one's neighbour through the love of God, does in effect teach civic duty and obedience to the state. He has no discussion of the merits or otherwise of various types of constitutions, although he does describe the qualities of a good Christian king. But no earthly kingdom can ever be a permanent peaceful refuge. However, drawing on his experience with the Donatists, he argues for the unifying role of the civil power even to the extent of coercion of dissenters, and justifies the use of force as an educational persecution for the good of the soul. The civic duty is one within the larger Christian duty to providence. The state keeps the peace and extends the province of the kingdom of God on earth.

The traditional pagans accused Christians of pacifism and of withdrawing from public affairs. Augustine's very life was a refutation of this charge, for his own episcopal power was wielded with the support of the imperial administration. And he preached in North Africa unambiguously about the need for the public enforcement of morality. The ancestral way of life was empty; just laws, revealed to men by divine authority, were to be actively enforced in a Christian empire. The human race as a whole required discipline by frequent and unwelcome crises. Rome fell as one episode in the tragic history of human disasters issuing from the deep guilt of the race, for which this tribulation was a quite sufficient cause. There will be an end to every earthly kingdom, and Rome had no special place in providential history.

Not only patriotic and conservative pagans, drawn to the 'myth' of Rome's past, but those drawn to the Platonist literature of Porphyry were also shown to be on the wrong track. This Neoplatonist philosopher's quest for a universal way to set free the soul was a failure, for he had said that a universal way to salvation was unknown to historical knowledge. Augustine disagreed. And yet his respectful treatment of Porphyry shows the extent to which the philosophical pagan past was still important to Augustine and would remain so until his death. The moral history of Rome and the moral qualities of men like Cicero had, he recognised, made the empire great, for such men were devoted to the common good. They were misguided, however, in not seeing that this involved a higher allegiance to God. Instead, they glorified the wrong city, the earthly city of self-interested achievement. Here he passes to writing more than a *livre de circonstance*, and he sets out the distinction between the *civitas terrena*, the city of men and the *civitas dei*, the city of God.

Augustine argues that since the fall of Adam there have been two cities, distinguished by their two loyalties, one to self, the other to God. One city served the rebel angels, the other those loyal to God. The two cities, in history, were inextricably mixed; but while Cain founded a city, Abel was a sojourner. Babylon and Jerusalem crystallised in symbolic form the reality of these two cities, even before the coming of Christ. The Bible told men all the history they needed to know. The Bible was God's chosen words of history. The 'facts' of more recent history were merely the new-born ousting the dying. The latent pattern of history was set at the Creation, inaccessible to rational man but clear to God. However, hints of the two cities could be seen throughout the tragic history of the human race. Augustine's understanding of history is prophetic and concentrates on a few scriptural moments of significance beyond their time. The seeking of the social good of peace in an organised city typified the historical quest of all civilisations. The tension between Cain and Abel, or Romulus and Remus, is universalised. All men desire to share peace, resolve tensions and control discordant wills in social life, but members of the city of men regard earthly political peace as a sufficient closed system. The city of men is founded on a fratricide and is transient. But some men 'know' that they must preserve their identity as citizens of Heaven, and they are resident strangers in all other cities. They live according to the customs of the land but are like pilgrims desiring a distant country. They have, like all social men, common business to pursue, but they are not ultimately lovers of this world. They must take on the role of magistrate, taxpayer, good citizen with the idea that theirs is a measured paternalism desired by God who had instituted cities amongst fallen social men. Augustine exhorts men to love the good things of the city of men, created things, human achievements, but because they are gifts from God and given utterly gratuitously rather than merited by men. Men are overwhelmingly dependent, but pride prevents them from admitting dependence. Men had been collectively punished for Adam's sin and consequently death was instituted as penal rather than inevitable.

In response to the schisms in the North African Church, Augustine developed his idea of the unity and universality of the Church. Since God is the *summum bonum*, then temporal felicity is irrelevant; furthermore, it cannot be permanently achieved. The chief end of man is to glorify God and enjoy him for ever. God is, however, the giver of all kingdoms and determines their end, an end not always apparent to human rationality. Members of the city of God, intermingled with those of the cities of men, use the peace established by governments wherever they may be, in the hope of an enduring peace in the life beyond. But the city of God, thus intermingled in history, was not strictly to be identified with the visible Church.

Because men are uncertain of membership in the true trans-historical church, and because Augustine argues that only a few can be saved from damnation, the city of God can never be realised in a coherent society on earth. The progress of the two cities is a confused progression throughout history. Only at the Last Judgement will membership of the city of God, the true Church, become clear. The promised millennial kingdom is not the future reign of Christ in the world but the present kingdom of the Church comprising the tares among the wheat. The Church militant in history is no more free from perils than is the secular state, but the Church's sacramental function, as a dis-penser of grace without which man can do no good, makes religion a collective means to salvation. Baptism and communion do not ensure salvation but they are the *sine qua non* conditions of salvation. And because Augustine believes in the fundamental equality of all peoples, in that all men suffer the stain of Adam's sin, the sacramental Church must be universal. His doctrine of original sin and his teaching that election to salvation is seem-ingly arbitrary and not dependent on merit can only be re-conciled by inscrutable divine justice before which men are essentially helpless and dependent. Those who escape damnation where all men belong after the fall, have no merit. Not even a conscious turning of the will to God is sufficient for salvation, for this is the work of gratuitous grace and God's mercy. Here he was arguing against the British monk Pelagius, who placed greater emphasis on man's ability to meet God half-way by consciously doing the good unaided by supernatural grace.

Augustine tries to argue against what some interpret as a con-sequent fatalism in his doctrines. He says that although God foreknew Satan's prideful fall and Adam's sin, their individual freedoms to take these decisions were not hindered by God's knowledge. God is free as man is free by nature. Adam's sin was not predetermined by God, although it was foreknown. Moral evil arrived in the world by the conscious decision of Satan and Adam to misuse their free will. And after these first evil acts the human will is forever dominated by pride and concupiscence. God's world will move ineluctably towards its foreknown end, but by means of real, concrete and active persons choosing between contingent alternatives in their societies. For Augustine, social men are responsible for making wrong choices, but when they make good choices they do so with divine aid through grace.

So too it is with governments of men, divinely instituted as means of keeping order and civil peace. He condemns the notion of imperialism, dislikes tyrannies of strong nations over the weak, and conjectures that the world would be happily governed if it consisted not of social aggregations secured by wars of conquest and despotism but of small states. His model is that of the family; as many small states in the world as there are families in a city. But these small states must be governed to keep the peace. In contemplating a union of families to create a city and a union of associated governments operating in harmony, he imagines a condition in which compulsion will not be needed, any more than it is needed in a well-governed family. For law is not a mere expression of force but has its origins in consent. In so far as it is possible among fallen men, the ruler of the true commonwealth will provide warning and counsel. However, in realising that there will always be those who choose evil, the state will have to step in as the public executioner. And those in a position of governmental power will have to take decisions to kill criminals, although they will always remember that their knowledge of any case is fallible and that they may have tragically misjudged the situation. Augustine's parallel of the patriarchal family rule with that of the state was a rejection of Aristotle's understanding of the family as pre-political, serving as no model for government among political men, who were free and equal. Augustine's patriarchal family model of government was to exert great influence on theories of monarchy throughout the Middle Ages and beyond.

What precisely did he find inadequate in the Roman republican theory of government as set forth by Cicero, whose ideas provided the theoretical justification of the Roman commonwealth? Cicero had argued that a just commonwealth was a *res populi*, a thing of the people. Augustine saw a problem with this notion of a 'people'. According to Augustine, if justice is the essence of the state, then justice as he defines it, including God, is necessarily remote in pagan commonwealths, which are, consequently, like great robber bands. There is indeed a social contract even among criminals against the outside world, and therefore, even these unjust societies display a kind of unity. Instead, Augustine redefines a 'people' by saying that they constitute a rational multitude united by a common love. Cicero's *populus* was united by a common love of the things of the state, the material well-being of the social order. Augustine believes that a true commonwealth can be united only when people love one another grounded in their higher love of God, for this rather than material well-being is the greatest bond of union among men.

His true state is, therefore, a true Church which will be realised only after history. No true commonwealth has existed or will ever exist in time. The good at which imperfectly just societies aim, being peace and security, is not a final end but must be used by the city of God's dispersed members. Civil authority must not be destroyed. But it must always be remembered that what is morally right for a nation to do is quite distinct from saying that if it fails to do the right it ceases to be a nation: it is simply not a true commonwealth based on love of God uniting its members. Augustine has, therefore, distinguished between positive law and moral right. Although we do not have a clerical definition of the state, worldly states can choose to do what is morally right. Because civil societies can be perverted by evil, self-regarding wills, an opposing state can decide to defend itself against such evil by justly going to war with those perceived as evil. It is a tragic necessity, but the lesser of two evils, to wage a just war, fighting the greater injustice of the opposing side. There is no pacifism recommended here. Defence is not condemned, merely the animus of revenge.

The city of God on earth is therefore not the visible Church. Rather, it is the invisible, non-cohesive communion of saints, the body of the elect who will be united only after history. The visible church's peace, unity and relative coherence lives only in *hope*, not in realisation. Eventually, the elect will include, among the 144,000 (Revelation 14:1–3), all men of all nations and of every age. In this life the Church cannot be pure and uncompromising; it is merely serving God as a human agent of divine sacraments. The visible Church must be a universal, world-wide polity opposed to exclusionist, particularist and nationalist tendencies.

It was this universalist language that inspired later ages to develop a doctrine of the Church as a perfect society with powers necessary to any self-sufficient community in the realm of property and governance. Although Augustine never quite said that there was no salvation outside the Church, he implied it in principle, and thereby inspired a theory that emerged in the medieval notion of a universal political Christianity exercised by rulers of the Church hierarchy. Augustine may have insisted that political, secular recognition of the Church was 'a thing indifferent', and he did not think civil and ecclesiastical authorities were two distinct co-ordinate powers occupied with governing, but his views were interpreted to imply a two-swords theory of world rule. He would later be used to justify the notion of a universal Catholic commonwealth with two heads, pope and emperor. Some have seen in his theory of the visible and in-visible Church the seeds for the later development of a doctrine which completely subjugates the state to the Church, but it is doubtful that this was Augustine's meaning. The state was not merely the secular arm of the Church, either in fifth-century conditions or in Augustine's thought. But the visible Church was an adviser of the civil governor, and this led easily to the concept of a religious tyranny and a theocratic state that controlled the law for spiritual ends.

With the increasing development of the vast ecclesiastical machinery of spiritual governance, and given the historical fact that the Church became to conquering barbarians the symbol and source of Roman culture and organisation, we can see already in the later fifth century how the conception of Church power as a *plenitudo potestatis*, a fullness of power, would develop into the ideology of a strong papacy in the high Middle Ages.

Augustine's influence in moulding the mind of the medieval west is immeasurable. His theological doctrines of grace and predestination, his radical understanding of history, his dis-cussion of the city of God and the city of men, were of immense significance, and he prepared the way for the *civitas dei* to be interpreted as the earthly Christian state. His other-worldly emphasis was somewhat underrated in the Middle Ages. Imperialist and papalist theories drew upon his writings to justify their social and political views. Whether they rightly interpreted him is another matter, as so often in the history of political thought. But Augustinianism was at the heart of the future revivals of theories of true governance and dominion founded on grace, both in the later Middle Ages and during the Reformation. That his mind and his experiences were fundamentally 'antique' was irrelevant to later ages. He said so much and so diffusely in *The City of God*, as in his sermons and other tracts, that he was mined as a source for all sides in the later controversies between Church and state. He gave us an encyclopaedia of his mind.

Scaling up his experiences to apply to world history in general, he never produced an organised system, and it is precisely his divergencies and his inconsistencies that have enabled different views to justify themselves under his name. However, his arguments that man needs to accept all governments as legitimate, that all revolt is inexcusable, that man is so essentially helpless and corrupt as a consequence of Adam's original sin, served as a legacy to political Christians. It led them not necessarily to pacifism, which Augustine rejected, but to a painful quietism of acceptance that evil conditions created by men perhaps ought not to be reversed because they were, after all, deserved. Furthermore, his personal asceticism and repulsion from sex, developed in his controversy with Pelagius and as a rejection of his own wayward earlier life, were turned into a generalised inheritance for the west. This further undermined men's optimism to act positively in creating a more humane polity. Augustine argued, as we have seen, that the entire race fell in Adam, and that the transmission of hereditary sinfulness is bound up in the reproductive process. He developed the Pauline notion that virginity was a higher state than marriage, and asserted that the sexual impluse could never be free of some element of concupiscence. His insistence on infant baptism in a fifth-century Christian world that was still practising adult baptism presupposed that all infants arrived polluted by sin, the fault existing already in their fallen natures. Babies who die unbaptised are damned. This was a correlate of his view that mankind was a lump of perdition, incapable of any act of pure good will without unmerited redeeming grace. It would be only strict justice if all mankind were consigned to hell.

The only element of hope in this picture is Augustine's faith in God's mercy in having chosen a minority of souls for salvation by an inscrutable decree of predestination prior to all acts and all merit. He pictured a man so corrupt as no longer possessing the free will to do any good: thereafter grace must do all. For Augustine it was empirically obvious that the man who persevered in consistent goodness throughout his life, did so through the operation of grace as a fore-ordained irresistible gift of God, a gift given independently of merit or works. This rigorous predestinarianism met vigorous reaction in his own time.

His model of man would be adopted and then rejected in turns as future conditions created possibilities to define men otherwise – as consenting self-governors in a world that would be seen as open to man's making. There is still operating in our world an Augustinian notion that freedom – by which we mean the power to choose the good and do it – is precisely what fallen man's nature is incapable of achieving. In this, our post-Enlightenment world, it is probably a minority view. Already in the Middle Ages Thomas Aquinas, with the help of Aristotle, would provide a more positive model of man which would enable Christians and others to endow man's use of reason with the powers to establish just polities rather than to accept the unjust.

St Thomas Aquinas:
the state and morality
Antony Black

After the collapse of the Roman empire in the west (AD 476), political power fell into the hands of local chiefs and nobles who offered 'protection' in exchange for fealty and service. By the eleventh century the empire had been restored under a German dynasty, and France and England were beginning to develop as nation states under powerful monarchies. By the time Aquinas was born in the early thirteenth century, Europe had become a dynamic and outward-looking society of feudal, civic and national states. Commerce was thriving and the Church was wealthy and influential.

Aquinas was born in 1224 or 1225 near Naples in Italy. In 1243 he joined the recently founded Dominican order and spent the next fifteen years studying and teaching in Paris and Cologne. From 1259 to 1269 he taught in Italy and acted as adviser to the papal court. His last years were spent at Paris and Naples completing his greatest work, *Summa Theologiae*. He is regarded as the classic exponent of medieval 'scholastic' (academic) thought, based on the dialectical method.

St Thomas Aquinas (1224/5–74) was one of the outstanding philosopher-theologians of the Middle Ages. The combination of rigorous and often profound intellectual analysis with impeccable orthodoxy led to the later adoption of Thomism, in many quarters, as the Catholic philosophy *par excellence*. Aquinas's major achievement as a political thinker was to gain acceptance in Europe, at a time when people thought about politics in religious and legal terms, for Aristotle's idea of man as 'by *nature* a political being'. At the same stroke, he gave Christian ideas on ethics and human destiny a central place in what was really a new theory of the state. It was probably thanks to Aquinas, more than to any other individual, that European politics became less dominated by religious dogma and legal traditionalism, yet retained, on the basis of God's universal fatherhood, the notion that all men have dignity and rights.

Aquinas's family belonged to the lower nobility of southern Italy. They intended him, as the youngest son, to enter the Church, earmarking the important abbacy of Monte Cassino for him. But he was determined to join the newly formed Dominican order of friar-preachers, impressed by their poverty and dedication, and, in fact, throughout his life he rejected all offers of ecclesiastical preferment. His brothers even kidnapped him and attempted to have him seduced, but he was not to be tempted.

Aquinas studied at Paris and Cologne under Albert the Great, and became professor of theology at Paris. Between 1259 and 1269, he lectured at Dominican colleges in Naples, Orvieto, Rome and Viterbo; he was befriended by Pope Urban IV and had close contact with the Curia, the Papal bureaucracy. He moved to Paris in 1269, and in 1272 back to Naples. In 1273 he suffered a breakdown, accompanied by a mystical experience. Pressed by his close friend to continue work, he replied, 'Reginald, I cannot, because all I have written seems like straw to me.' Aquinas devoted his life to study, writing (or dictating) and lecturing; his work schedule overwhelmed him. Stories abound of his taciturnity and wit. For a man who died at the age of forty-nine, his output was prodigious: his chief work alone, the encyclopaedic (and unfinished) *Summa Theologiae*, runs to sixty volumes in a modern Latin–English edition.

Scholastic theology was highly abstract but also concerned with the everyday application of Christian ethics. The dialectical method encouraged consideration of every question from two sides. Aquinas was familiar with the politics both of the rapidly-developing Italian city-states and of the feudal monarchies in northern Europe. His political ideas are contained in the *Summa Theologiae* (1266–73), a handbook called *The Rule of Princes* (1265–67), and his commentaries on Aristotle's *Ethics* (1271) and *Politics* (1269–72, unfinished).

In the thirteenth century, governments were faced with a more complex society in which population was growing fast, commerce and manufacture were expanding, and towns were developing. The religious ferment of the late eleventh century Investiture Controversy, when the popes with some success challenged the secular rulers' right to appoint bishops and so gave the church greater independence, had resulted in a dynamic papacy and revitalisation of religious life. Churches became wealthy and churchmen held high posts in government. The empire was weakened, but national kings were expanding their power and

St Thomas Aquinas (1224/5–74)

cities like Venice and Florence developed republican constitutions. In the twelfth and thirteenth centuries, numerous previously unknown works by Aristotle on logic, philosophy and science percolated into Europe via Moslem Spain and were translated into Latin. These contained clearly superior scientific knowledge and philosophical analysis but diverged from Christian belief on matters such as the Creation and the immortality of the individual soul. There was an intellectual crisis comparable to that produced by Darwin in the nineteenth century. Some wished to ban Aristotle, others accepted his ideas wholesale. Aquinas sought to achieve a synthesis between pagan philosophy and Christianity. Faced with Aristotle's pre-Christian ideas about God, the universe and man, Aquinas insisted that a good pagan could grasp much of the truth, and tried wherever possible to show that Aristotle's opinions did not conflict with those of Scripture. He also felt that he and his generation had much to learn from Aristotle.

In Aquinas' view, man's original nature, his physical and mental abilities, were vitiated but not destroyed by the Fall; the 'new being' offered by Christ involves a partial restoration of man's original status as well as a new life of divine grace. 'Grace does not take away nature but perfects it.' Man's essential quality is reason, which differentiates him from other animals. In spite of the fall, all men retain the use of reason, so that, though prone to error, they are capable of knowing the truth and practising virtue. Many pagans practised the 'natural virtues' of justice, courage, temperance and prudence; Christians must attend to these as well as the 'new law' of love towards God and neighbour. Aquinas here extended Aristotle's vision by saying that all men, not just 'Greeks', possess reason, at the same time interpreting the Judaeo–Christian doctrine of man made in God's image to mean that all men are rational. Although he followed Aristotle in accepting slavery, he did not see slaves, as Aristotle did, as lacking truly human qualities. 'The light of natural reason . . . [is] the impression of the divine light upon us . . . by which we discern good and evil'; 'the light of reason is implanted by nature in every man, by which he is guided in his actions to his goal'.

All this was a great change from Augustine, who saw non-Christians as incapable of true wisdom or virtue; it was Aquinas's contribution to the humanist revolution in thought. This much more optimistic view of human nature affected Catholic attitudes to non-Christians, and European attitudes to the common man.

A distinctive feature of Aquinas's God-centred notion of man is the way he internalised the divine spark of reason; man is called to co-operate with God through his own understanding and will. Faith and reason are inward guides by which autonomous, responsible individuals make their own decisions in the manifold situations they face. Man is not, as much earlier theology implied, a soul temporarily inhabiting a body, but a 'composite whole' in which the soul vivifies the body. Soul and body are inseparable and interdependent. Man has two goals – earthly and heavenly felicity – and earthly happiness requires a suitable material environment. Whereas other animals are provided by nature with the equipment they need for survival, man has 'reason and hands' by which he must make his own tools, clothing and so on. He has to exercise effort (*industria*) and skill (*ars*). Finally, man is 'by nature a social and political being'. Aquinas added to the Stoic–Christian notion of man's natural sociability the Aristotelian idea that man's natural fulfilment lies in the state (*civitas, polis*). This is because society itself requires some form of directive authority; and, while family and village enable man to 'live', the state alone enables him to 'live well'. Coercive power provides security, the division of labour provides material comfort; political society is the milieu for mental and moral development.

Aquinas thus established that, contrary to Augustine's view, political authority is not solely a corrective for sin or a consequence of man's 'lust for power', but is natural to man and would have existed in the pre-fall 'state of innocence'. Here he used Aristotle's distinction between the authority of master over slaves and of ruler over free subjects. The ruler, unlike the master, directs subjects to their own proper good. Such consensual authority is appropriate and necessary both for natural man in his perfect state and for the redeemed sons of God. Political societies are the creation of men acting out their God-given nature; they require both rational calculation and the communion of friendship. Thus pagans can have legitimate states, and Christians are by nature members of a polity as well as members of the Church by grace.

Here, however, Aquinas adapted Aristotle to contemporary European conditions. In Aristotle the state (*polis*) meant specifically the Greek city-state; in Aquinas it means rather, political association in general ('state' in our sense), large or small, feudal monarchy as well as (and perhaps more typically than) city-state. He thus lost Aristotle's notion of a specific and rather intimate cultural milieu in which participation in collective provision for the common good promotes the development of human virtue. For Aquinas, moral teaching and spiritual formation are the Church's province.

Aquinas examined political justice and obligation in the context of a detailed analysis of law. He defined law in general as the rational regulation of action through public proclamation, by a people or its representative, for the purpose of achieving human felicity. God regulates the universe through 'eternal law', which is 'impressed' on all beings and 'inclines' them to fulfil their proper destiny. A rational creature like man, however, 'is subject to divine providence in a more excellent way, in that he shares in providence itself, providing for himself and others'. Some goals, such as self-preservation, man shares with all substances and pursues automatically. Others, such as procreation and rearing of young, he shares with animals; these he pursues instinctively. Yet other goals are properly human, such as 'to know the truth about God and to live in society'; here the pursuit of natural inclination requires mental and moral effort.

This 'participation in the eternal law by a rational creature' is *natural law*. Natural law tells man both what he ought to do and how to attain happiness; for right action leads to happiness. 'All things, towards which man has a natural inclination, reason perceives as good ... and their opposite as bad.' It is a law of development: it tells us how to achieve human felicity for both individual and society. By combining this idea of natural law with the idea of man as 'by nature a social and political being', Aquinas retained some connection between the state and man's moral life. Family and state are natural to man both because they serve his basic needs and because they provide the material and moral environment in which he can achieve virtue and happiness. This 'natural-law theory of the state' dominated European philosophy and jurisprudence until the eighteenth century.

All men can know right and wrong through 'practical reason', and the basic principles of natural law are 'self-evident (*per se nota*)'. They are to avoid ignorance, not to offend those with whom one must associate and to harm no one. These principles are common to all men, and are always to be followed; but the way in which they are applied, 'the proper conclusions of practical reason', are not known to all and are not immutable. Some peoples do not know that brigandage is wrong. A 'proper conclusion' from the principle 'act according to reason' is that debts should be repaid; but one should not repay someone preparing war against one's own country. Circumstances are crucial in moral reasoning.

This is akin to the biblical concept of a law 'written on men's hearts'. It is not legalistic nor indeed moralistic. Its more precise formulations, such as 'thou shalt not kill. . . . thou shalt not steal', while generally binding, have to be understood according to circumstances and sometimes modified: war and execution of criminals can be justifiable; the starving man can rightly take what he needs from the wealthy. This is the difference between Aquinas and Kant: the sanctity of oaths and of political allegiance, which posed *in extremis* such a problem for the German generals under Hitler, would not have worried a Thomist. 'Good morals meant human activity keyed to true happiness, discovered by experiment, reflection and inference, not by an unearthly intuition of right for right's sake.'

Aquinas's theory of natural law rests upon his notion of God's relationship with creation: the idea of a moral law implanted in man by nature would be difficult to justify otherwise. Wider knowledge of human societies and theories like Darwinism have done much to discredit it. On the other hand, natural law had the advantage of basing morality on humanity: it tells us how we should behave towards *all* men, and thus (if taken seriously) makes one reject exclusive nationalism and cultural chauvinism. It provided a link between Christian and pagan; sixteenth-century Thomists used it to condemn the slaughter and enslavement of American Indians. Similarly, the later doctrine of natural or human rights prescribed how men in general, not just Christians or Europeans, should be treated. Phenomena like Nazism have indeed led to a partial revival of natural-law theory in our own times.

Natural law provided the standard by which all human, man-made laws are to be measured. It is woven into Aquinas's concept of the state's legislative and judicial authority, giving a guide to both rulers and subjects. The purpose of statutory and customary law is to restrain by fear and coercion those who are prone to vice; it is an enforced learning (*disciplina*). Human law is a series of still more detailed specifications as to how the general tenets of natural morality are to be applied by particular peoples in particular territories. Murder must be punished, but what form this punishment takes is a matter for the legislator to decide. To qualify as law at all, human law must be just, that is in accordance with reason and natural law and aimed at the common good. This is what makes a law valid and gives one a moral obligation to obey it. An unjust command is not just a bad law, it is not even law. Enactments contrary to the common good – for instance, those which impose 'burdens' (such as taxes) for the sake of the ruler's 'cupidity or glory', or distribute them unfairly – are 'acts of violence rather than laws'. This theory, which also lay behind the American Declaration of Independence, makes civil disobedience easier to justify than does modern positivism, which defines law simply as the formal command of a recognised sovereign.

Aquinas, however, also recognised the difference between law and morality, crime and sin. For law 'does not enjoin every act of virtue, but only those acts which serve the common good'. Human law does not punish all vices, but only those graver ones 'from which it is possible for the greater part of society to abstain, and especially those vices which are harmful to others'. In trying to prevent all that is evil, human law would render impossible also much that is good. This implicit distinction between other-regarding and self-regarding acts would have been appreciated by J S Mill.

The 'common good' meant the welfare of the whole community as opposed to the sectional advantage of ruler or group; Aquinas would probably have endorsed the principle that, in calculating the common interest, each individual must count as one. 'Common good' included defence and 'material affluence'. Finally, it meant the promotion of virtuous living. In both the material and the moral spheres, the ruler must be concerned with *improvement*. All this amounted to a considerable expansion of current teaching on the scope of government, which was confined to defence and prevention of injustice. Aquinas also used 'common good' to justify extraordinary taxation. Here he accurately reflected the city-states' conception of their political functions, which included economic regulation and social welfare.

Aquinas adopted Aristotle's view that the ultimate purpose of political association is not material welfare but the virtuous life. The state must help subjects achieve their own virtue. But, unlike Aristotle, he says nothing about the state's role in education; he appears to have modified Aristotle so as to leave the Church as the institutional source of moral instruction. Laws are to make subjects virtuous, and the ruler's function is to promote the good life; but what the good life consists in he learns from priests, and he must promote earthly felicity 'in such a way that it leads fittingly to the happiness of heaven'. As a Christian, Aquinas could never allow the state to become the all-embracing association it was for Aristotle, nor could he allow it to be the source or primary custodian of moral values.

The relation between Church and state – between the papacy or clergy and secular governments – was the most hotly debated political issue in Aquinas's day, and he had surprisingly little to say about it. As used by others, his theory of the state soon gave secular rulers more convincing arguments in support of their independence from clerical intervention in 'temporal' affairs. But his own treatment of the topic was evasive. Having explained 'render unto Caesar . . .' as meaning that spiritual authorities should be obeyed in matters of salvation, and temporal authorities in matters of civil welfare, he added that the pope occupies 'the pinnacle of spiritual and secular power'.

On the relation between individual and state (more crucial, certainly, to us than to him), Aquinas also contradicted himself. He 'spoke in two parts, as a theologian for the supremacy of the person, as a social philosopher for the supremacy of the community'. The citizen is a 'part' of the community, and depends upon it for his welfare, so that his claims, interests and goods must be subordinated to the requirements of 'the common good'. On the other hand, 'rational beings are not made for anyone's utility'; each person is an end in himself. 'Man's whole being and everything he has are not orientated solely towards the political community. . . . The whole man is orientated solely towards God.' Perhaps the very rivalry between Church and state did something to protect Europe from totalitarianism.

Neither Aquinas nor his medieval successors showed any real interest in Aristotle's scientific method for comparing and classifying states, nor did they investigate political functions or social behaviour empirically. His sole concern was with right order: which constitutions are legitimate, and among these which is best? Aquinas employed different criteria side by side. On the one hand, following Aristotle, he said that, provided it aimed at the common good, any of the main forms of government (rule by one, the few or the many) is just. More tersely, legislative power belongs either to the whole people or to a 'public person' acting on their behalf. This itself marked an important change in attitude; previously, monarchy had been generally regarded as the only legitimate form.

Aquinas followed conventional wisdom in saying that the *best* constitution is a mixture of the three good forms. His supporting argument is interesting. Although kingship and aristocracy are 'the principal forms of government', it is desirable that 'all have some share in sovereignty' because then all will 'love and guard the constitution', and the people will be at peace. The popular element consists in princes being chosen by the people and from the people; this was the constitution 'established by divine law' for the Old Testament Jews. There is thus a blend of dogmatic and prudential reasoning: elections are sanctioned by scripture, popular participation produces stable government. However, there was a further reason why Aquinas advocated an element of democracy: for elsewhere he said that 'every man in so far as he is rational, participates somehow in government according to the judgement of his reason'. Nevertheless, the prudence of the prince, he went on, differs in kind from that of the subjects: he is the architect, they are the masons, intelligently carrying out the design they are given.

In *The Rule of Princes*, however, Aquinas argued that monarchy is best: here again he combined argument from experience, that monarchy is most effective in securing law and order, with the dogmatic argument that one king mirrors one God in the universe. One might reconcile these passages by regarding his mixed government, as, in effect, elective monarchy with a consultative parliament. However, Aquinas's constitutional views appear to have been developed rather haphazardly, and he may be accused of contradicting himself. He was acquainted with Louis IX, the saintly and effective King of France, and probably approved of centralisation in the interests of fairer and more efficient administration. The good king submits himself voluntarily to the laws.

One of Aquinas's most notable contributions to political thought concerned the limits of civil obligation. Germanic tradition and the feudal contract enabled barons to resist and depose any 'unjust' king, but the New Testament appeared to teach non-resistance. The Middle Ages were not notable for political quietude; revolution was endemic in Italian cities, and the papacy had sanctioned and encouraged rebellion against the emperor. The prevailing chaos made writers emphasise order and authority.

Aquinas accepted that 'the prince is released from the laws', thus implicitly following Roman–imperial absolutism against Germanic constitutionalism. Peace is the first aim of government: we have seen how he elevated the state and expanded its scope. Against this, God is to be obeyed rather than man, and divine and natural law override any contrary human command. Aquinas concluded that the scriptural injunction to obey the authorities applies only so long as they are just. Power does not come 'from God' if it is acquired by violence or corruption (*simonia*). In such cases, unless they have subsequently been legitimised by popular consent or superior authority, rulers may be overthrown: indeed, 'he who kills a tyrant to liberate his country is praised'. Later, however, Aquinas modified this. Rebellion leads to factionalism; a private right to depose or kill a tyrant would lead to the murder of many good kings. Therefore, he now argued, action may be taken only by public authority – that is, by the community or its superior, whichever appointed the ruler in the first place.

Although private individuals may not depose a ruler, their obligation to obey him in specific instances is conditional upon the justice of his commands. One is not bound to obey a ruler acting *ultra vires*; and, if one is commanded to commit sin, one is 'not only not obliged to obey, but obliged not to obey'. It was for these doctrines that Acton, a nineteenth-century proponent of Christian liberal ethics, called Aquinas 'the first Whig'.

One of the characteristics of Aquinas's political thought was the formulation of middle-range principles. He was rather weak on detail, but he knew how to combine principle with flexibility. For him expediency and results play a more prominent part in political calculation than for his predecessors. Governments, laws and policies are measured in accordance with their purpose, the good life. For example, war is justified if it is waged on the authority of the sovereign, for a 'just cause', and with the 'right intention' of preventing injustice. Such formulas are vague, but they reflect Aquinas's conception of practical reason and 'political prudence'. Rulers and subjects *have* to use their own judgement in each situation; that is what it is like to engage in morality and politics. This was the common ground between the anti-legalism of the gospels and Aristotle's situational ethics.

Aquinas's theory of natural and human law may be seen as an attempt to capture the degree of secularisation initiated by the Gregorian reform movement two centuries earlier, when the papacy went a long way towards desacralising politics. The genius of medieval Catholicism was to redraw the line between the sacred and the profane. Biblical teaching on God and man, and the Church's hierarchical structure remain inviolable; but mundane affairs can otherwise be dealt with rationally, as circumstances permit. Governments and social structures are neither sacred nor immutable. For the Germanic peoples, the 'good, old law' had a sacred quality and was deemed immutable and just, but Europe was experiencing rapid economic and social development. Here Aquinas's political theory filled a need by making rational adaptation to circumstances morally and intellectually respectable. It offered an appropriate ideological basis both for legislative innovation and for the expansion of government. It provided rational criteria for the evaluation and improvement of laws and institutions.

Aquinas's theory of the state put European political thought on a new plane. It legitimised the autonomy of secular rulers and a prudent rationality in decision-making. It influenced an increasing number of thinkers from the fourteenth century onwards. Thomism was revived in sixteenth-century Spain and again (among Roman Catholics) in nineteenth- and twentieth-century Europe and America. Its merits and its modernity have sometimes been exaggerated. However, the theory of natural law, of which Aquinas was one of the most influential exponents, helped lay a foundation for the theory of international law in Suárez and Grotius. John Locke owed much to the Thomist theory of authority as based upon, and delimited by, natural law and the common good. The marriage of the classical civic polity to the Stoic–Christian ideal of universal human dignity was of profound importance for the development of the modern state, of democracy and the rule of law. It is for his underlying perception of what the state and politics are about that Aquinas deserves to be read today. Men need states; but states serve men, each of whom carries within him the spark of divinity. The state promotes morality; but the morality it promotes is not of its own making. Such was the message of Christian Aristotelianism.

Niccolò Machiavelli: the anatomy of political and military decadence

Sydney Anglo

Niccolò Machiavelli (1469–1527) lived during a period of constant European war and territorial fragmentation dominated by rulers bent on aggrandisement. In England, Henry VII and his son, Henry VIII, held sway. France, especially under the bellicose Francis I, assumed European significance, and Habsburg power in Spain, the Low Countries and Germany was personified in the Emperor Charles V. Born in Florence during its Republican period, Machiavelli was employed as a diplomat on various missions abroad and was also involved in the organisation of a national defence militia. When the republic fell in 1512 and the Medici family returned to power, he was deprived of office and thereafter devoted his life to political analysis, military theory and the study of history. He slowly won acceptance with the Medici, but when their regime suddenly collapsed and a republic was re-established, Machiavelli was passed over and died soon afterwards. He has been variously assessed – as malodorous amoralist; inspired founder of modern political science; monster of iniquity; and prophet of Italian unity. This ceaseless debate and the unfailing magnetism of his writing together constitute his principal achievement.

In the summer of 1498, Niccolò Machiavelli was appointed to a post in the Florentine civil service, Chancellor to the Second Chancery, with special responsibility to the committee which dealt with military and foreign affairs. He was just twenty-nine years old, from a modest but well connected family, and he had received something of the classical education then regarded as essential both for thinkers and for men of affairs. How far a knowledge of Latin literature furthered his career is impossible to determine: but it certainly enabled him to come to terms, both emotionally and intellectually, with the political turmoil into which he was plunged – with a hapless Italy serving as battle-ground for the European nation-states.

Four years previously, the French King, Charles VIII, had invaded Italy in pursuit of his claim to the kingdom of Naples, and this had, in the words of Machiavelli's young contemporary, Francesco Guicciardini, 'opened the door to innumerable and horrible calamities'. The bubble of Italian self-esteem had burst. Generations of Italians had deemed themselves politically, militarily and culturally superior to the 'barbarians' of northern Europe. Now the trembling balance between the Papacy, Naples, Venice, Milan and Florence – so long maintained by subtle diplomatic manoeuvring, and by wars in which citizens stayed at home while their mercenary armies elaborately postured in the field or at siege – was destroyed in a moment. Everything was turned upside down as if by a storm, for the French were followed into Italy by Spanish and Imperial armies and, worst of all, by the dreaded Swiss and German infantry who introduced a degree of military frightfulness and dedication to slaughter which terrified their unwilling hosts.

The city of Florence had always regarded itself as a republic, and its propagandists used the word 'liberty' as if it were their special prerogative: though, in fact, Florentine liberty had never extended very far down the social scale, nor was it very readily offered to those whom the city had been able to subjugate. Moreover, for most of the fifteenth century, Florence had been an oligarchy dominated by the interests of one banking family, the Medici. When the political whirlwind of 1494 drove the Medici into exile, their comparatively benevolent rule was replaced by the fanatical theocracy of Savonarola, which endured until that religious firebrand and book-burner was himself publicly incinerated in 1498. It was to the resulting administrative re-shuffle that Machiavelli owed his appointment.

The very name of Florence is synonymous with many of the greatest artistic and literary achievements of the Renaissance; and politically it had been one of the foremost Italian states. Now the ugly realities of power politics exposed its weakness. Machiavelli found himself scurrying about on diplomatic missions on behalf of a weak and vacillating republic whose grandiose pretensions were treated with unconcealed disdain not only by its avowed enemies but also by the French whose cause Florence had, unhappily, been constrained to espouse. It was a humiliating experience: but it was also the most rigorous possible political education.

Machiavelli visited France on four occasions between 1500 and 1511, and had to endure insults, neglect and hearing the Florentines dismissed as 'Signor Nothing'. He was present at Cesena when the drastic Cesare Borgia rewarded his lieutenant,

Niccolò Machiavelli (1469–1527)

Ramírez de Lorqua, by having him cut into two pieces and displayed in the town square; and he was likewise present at Sinigaglia when Cesare reconciled himself with his disloyal captains by the simple expedient of having them strangled. Cesare's implacable energy remained a lifelong memory; but Machiavelli was also present at Rome with the belligerent Pope Julius II to witness Borgia's own degradation. Machiavelli negotiated with several petty Italian tyrants and mercenary captains and learned, at first hand, the extent of their brutality and treachery. He even visited the Holy Roman Emperor, Maximilian, in Germany, and acquired a lasting contempt for the Emperor's irresolution together with an exaggerated respect for the liberties, public spirit and martial prowess of the German cities.

Throughout his diplomatic career Machiavelli – who was not of sufficient social status to be appointed by the republic as a full ambassador – was plagued by poor pay, poor bargaining power and poor briefing. Messages so long hidden in a courier's boot, or in a damp loaf of bread, that they proved indecipherable were scarcely less typical of the ineptitude and deviousness characterising Florentine diplomacy than were the contradictory and indecisive missives which, though legible, left unfortunate legates such as Machiavelli in a hopeless position.

A second significant aspect of Machiavelli's work was his ever-growing concern with military affairs. Florence's persistent failure to reduce the little town of Pisa had become a scandal, and – though the craven republic was terrified that a national army might pave the way for dictatorship – the time was ripe for military experiment. Machiavelli was empowered to produce a small-scale model militia; and, by the end of 1506, he was able to report favourably in his *Discourse on Florentine Military Preparation*. A new magistracy, the Nine of the Militia, was created; and in January 1507 Machiavelli was appointed its Chancellor. He toiled with boundless zest; his troops performed wonders on the parade ground; and, coincidentally, in June 1509, Pisa finally succumbed – through blockade not battle. Machiavelli was asked to organise some experimental cavalry units to complement the infantry, and he was also entrusted with other military responsibilities, including the inspection of fortifications. He had become something of a military specialist, and his public career was at its zenith.

Events, unfortunately, rapidly overtook him. The fortunes of France, to which Florence was inextricably linked, declined miserably, and, in the summer of 1512, the republic was abandoned to the mercies of a Spanish army. The vaunted militia turned tail; the republican leader, Soderini, fled; the Medici returned; republican institutions were abolished; and by November Machiavelli was out of a job and banished from the city. Worse was to follow. He was wrongly thought to be implicated in an anti-Medici plot, and, though released after torture, he remained under suspicion. Seven years passed before he was trusted with even a trifling transaction; and it was not until May 1526 that he was again eligible for public office and was elected Chancellor to a new magistracy dealing with the city's fortifications. Any pleasure which Machiavelli may have derived from that congenial task was short-lived for, precisely one year later, the Medici administration collapsed. A republic was re-established, and Machiavelli, who had spent nearly fifteen years ingratiating himself with the tyrants he abhorred, was again out of office. In the subsequent re-shuffle, he was ignored. This last disappointment was, however, of little moment, for Machiavelli was mortally sick and died on 21 June 1527.

For Machiavelli, who was prepared to do anything to gain employment – even if, as he wrote, the Medici began by making him 'roll a stone' – the years of rejection were almost the worst fate that could have befallen him. Yet it is to his dismissal from office, his exile and his leisure that we owe the books on which his fame rests. During his period as a bureaucrat, his writings, apart from some minor literary works, consisted of diplomatic correspondence, often prepared in conjunction with senior colleagues, and miscellaneous military and political reports. These papers, full of passages later incorporated into his books, and especially revealing of the author's analytical temper, are of considerable value to the student. None the less, were they the sum total of Machiavelli's literary legacy, his name would now be forgotten by all but a few professional scholars. Compulsory retirement enabled Machiavelli to ponder, bitterly, the catastrophes which had befallen Italy in general and Florence in particular; to rehearse past diplomatic lessons; to recall men of action; to analyse the efficacy of the various armies he had observed; and to conduct a *post mortem* on his own ill-fated militia.

The results of these deliberations were embodied in four major works. *The Prince*, written about 1513, was designed to show the 'new' prince of the Medici how to gain, hold and increase political power. The *Discourses*, written between 1513 and 1519, examined Rome's political and military institutions on the basis of Livy's account of Roman history. The *Art of War*, written about 1519/1520, reviewed military techniques; and the *Florentine History*, written between 1520 and 1527, set the history of the republic – up to the death of Lorenzo the Magnificent in 1492 – within a broad Italian context.

Machiavelli's continuing appeal to readers arises from a series of all-pervasive and unresolved tensions in his work. His style is paradoxical, provocative and heavily disjunctive. States are either republics or princedoms; they are either accustomed to live under a prince or they are used to being free. Princes have to choose between love or fear, clemency or cruelty, liberality or meanness. Soldiers in battle have either to conquer or die.

Subject peoples have either to be treated well or crushed. Extreme measures may be either well or ill used. Memorable phrases and brilliant aphorisms abound. An air of precision is constantly created. Judgements always seem firm and final. Yet the detail of Machiavelli's meaning often remains obscure. He uses the same historical examples to assert contradictory positions. He employs a limited number of key words to convey more meanings than they can comfortably carry. He is, for all the rigour and vigour of his magnificent prose, difficult to pin down; and debate concerning his intentions has continued to the present day.

His ideas are a tissue of contradictions. He despaired of modern Italians and their rulers; yet he hoped for national regeneration under a Messianic leader. He despised the dilatoriness and debility of the Florentine republic; and he struggled to gain recognition from the nepotistic Medici. Yet he retained his republican idealism, and even suggested to the governing family that, once they had established good order, they should educate their citizens for republican rule, create free institutions and then voluntarily relinquish the reins of power.

Machiavelli's fundamental contrariety resides in his view of human nature. His work teems with dismal pronouncements on his fellow men. They are fickle, selfish and evil. They do good only under constraint. They are both deceitful and easily deceived. They are envious, more prone to evil than to good, inefficient, discontented and ambitious. Human nature is an unstable amalgam of stupidity, cupidity and malice. And the rulers are no better than the ruled. Yet, despite this profound pessimism, Machiavelli clings to a belief that princes and their subjects are redeemable. It is, he feels, possible both to devise and to teach rules for effective political behaviour; to persuade men to eschew wickedness; to inspire them to selflessness; and to awaken in them a civic spirit. This is why he bothers to write at all.

Parallel to this ambivalence concerning human nature was Machiavelli's assessment of men's capacity actively to influence the course of their own destiny. Two sets of polarities recur throughout his writings, and, although they are never defined, their meaning becomes clear from their frequent reiteration in a wide variety of contexts. The first set, *fortuna* and *virtù*, relates to whether affairs are completely dominated by chance or whether they may be affected by human skill and effort. The seemingly inexorable despotism of *fortuna* renders Machiavelli pessimistic, for men often appear nothing better than helpless victims of circumstance. On the other hand, he can discern in individual men a quality which he calls *virtù*. This is certainly not merely moral virtue, though it frequently connotes public spirit, selfless service and good citizenship. Usually it is a complex endowment comprising skill, courage, decisiveness, adaptability and ruthlessness. It is, above all, the ability and resolution to pursue whatever course of action is expedient to achieve precise political objectives. Thus, while mankind in general remains subject to the whims of *fortuna*, it is possible for some men, at least, to control a part of their fate.

The other polarity – equally important to Machiavelli – is that between *virtù* (now conceived as a corporate rather than a personal quality) and corruption. These stand at opposite extremes of the historical process, for states, like men, have a life-cycle: birth, growth, maturity, decay and death. Responding to the challenge of disorder, a young state becomes warlike and full of *virtù*. *Virtù* brings tranquillity; tranquillity, laziness; laziness, disorder; and disorder, corruption and ruin. Theoretically the whole process could begin anew – ruin leading to order; order to *virtù*; and thence on to glory and good fortune – but, unfortunately, states in decline invariably fall prey to others in the ascendant.

Empires rise and fall. *Virtù* is both cause and effect of their success. Corruption is both cause and effect of their downfall; and its symptoms are multiform. Lack of unity; irreligion and bad faith; the advancement of evil men and the rejection of good; lasciviousness and debauchery; avarice and a desire for empty honours; incessant quarrels and factions; and the pursuit of party interest at the expense of the common weal – these are the visible marks of political decadence. Corruption is manifest where the laws are made not for public but for private advantage; where war, peace and alliances are decided upon not for common glory but for the satisfaction of a minority; and, most flagrantly, where prince and populace alike have lost the will and the ability to defend themselves against their enemies. This, in Machiavelli's view, was (with the exception of Switzerland and Germany) the current state of Europe; and, floundering at the bottom of the heap, was Italy where corruption was complete. The Italian princes lacked personal *virtù*. The Italian cities were devoid of civic *virtù*. They were, accordingly, mere playthings of the cruel goddess, *Fortuna*.

Machiavelli's concern, as a political thinker, was to document this corruption; to explain it; and to establish whether or not it could be remedied. He pursued a comparative method throughout his works; studying past and present behaviour on the basis of his reading of ancient histories and his own practical experience of affairs. This procedure, he believed, would yield positive results because human behaviour has remained the same throughout history. Since men have always entertained identical desires and passions, the analysis of parallel problems would reveal previously successful solutions, lay bare the reasons for failure, and indicate the most effective political practice for present circumstances. The unrivalled thesaurus of political wisdom was, for Machiavelli, the history of the Roman republic; while the brimming cesspit of ineptitude was modern Italy and, especially, his own, unhappy but beloved city of Florence.

What did Machiavelli discover in this confrontation of ancient excellence and modern degradation? First, and last: corruption cannot for ever be held at bay. Even Rome degenerated from republican *virtù*, by way of imperial corruption, to ultimate ruin and disintegration. Nevertheless, Machiavelli also discovered that the decaying process in Rome had been considerably retarded by the regular rejuvenation of political institutions; strict religious observance; ruthless punishment of malefactors; rewards and honours for good citizens; and the inculcation of civic consciousness and disciplined obedience to the laws. Here his findings seemed congruent with his own experience – or, rather, his preconceptions. Good laws arose from, and were dependent upon, good military institutions. Without good arms there could be no good laws. And good arms could be established only through the militia system: an army of citizens regularly training in time of peace so that they were always ready for war; an army of men prepared to fight and die for their friends, family, countrymen and fatherland. Dependence on hired thugs, whose sole concern was personal safety and profit, had been the curse of Italy. Mercenaries were the very source of Italian cowardice and feebleness; and their role in Machiavelli's great historical drama was one of unmitigated villainy.

Cool reason and fiery emotion; concise style and imprecise vocabulary; clear ideals and confused arguments: Machiavelli's writing is richly ambiguous. Yet each of his works forms part of a coherent historical and political enquiry; and all are so closely interrelated that they cannot be appreciated other than as an entity.

The *Discourses* isolate the factors underlying the long-continued success of Roman institutions, and suggest remedies for corruption, derived from the contrast between Roman fore-sight and modern folly. The ideal solutions are, of course, republican: but Machiavelli does raise the problems posed by extreme corruption, and concludes that in such circumstances an 'almost royal hand' is required. Only the *virtù* of one great man can re-establish order; and only the most violent measures will suffice. These Machiavelli had already dealt with in *The Prince*, which was concerned exclusively with conditions of total corruption – that is, with an Italy ruled by the inept princes of his own day, and shamed by barbarian invaders. The answer to these problems had been dire. Only a ruthless prince, prepared to violate all ethical norms, could possibly succeed. *Fortuna* had to be overcome by this leader's *virtù*, which is here equated primarily with military expertise, the rejection of the mercenary system and the training of native troops. This prince can triumph only if his energies are devoted to war. Nothing less can unite Italy. Nothing else can expel the foreigners.

Precisely what does constitute ideal military practice is the subject of the *Art of War*, which is thus the central text among Machiavelli's political works. Here, expanding the military discussion of his previous two books, Machiavelli constructs a model army based upon his interpretation of Roman institutions, slightly revised to take some account of recent technology, but with undimmed enthusiasm for ancient *virtù* and unrelieved contempt for modern corruption. Moreover, although his emphasis is necessarily upon martial techniques – recruitment, armament, organisation, movement, battle and encampment – Machiavelli's ultimate and explicitly declared aims are once again the inculcation of good citizenship through military discipline; the affirmation that good laws are established and maintained by good arms; and a closing appeal, echoing the patriotic fervour of *The Prince*, that the rulers of Italy heed his advice and thereby liberate their oppressed native land.

There is, however, no such rousing call to arms in the *Florentine History*. This constitutes Machiavelli's last and most elaborate account of the process of Italian corruption in which decadent political institutions had followed hard upon the loss of martial prowess and a disastrous dependence, throughout the fifteenth century, on mercenary armies. Here Machiavelli provides the historical bases for many of the purely theoretical assumptions of his previous books; and once again Roman *virtù* is the measure of modern misery. The only marked difference between this and Machiavelli's earlier writings is an increased sense of the author's despair. The *Art of War* had been published in 1521; but Italy remained indifferent both to its plans for regeneration and its doom-laden warnings.

The *Art of War* was the only major book by Machiavelli to appear in his lifetime. The rest of his works were first published in 1531–1532; and from that time onward they have circulated both in their original Italian and in vernacular and Latin translations. They have always been readily available, widely read and greatly admired; yet Machiavelli's reputation has rested upon a very small fragment of his writings. To some extent he was himself to blame for this. He loved to challenge his readers; to shock them into re-examining conventional attitudes; to stimulate them with his arresting, aphoristic prose; and, in particular, he provoked debate in two sensitive areas.

In *The Prince*, he not only declared that, since his intention was to write something useful, he would avoid the conventional wisdom which enjoined moral virtues upon princes; he did, in fact, stand tradition on its head. For centuries, thinkers had exhorted rulers to be liberal and merciful, to be loved by their subjects and to keep their word. This would be very laudable, admitted Machiavelli, were the world virtuous. But it is not, and a prince could only survive by meanness and cruelty, by inspiring fear, and by keeping his promises just so long as it was advantageous for him to do so – and no longer. This was how the rulers of the world did behave. If they did not, they would soon be destroyed. Machiavelli, therefore, deliberately divorced political morality from Christian ethics – specifically in the case of a new prince striving to preserve his state intact amid the seething corruption of early sixteenth-century Italy. However, Machiavelli's precise context was quickly forgotten, and those chapters of *The Prince* in which he sets forth this topsy-turvy morality have been treated autonomously – as though they themselves advocated the autonomy of political behaviour in all circumstances.

The second area of provocation occurs in the *Discourses*, where Machiavelli offers a dispassionate assessment of religious faith as a valuable political tool; bitterly blamed the Papacy for Italian disunity and moral turpitude; and compared Christian elevation of the meek, weak and humble unfavourably with pagan regard for men of *virtù*. For Machiavelli, a pusillanimous religion was politically useless. Arguments such as these raised unavoidable difficulties. Was it morally justified for rulers to preserve traditional probities and thereby jeopardise the safety and well-being of their subjects? What is the role of religion in society, and what is its relationship with secular authority?

From the beginning, the innate tensions of Machiavelli's work elicited widely diverse reactions. There have always been attentive readers who have praised his political acumen and powerful style. Equally, hostility has always been stirred by questions of morality and religion. Such hostility has generally been less cognisant of Machiavelli's work as a whole, proportionately more shrill and insistent, and undeservedly better known than more favourable comment. The mould was cast long before the close of the sixteenth century. In spite of the popularity of his books – perhaps because of it – Machiavelli was among those authors whose work was condemned *in toto* in the papal Indexes of Prohibited Books in 1557 and 1559. Then Protestant hostility was violently stirred in the pamphlet war following the massacre of Huguenots on St Bartholomew's Day, 1572. Ill-considered Catholic polemic exulted over the destruction of the heretics, and the main response came from a Huguenot lawyer, Innocent Gentillet, who defended French chivalric values against foreign contamination. Among foreigners, the Italians were most execrated; among Italians, the Florentines; among Florentines, the Queen Mother, Catherine de' Medici and her advisers; and among the advisers, the long-dead but still dangerous Machiavelli, whose writings had furnished the theoretical justification for the perfidious massacre. To prove this thesis, Gentillet set forth Machiavelli's doctrines in a number of 'tyrannical' maxims, reducing the complexity of the original to a series of simple, immoral propositions. The *Machiavel* stereotype had emerged.

The Florentine's name became a label for anything of which one disapproved; and the process was completed when, in 1611, Cotgrave's famous *Dictionary of the French and English Tongues* defined *machiavélisme* as 'subtle policy, cunning roguery'. Of course, the greater part of Machiavelli's writings have nothing whatever to do either with subtle policy or cunning roguery: but his reputation had finally parted company from his books – and, notwithstanding the loving labour of scholarly cohorts during the past century, that separation has persisted.

Machiavellian, machiavellico, machiavellistisch, maquiavélico, machiavélique: we can never erase Machiavelli's imprint on modern languages, nor free it from its sinister connotations. And this is, perhaps, no bad thing. Some readers, lured to his books by the seductive scent of naughtiness, may linger to savour more substantial matters of continuing relevance to human societies: the nature of public morality; the limits of authority; the need for merited reward and condign punishment; the role and control of ideological fervour; the relations between military discipline and civil order. And such readers may wonder whether Machiavelli was prophet as well as analyst, as they reflect uncomfortably upon his dissection of decadence exposing the cankers of self-interest and factional advantage pursued at the expense of the common good; the exaltation of moral perversion; nerveless reliance upon neutrality; supineness in the face of armed aggression; dependence on the arms of others in the struggle to maintain liberty; failure to recognise the monstrous disproportion between the armed and the unarmed. Machiavelli may have been uncertain in his dialectic, selective in his use of history and uncritical in his evaluation of sources; but he could recognise political corruption when he saw it.

Jean Calvin:
the disciplined commonwealth
Harro Höpfl

Jean Calvin was born in 1509 at Noyon in France, and studied at Paris, Orleans and Bourges. By 1535 his alienation from the official Catholicism of France made it necessary to leave the country and he eventually settled in Geneva. He became the prime mover of the Reformation in that city from 1536 to his death in 1564. Outside Geneva his chief concern was for the survival and solidarity of the new Protestant churches, and he corresponded with political and religious leaders of the Reformation throughout Europe. Intellectually he was indebted to the great German reformer, Martin Luther, and, like Luther, to the Church Fathers, especially St Augustine. The successive revised editions of his *Institution of Christian Religion* and his commentaries on Scripture were authoritative expositions of Reformed theology for generations.

His followers adapted his political and ecclesiastical thought to the circumstances of larger, monarchical states, usually in the face of determined royal hostility. They came to formulate doctrines of political 'resistance' (i.e. revolution) and limited government and it was partly in response to these doctrines that theories of absolute sovereignty were devised – notably, Bodin's *Six Books of the Commonwealth* (1576) and Hobbes's *Leviathan* (1651).

Jean Calvin was born in 1509 at Noyon in France, the son of an ecclesiastical administrator. At the University of Paris he studied scholastic philosophy and logic, and subsequently, in 1531, gained a law degree from the University of Bourges. He was to retain an abiding respect for Roman law, but his interest had already turned to Humanist (as opposed to scholastic) 'philosophy' – in other words, the cultivation of good literature, eloquence and good morals, for which Greek and Roman antiquity, both pagan and Christian, provided the exemplars. He was also learning Greek privately, at that time a language associated in France with the Lutheran 'heresy' as well as the New Learning. In 1532 Calvin published a learned commentary on the Roman moralist

Seneca's *Treatise on Clemency*. What interested Calvin about the work was not primarily its political content – it concerned one of the main princely virtues – or its moral sentiments (for Calvin preferred Cicero), but rather Seneca's technical skill as a practitioner of the art of persuasive speaking and writing, rhetoric. Calvin did not start out a political man.

At about this time Calvin underwent a conversion to Reformed religion. France became uninhabitable for him, and in 1535 Calvin settled in the Reformed city of Basel. Here, in August 1536, he published the Latin first edition of his theological masterpiece, the *Institution of Christian Religion*, an orderly digest of the main tenets of evangelical theology. He continued to expand and revise the work until the final editions of 1559–1560; its successive editions are the record of Calvin's life and thought. He also translated all the editions into splendid, vigorous French. That accomplishment was presumably learnt in the course of the preaching which occupied so much of his life; his education had been wholly in Latin. The book was a success, and on the strength of it Calvin was offered a post as preacher in Geneva in late 1536.

In co-operation with other ministers already there, Calvin set to work reforming the Church at Geneva, with such energy and already with such insistence on clerical autonomy that by Easter, 1538, Geneva expelled him and two other ministers. He was then summoned to be minister of the French refugee church in the important imperial free city of Strasbourg, where he was also involved in the international diplomacy of the Reformed states. In the autumn, 1541, a contrite Genevan magistracy requested his return, and accepted many of the proposals for a Reformed ecclesiastical order which he at once submitted. The rest of his life was spent converting these forms into a working reality. His achievements at Geneva depended entirely on his organisational skills, his personal authority and his capacity to persuade both his fellow ministers and an often hostile magistracy. His official status was simply that of a member of the 'Venerable Company of Pastors' and of the Consistory, an ecclesiastical court, on which both ministers and delegates of the magistracy ('Elders') sat. Until 1559, Calvin was not even a citizen. Because of his learning, he was called on to revise Geneva's civic ordinances in 1543. He and his fellow ministers – Calvin always insisted that an evangelical ministry must be collegial – secured from the magistracy the establishment of an exemplary moral as well as religious order. In 1559 Calvin at last attained the opening of the Genevan Academy, later the University of Geneva. For much of his life his health was poor. He died in 1564.

Jean Calvin (1509–1564)

Calvin wrote his *Institution*, the serried ranks of his *Commentaries* on scripture, and the pamphlets and books in which he defended true religion, as a theologian. The standard topics in law and government which philosophers, historians and men of affairs discussed concerned him only in so far as they might be treated by a theologian. In fact, he was reluctant to offer more than a mere outline of the civil component of a Christian commonwealth. But he was a theologian with a Church to manage, secular rulers in and out of Geneva to deal with, and the fate of fellow evangelicals, especially in France, to worry about.

And his experiences in all these roles, mediated by that sustained reflection on the Bible which is the proper study of the evangelical theologian, found their way into his writings.

Geneva, the locus of his activities, was a town with a not inconsiderable population (perhaps 16,000–18,000, including numerous religious refugees from all over Europe) but of little international standing. Its printing industry was established only in Calvin's time; banking and watch-making came much later. It did not engage in the lucrative supply of mercenaries to foreign princes, unlike the cantons of the Helvetic Confederation, to which in any case it did not belong. Yet Geneva, having recently expelled its former overlord, the Prince-bishop of Geneva, now acknowledged no temporal or spiritual superior. Further, it sustained a precarious independence by cautious diplomacy and armed vigilance: in 1534 the suburbs which had sprung up outside its walls were razed to the ground to facilitate defence. Living in a permanent state of siege, religious discipline and unity were matters of civic morale and survival as well as religious zeal.

The political arrangements of this free city-state or republic were complex. Its government was a sort of elective aristocracy of four 'Syndics' and a 'Small Council' of about twenty-five members, known collectively as 'Messieurs de Genève' or 'Magnifiques Seigneurs'. The Syndics were elected annually by the General Council of all the citizens, which met only twice a year. There was also a Council of the Two Hundred, which met monthly and which elected the Small Council, also for one year. There were no professional politicians, judges or civil servants, although the same family names tend to recur in the public records. The government of Geneva was thus both a town council and an independent sovereign, and it concerned itself with everything from street cleaning to criminal trials and the conduct of foreign policy. Latterly, Messieurs had taken the doctrine and worship of their citizens under their tutelage. As elsewhere, religious reformation was completed by governmental decree, the result being a net increase in the power and jurisdiction of secular rulers. Here lay Calvin's problem.

As the time understood it, a commonwealth or polity (*civitas*; the term 'state' migrated northwards from Italy only after mid-century) was both a religious and a secular collectivity. It was composed of subjects who were Christians and rulers who acknowledged duties to souls as well as bodies. Having by decree terminated the spiritual and temporal authority of the Papacy over their subjects and such clerical immunities and jurisdiction as had survived, the governors of Reformed states simply assumed to themselves the supreme headship over 'their' Churches. The early Reformers had not intended this. They aimed to abolish the spiritual tyranny of popes and prelates, to rid the Church of worldly wealth and contaminating secular power, and most of all they intended a return to the pure, internal, unmercenary spirituality of the gospels, as opposed to the ritual 'outward observances' which now passed for religion. Since princes and magistrates appeared willing to use their power to advance this work, which in any case could not be done without their assistance, well and good. The Reformers were at first not greatly concerned about ways and means or about organisational matters and forms: godly preaching, the vernacular Bible and the abolition of corruptions seemed of infinitely greater importance. And shortly thereafter, sympathetic governors became indispensable protectors against civil disorder, the menace of sectarianism and the enmity of Catholic princes and emperors. It rapidly became clear that the price to be paid for such 'protection' was too high, but by then it was too late to recover even a portion of the ecclesiastical autonomy, limited as it had been, which had been jettisoned in the first flush of anti-papal and anti-prelatical enthusiasm.

The only political doctrines that Reformers enunciated unequivocally concerned the duty of all men to obey the powers that be (Romans 13: 1–7 and 1 Peter 2: 13–14 being the most commonly quoted texts) and the right of godly princes and magistrates to take a hand in reforming doctrine, worship and morals. In the later 1520s, the duty of magistrates to protect their subjects from the contagion of 'heresy' (that is, popery and sectarianism) and to uphold the honour and glory of God against public scandals and blasphemy was added to the list of standard topics. These teachings served merely to reinforce the dominance of princes over churches.

The 'political' (last) chapter of the first *Institution*, written shortly after the notorious Anabaptist insurrection at Münster, if anything re-emphasised those features of evangelical doctrine which made for the dominance of secular governors over the Reformed churches. Calvin insisted that secular government *is* a divine ordinance and *is* of vital importance to Christians, not merely to worldlings; that private men have no business meddling in public affairs; and that the competence of secular government extends to the enforcement of outward godliness (*pietas*) and the repression of heresy, as well as to outward justice and other worldly concerns. And against Luther's doctrine of the 'liberty of Christians' with respect to laws and outward observances, Calvin stressed that Christian liberty could never override Christian duty, and that the mainstay of churches is good order and concord, which are the fruits of obedience, law and duty.

Calvin was here arguing as if the only enemies the Reformation confronted were Papists and sectarians. He was never to withdraw these doctrines. But in the light of what he later learned as a minister about the threat to religious truth posed by the dominance of secular rulers over Reformed churches, the balance of his political doctrine was to change. Whereas in the first *Institution* he had only defined the true Church by what it was *not* (it was not Papist or sectarian), on his return to Geneva in late 1541 he was able at once to draft a comprehensive constitution for the Genevan Church, and in the editions of the *Institution* from 1543 onwards he spelt out the principles of ecclesiastical polity, which he took to be imperatively laid down in the Word of God, and with which secular rulers were consequently not entitled to meddle. He acknowledged too that political thinkers and statesmen had come to very similar conclusions about the principles of good order in the *civil* polity, without the aid of scripture. He was thus able to offer, at least in outline, a model of the order of a Christian commonwealth.

This model presupposes that fallen human nature is dominated by pride and insubmission, which make for chaos. The source of order in the world is the will of God, still dimly perceived as 'natural law' (the moral rules recognised as valid by the unaided human intellect, for example by the pagan philosophers and polities of antiquity), but clear and explicit in divine law, revealed in scripture. The custodians of the scriptural 'rule of life' are the ministers of God's Church. What God's law ordains, what the life and death of Christ exemplifies, and what the twin ordering institutions of the Christian commonwealth (secular and spiritual government) are set in the world to foster, is a willing and zealous, energetic obedience to God. And precisely because all rightful authority, whether in the Church or the civil commonwealth, is derived from God, it must be limited and conditional authority, subordinate to God's law. In the *De Clementia Commentary*, Calvin had still accepted the conventional concept, based on Roman law, of the *princeps legibus solutus*, the prince who is above the law because (and in so far as) he must be able to reform, dispense from and unify the law of his kingdom. Even then Calvin's endorsement of 'absolute' authority had been reluctant and qualified. Now, as an evangelical, he recognised only one 'absolute' legislator in the universe, namely God. Calvin now compared the authority of the spiritual governors, the clergy, to that delegated and circumscribed authority which ambassadors, provincial governors, vice-regents and legates derive from a Roman emperor. Secular authority was equally limited by the law of God, although that law gave to secular government and civil prudence somewhat more freedom of movement than it allowed to the ministry. And because he associated monarchy with unbridled authority, power arbitrary and intolerant of restraint – a government of disordered human will – he allowed it no place at all in the Church; the most he would recognise as legitimate was the presidency of a 'first among equals'; that indeed was in his view a requirement of good order anywhere.

It was Calvin's habit to claim to have derived his ideas of a well-ordered Church directly from scripture, whereas he denied that there was an equivalent biblically authenticated model for the order of the secular polity. Here his previously formulated doctrine of political obedience took over, so that in effect *any* established political order had divine authorisation – even established monarchies, however deplorable the actual conduct of princes past and present. All the same, there could be no justification for 'absolute' monarchy. In the *Institution* from 1543 onwards, Calvin acknowledged his agreement in principle with the conclusion of philosophers that an aristocratic form of government with perhaps some admixture of democracy (*politia*, the Aristotelian non-corrupt form of democracy) is the best form of all, in view of human imperfection. It was a conclusion he had first arrived at with respect to ecclesiastical government. Elsewhere in his writings he also made clear his disapproval of large states, which he associated with belligerence and tyranny: the governors of small states deal more civilly with their subjects.

Since God independently authorises both spiritual and temporal government, there can be no question of one authority being entitled to subordinate the other. They must consequently be related co-operatively, as partners in a common enterprise, yet maintaining some independence. Even this was perhaps more than might be hoped for under current circumstances, but Calvin spoke from principle as well as expediency. Governors occupy an exalted office and are entitled to be convinced by the evidence of the Word; they are not simply to be dictated to by the ministers in virtue of the latter's spiritual authority.

Calvin persisted in using the terminology he had derived from Luther, who had (in *On Secular Authority*, 1523) attempted to protect religion from governors by establishing separate areas of jurisdiction and distinctive ends for secular and spiritual governments respectively. Calvin almost completely abandoned any such attempt: he assigned to both a common enterprise, the same aim. It is of course not the business of magistrates to preach the gospel (though in fact Genevan magistrates were notably sententious in the hortatory preambles to their edicts). Conversely, ministers of the Word are debarred by scripture itself from using physical coercion, and the ordinary administration of civil and criminal justice and the conduct of foreign policy are not *per se* their business. But in teaching godliness and administering spiritual correction, the Church contributes to the justice and concord of civil relations. And by enforcing civil peace, sustaining ministers against 'scorners' of religion, and repressing heresy and vice, magistrates in their turn serve the growth of godliness, the building of God's kingdom on earth.

It is Calvin's concept of 'godly discipline' which best sums up his view of the task of spiritual and temporal government. Yet that concept is easily misunderstood, in view of Calvin's and his Puritan followers' later reputation. 'Discipline' for Calvin never *merely* meant constraint or regimentation. He used the term in the older sense, which it still retains in 'academic discipline', for example, to mean instruction or training (*institutio*, the title of his masterwork). Spiritual and temporal governments are established by God to train their congregations/citizenry in the punctilious and willing performance of their duties to God and to each other.

Whether the emphasis in the choice of methods of training is on constraint, punishment and severity, or on benevolence, encouragement and leniency, depends on the tractability and willingness to learn of the 'pupils'. Equally, whether government is by way of general rules which individuals are left free to interpret or whether it is by way of detailed commands and intrusive surveillance, depends on the degree of godliness and righteousness already attained. But since even Genevans were unreceptive and hostile to being 'trained', severity and detailed regulation tended to be the ordinary, if not the only, means of discipline.

In exemplary Geneva, there seemed to be nothing which was

immune from the attentions of either magistrates or ministers or both – not even the choice of Christian names, hair-styles, personal ornamentation or the number of courses at banquets. For Calvin there were only private *persons*, not private *matters*. The sixteenth century in general was careless about distinguishing sins and crimes, and, on Calvin's terms, the only relevant distinction was between offences of which a this-worldly tribunal, lay or clerical, could take cognisance, and those hidden sins of the spirit known only to God. And of course a profession of Christian belief and participation in public worship were conditions not merely of citizenship but of mere residence in the godly commonwealth.

Training or instruction requires trainers and instructors, and God has cast magistrates and ministers in this role. However, Calvin never for a moment supposed that the personnel of either government anywhere in this world would be composed of perfectly reliable servants of God's law. His guiding thought here was that no individual governor should be left free to do as he pleased. And Calvin devised for the Genevan Church, and partly articulated doctrinally, an intricate system of mutual restraint and animation. Not only do ministers and magistrates stand to each other in a relation of partnership, but they are also mutually subject: ministers are citizens of the commonwealth, and magistrates are members of the Church, and each group is liable to the other's discipline.

Furthermore, Calvin saw scripture as ordaining a collegial ministry (the 'Venerable *Company* of Pastors'), which itself attends to its own recruitment and the maintenance of high standards of conduct and learning; discipline means animating to good works as well as restraining from bad. We have already seen that the possibility of an equivalent system of mutual restraint of a corporate magistracy by its own members underpinned Calvin's preference for an aristocratic form of civil government.

Finally, Calvin conceded, at least in principle, a right of Christian congregations to a say in the choice of their spiritual governors, provided that everything was done 'decently and in good order'. In much the same way, the more scripturally literate the members of congregations, the more discussion took the place of instruction: discipline aims at understanding and conviction, not rote-learning. It is true that the Genevan congregations' role in ministerial appointments was in fact merely to rubber-stamp, and that ministers resisted magisterial intervention consistently, and ultimately with success. However, in 1560 provision was made for congregational objection to candidates to the ministry proposed by the Venerable Company. In the *Institution*, Calvin had already acknowledged the desirabilty in civil polity of a measure of citizen participation, and in other writings he made it clear that civil liberty – that is, a right, albeit a circumscribed one, to choose rulers (such as Genevan citizens enjoyed) – was a great blessing of God; he explained the prevalence of 'tyrannies' by the fact that this liberty had so often been misused. We may see in Calvin's endorsement of such guided participation in the government of the Church and the polity his recognition of yet another instrument to restrain arbitrariness in rulers and to subordinate them to divine law.

Nevertheless, as before, Calvin was unprepared to license political innovations, especially by private persons. In the ordinary way, Christians are not entitled to construct a new civil order for themselves, however intrinsically desirable that order might be. In this respect, Calvin's disciples proved less hesitant. As Calvin himself left the matter, the possibility of an ungodly magistracy or prince spreading chaos and tyrannising over the Church could not be excluded; still less could tyrants be resisted by force. Tyranny too has its place in the providential economy: it is a stern and searching spiritual 'exercising' of Christians in the virtues of patience and obedience. At any rate, tyrants would get from Calvin no 'courtier's theology', no 'flattery of princes' to legitimate their enormities.

Further, in one place in the *Institution* Calvin guardedly asserted that established political orders often already provide for 'popular magistrates' empowered to restrain tyrants; for example, the Spartan ephors, the Roman tribunate and the estates general or parliaments of modern kingdoms. It was the duty of Christians actively to support such 'popular magistrates', where established, in their resistance to 'tyranny'. This was as far as he was prepared to go, but his disciples abroad seized on this opportunity for legitimate political 'resistance'.

The legacy which Calvin left to his disciples was in some respects ambiguous. He had protected Reformed religion from reduction to an instrument of statecraft, without at the same time reducing it to a merely private and apolitical piety. Moreover, in his printed works and in the Genevan model he had provided one of those 'examples of the best reformed Churches' to which later generations of Protestants liked to appeal. Again, Calvin's disciples in France, the Netherlands, Scotland, England, Poland

and America found little difficulty in converting his doctrine of government limited by divine and natural law into a doctrine of constitutional government limited by 'fundamental laws', and his doctrine of the 'reciprocal obligatedness' of rulers and ruled into a contractual theory of the polity. They were more than faithful to their teacher in their hostility to absolute monarchy, and the debt which 'liberalism', as it came to be called, owes to Calvinist antecedents is clear.

Equally, however, the view of the state as an institution for the enforcement of virtue, and instrument of 'education', has little connection with limited government; in particular, it made for religious intolerance. It was the heretics within Calvinist ranks, not Calvin's orthodox followers, who insisted on separation between Church and state as a matter of principle, rather than as a *faute de mieux*, and it was they who cleared the way for a principled religious and political liberty.

Thomas Hobbes:
the sceptical state

Richard Tuck

Thomas Hobbes was born in 1588 at Malmesbury in Wiltshire; he was educated at the grammar school there and at Magdalen Hall, Oxford. The rest of his life was spent in the household of the Cavendishes, Earls of Devonshire, as a tutor and secretary. He began writing philosophy in the late 1630s, and is most famous for his *Leviathan* (1651), in which he set out his ideas on how the state overcomes radical interpersonal conflict. He died in 1679.

The period between Calvin's death and the publication of *Leviathan* had seen continuing effects of the Reformation. The Dutch republic was established after a rebellion (mainly by Calvinists) against the ruling Spanish monarchy, while France was engulfed in a protracted religious war. Although by the end of the sixteenth-century strong and secure states had emerged in the west, central and northern Europe were plunged into the Thirty Years War, which ended in 1648. The end of this period of international conflict saw civil wars, or revolts, in many countries – most famously, in England, where a republic was declared in 1649 and the king executed. War and revolution had become the central concern of political theorists, and are the major themes of *Leviathan*.

In the year in which Thomas Hobbes was born, there occurred a most dramatic demonstration that henceforward Europe would have to live with fundamental and irresoluble ideological divisions. He was born on the day when news reached his parents at their home in Malmesbury, Wiltshire, that the Spanish Armada had set sail: on 5 April 1588. He remarked later that 'my mother dear did bring forth twins at once, both me, and fear'.

The Armada's defeat, together with the associated success of the Dutch rebels and the inconclusive end of the French wars of religion, ensured that the Counter-Reformation would never recover the ground lost at the Reformation, and that most major European states would now contain within their borders groups of Christians who had fought one another to an ideological and political standstill. The new fact of this radical pluralism could not easily be ignored, and though many people clung resolutely to the truth of their own convictions, many others (particularly those involved in authority) were increasingly attracted to a kind of moral relativism. The revival of ancient scepticism in the work of Montaigne and his follower Pierre Charron was tremendously influential, and its central message in ethical matters for the late sixteenth century (as it had been also for the equally pluralist world of the Hellenistic and Roman empire) was that 'there is not so much one moral law to be found, which the fortune or temerity of chance hath granted to be universally received, and by the consent of unanimity of all nations to be admitted'. Montaigne summed it up: 'what truth is that, which these mountains bound, and is a lie in the world beyond them?'

This message was delivered principally to the Aristotelians entrenched in all contemporary European educational institutions. The Aristotelian (whether of a medieval or a renaissance variety) had believed in the possibility of genuinely objective moral standards, capable of being ascertained by men of 'practical wisdom' thinking systematically about the nature of the virtues. Against this, the sceptics pointed to the absurdly local character of the classical virtues – many societies had practised neither temperance, nor courage, nor prudence, and some had not even exhibited any justice. As Charron said, Aristotle 'had uttered more gross absurdities' than all other philosophers.

The sceptical attack on Aristotelianism was extended to physics, for the sceptics insisted that whereas Aristotle had argued that observation of the world could tell us what it was really like, in fact illusion was commonplace and universal. There could be no confidence in our perception of size, shape or colour, and hence no confidence in any physical theory. This subversion of objective standards, particularly in ethics, struck a chord with many contemporary rulers. Richelieu, for example, fostered the careers of many of the French sceptics, and was not above making the most relativist utterances himself – 'in matters of state the weakest are always wrong', he once remarked, chillingly.

Hobbes began his intellectual life in the world of high politics and among the rulers of England, though his family background was far from grand. His father was a minor clergyman and an alcoholic, his mother of 'yeoman stock'. But like many bright boys from that kind of lower middle-class background, he was propelled upwards by the educational system. Recognised as able by the master at Malmesbury grammar school, he was sent to Oxford (though not to a smart college), and was then found a place by the Master of his college as a tutor and (in effect) secretary to the family of William Cavendish, first Earl of Devonshire.

This was a *carrière ouverte aux talents* for many people like him in seventeeth-century England. The universities were educating a huge proportion of the age-group (comparable to the levels of the 1930s), though in ways which many people including Hobbes found deeply unsatisfactory, and aristocratic households offered employment and a career independent of the traditional structures of Church or Law. From them, intellectuals such as Hobbes (or John Selden, or John Locke) could survey the politics and society of seventeenth-century England with a remarkable degree of detachment. It is striking how all these three, for example, were exempt from customary familial relationships, and lived a life more of contract than of affection.

Until the late 1630s, Hobbes wrote very little. His only publication before then was a translation of Thucydides, a work to which he was presumably attracted by its grave vision of conflict between men, all of whom were convinced that they were doing the right thing. His reading (we know from a catalogue of the books in his study at Hardwick, the Cavendishes' house) was largely in humanist works of history and politics. But from 1628 onwards he spent much of his time on the Continent, accompanying his noble protégés on their grand tours, and during the 1630s he became friendly with a group of French writers who saw their task as transcending the scepticism of the late sixteenth and early seventeenth centuries, and creating new sciences. At the centre of this group was the intellectual entrepreneur Marin Mersenne, and around him gathered Pierre Gassendi (Hobbes's constant philosophical companion) and, most famously, René Descartes.

Their sense that new sciences were possible in all branches of human enquiry, and particularly in ethics and politics, seems to have been engendered by various developments in the 1620s. The most spectacular was the work of Galileo, culminating in the publication of his *Dialogue on the Two Chief World-Systems* in 1632. What Galileo showed was that while Aristotelian physics was indeed false, the sceptical objections to Aristotelianism equally missed the point. Observation alone could not determine the truth of a physical proposition (his main example was the

Thomas Hobbes (1588–1679)

rotation of the earth, which could not be established by an observer on earth), and therefore the fact of illusion did not directly overthrow the possibility of a true science. A genuine physics was possible which went beyond observation, and employed very general notions of simplicity and elegance to decide between competing theories. Galileo not only suggested what a new physics might look like, he in effect provided one – all the great physicists from then to Einstein worked within the framework which he had set up.

Most subsequent historians have seen how spectacular this achievement was, but they have not seen how equally spectacular at the time was the achievement of another writer, in ethics – Hugo Grotius. Until the late eighteenth century he was classed by historians along with Galileo and Bacon as someone who had founded a wholly new science, but for various reasons since then he has been relegated to the backwater of the history of international law. However, it is clear that for his readers in the 1620s his main work, *The Law of War and Peace* (1625), offered the same kind of possibility of an ethical science as Galileo's offered of a physical science. For in that work Grotius explicitly attacked both the Aristotelians and the sceptics (in the person of Carneades, the ancient sceptical philosopher), and proposed what amounted to a resolution of the relativist's dilemma. According to Grotius, there are moral universals, but they are minimal by comparison with those of Aristotle – amounting in effect only to two: that all men have the right to defend themselves and to acquire possession of the necessities of life; and that no man has the right wantonly to injure another. If it is your life or mine, I am to prefer my own; but otherwise I am not to attack you.

Grotius presented these principles as functionally necessary for any society – that is, no society could be imagined in which these principles were denied. However, everything else was up to the members of the society to impose upon themselves; so to that extent the relativist was right, for, in Grotius's eyes, most strongly held and specific moral beliefs fell into the category of additions to the 'natural law' represented by these minimalist principles. So did most religious beliefs, for Grotius argued that in nature man's only obligation was to believe in at least one God who had a care for humanity, and no other religious propositions were to be established by natural reason. Although Grotius used this theory in *The Law of War and Peace* primarily to expound the relationship between states (which, by definition, had to be conducted along the lines laid down by this universal core to all human institutions, rather than according to some locally agreed set of principles), his readers immediately saw its general importance, and a great deal of seventeenth-century political thought is best understood as attempts to vindicate and systematise Grotius's ideas about a minimal but universal moral science.

Its attraction was that it enabled its advocates both to endorse the persuasive relativism of the sceptical generation, and to explain why it was universally right to combat the attempts by 'fanatics' to force all people into their ideological mould. Grotius's own life exemplified the need for such a theory, for he

had been forced into exile from his native Holland after the collapse of the attempt by his patron, Oldenbarnevelt (in effect, the
Prime Minister of the Dutch republic), to prevent Calvinist
churches from achieving a domination of Dutch religious life.
Oldenbarnevelt was executed for treason in 1619, a fate which
Grotius himself narrowly escaped, and their fall symbolised to
Protestant Europe the fact that religious pluralism needed both a
strong state and a coherent ideology for the use of state power if
the threat posed by Churches (of whatever persuasion) was to be
defeated. The – to our ears – disconcerting claim that intellectual freedom is best defended by an illiberal state was made first
by Grotius, when he argued for the possibility and perhaps the
desirability of absolutism, but it was a claim which was made
repeatedly throughout the century.

The group of writers associated with Mersenne seems to have
seen that theories of the Galilean and Grotian kind could be
made into new sciences, if they could be provided with the kind
of general philosophical foundations which their original
creators had neglected. Hobbes apparently developed his own
account of these foundations in the late 1630s, partly after reading Descartes's attempt in the famous *Discourse on the Method*
(1637), though the precise story of its genesis is still unclear. By
1640 he had circulated among his friends a draft treatise in
English, *The Elements of Law*, which contained the first full statement of his philosophy, and in 1642 he published in an extremely
limited edition his basic work of political theory, the Latin *De
Cive* (*On the Citizen*). This remained the principal work of
Hobbes on politics for many readers, particularly on the Continent, until the nineteenth century, but it was superseded at a
popular level in England by the English-language *Leviathan*.

Leviathan appeared in 1651 after a decade in which Hobbes
had lived in France, away from the Civil War, and had written a
great deal on the philosophy of physics (much of which
eventually appeared in print under the title *De Corpore*) and on
human psychology (which was embodied in the later *De Homine*).
The main point of *Leviathan* is contained in the two of its four
Parts which no one now reads, 'Of a Christian Commonwealth'
and 'Of the Kingdom of Darkness', for in these Hobbes explained in great detail how his account of politics related to the
urgent contemporary problem of ecclesiastical authority, an issue
which *De Cive* had only touched on. The fact that *De Cive*
remained an important statement of his theory is shown by the
fact that he translated it from the Latin into English at about the

same time as he published *Leviathan*. In a brief 'Review and Conclusion' to *Leviathan*, he also drew the conclusion from his theory that the new regime established in England after the execution of the King in 1649 was legitimate, and its publication (together with the absence of any strong ecclesiastical power in Interregnum England) enabled him to return to his native country and live in peace.

Ironically, although he had briefly been tutor to the exiled Charles (who later described him as 'the oddest fellow he ever met with'), he found the political conditions of post-Restoration England far less to his liking – largely because the restored Church of England represented more of a threat to his intellectual freedom than had the loose-knit Independency of the 1650s. He spent the last years of his life living still in the household of the Cavendishes, and engaging in extensive pamphlet warfare against all the groups whom he saw as stifling 'true philosophy'. These were mainly churchmen, but he also lambasted the early members of the Royal Society for forming a kind of professional clique and using the techniques of intellectual and political manipulation to secure the hegemony of their own scientific ideas, and the common lawyers for similarly indulging in a professional mystification of the public. His last writing on politics seems to have been a contribution to the Exclusion debate (1678/1679), in which his then patron's heir, Lord William Cavendish, was heavily involved (and during which Locke wrote his *Two Treatises*). His long life (for he was ninety-one when he died) thus spanned the period from the Armada to the Exclusion crisis, and he had something to say about every major political event it contained.

The central core of Hobbes's thought is contained in his purely philosophical or metaphysical writings. In them, he insisted (as Descartes also did) that all we can have absolutely secure knowledge of are the events inside our heads, our 'seemings' or 'fancies', as Hobbes called them. We do not even know without reflection that there is a world outside us, let alone what it is really like; for all our sense experiences may be wholly illusory, in the way we know some are (dreams, optical illusions and so on). He thus accepted the full force of the sceptical argument, but he nevertheless insisted that knowledge or science *of a kind* was possible. In particular, he argued that we know what form a decent scientific explanation should take, though unlike Descartes he refused to use a proof of God's existence as an answer to the sceptic. God for Hobbes remained (as for all sceptics) something to be apprehended by faith only, and never by reason.

Instead, his argument went as follows. If we reflect sufficiently, we can see that there must be moving material bodies in the universe. This is because our 'seemings' exhibit the property of change; no one gazes out over a static world. So we know there is change; but we can only conceive of change as alteration in spatial position, and space is what material bodies occupy. Moreover, no body can move itself, for if it could there would be no reason for it to begin moving at one time rather than another; so all motion is caused by the impact of other bodies. So we can have secure knowledge that a moving world exists, though its precise character will always elude us – an explanation of the occurrence within us of a particular 'seeming' can only be hypothetical, for the same phenomenon can always be brought about by more than one physical process.

Hobbes believed in fact that at the deepest level all science is ballistics (and his general theory was first published to the world, appropriately, as part of a volume edited by Mersenne entitled *Ballistica* in 1644). Because Galileo's physics could be stated in terms of ballistics, it was a possible science; because Aristotle's could not be, it was not. But even Galileo was not *necessarily* right; his was simply the most plausible hypothesis available which had the correct logical form. Hobbes also believed that any account of human psychology would have to be couched in the same terms: men's thoughts are the product of straightforward physical interactions, and are, in principle, capable of being explained like any other branch of ballistics. Traditional notions of free will thus disappeared, though Hobbes retained a distinction between rational or orderly thought and irrational or disorderly thought (word-associations, dreams, madness and so on).

Hobbes used this same metaphysical theory to show that a moral science of the Grotian kind is possible. The central point was that just as man's perception of the physical world is in itself an utterly unreliable guide as to what there is in the world, so there was no possibility of any direct perception of *moral* realities. There is no secure knowledge of anything outside an individual's own skull, and his own thoughts and desires are all that can guide his actions. This was therefore as far as a moral language could go:

... whatsoever is the object of any man's Appetite or Desire; that is it, which he for his part calleth *Good*: And the object of his Hate, Aversion, *Evill*; And of his Contempt, *Vile*, and *Inconsiderable*. For these words of Good, Evill and Contemptible, are ever used with relation to the person that useth them: There being nothing simply and absolutely so; nor any common Rule of Good and Evill, to be taken from the nature of the objects themselves.

But even though this is true, there are some generalisations that can be made about all men's attitudes; in particular, whatever else they disagreed about, all men (according to Hobbes) would agree that death was the worst evil that could befall them.

Hobbes then mounted a very subtle and much misunderstood argument. This general agreement that death is the greatest evil for anybody implied a number of other universal moral propositions – that is, propositions which would hold even in the absence of any superstructure of civility or custom. First, all men would agree that whatever a man did to preserve himself from death was right for him, and that he had a right to do it. This corresponded to the first of Grotius's two principles, the right of self-defence.

Second, there could be no argument of this kind about the rectitude of any other course of action, and so no one could be said (at least in the same universal language) to have a right to do anything else, which was not intended to protect himself. This is a point which has often been overlooked, but Hobbes made it clear repeatedly, particularly in some notes he added to a second edition of *De Cive* in 1647, where he summarised his position thus: 'if any man pretend somewhat to tend necessarily to his preservation, which yet he himself doth not confidently believe so, he may offend against the laws of nature' (that is, act without a moral right). Hobbes, it cannot be overstressed, was not a utilitarian: he did not think that anyone was *prima facie* entitled to maximise his own want-satisfaction when those wants were not directly related to the minimal objective of securing his own life. This aspect of Hobbes's theory corresponded to the second of Grotius's two principles, the prohibition on *wanton* injury to another.

Third, and in some ways most importantly, all men are by nature judges of what conduces to their own self-preservation. This follows simply enough from Hobbes's deep scepticism about the possibility of absolute knowledge of the world. There is a radical uncertainty in most cases about what course of action actually will preserve us, and no one can be said objectively to be mistaken in any sincere belief about his own best interests. In some cases the matter is of course obvious: if a stranger comes up and attacks us, it is clear what we must do. But in most situations there is far greater uncertainty. The first two implications outlined above would have straightforwardly confirmed Grotius's theory, but this third deeply compromised it: for it led Hobbes to conclude that in nature, when all men would act on the basis of their unstable beliefs, there would be an equal instability in their actions. Men would rightly or wrongly conclude that all other men represented a danger to them, and a state of war would result – in the most famous phrase in Hobbes's works, the life of man would be 'solitary, poore, nasty, brutish, and short'.

Hobbes thus produced a new kind of sceptical worry to set beside the ancient sceptical stress on moral relativism. Even if there is a minimal but universal moral code (as he conceded there might be, in the form of the right to self-defence and *only* to self-defence), there would not necessarily be any stability of belief or action, for the application of ethical principles to the real world was itself an uncertain matter. It was this new worry which forced him to go beyond Grotius, and it is one which anyone who takes scepticism seriously must still confront. But he also produced a solution to the worry, of a kind: for he proposed that knowledge of this instability would lead all rational men utterly to abandon their private judgement in areas of uncertainty. They would lose nothing of real substance by such an abandonment, for *ex hypothesi* they could not have certainty in the areas from which they were retreating, and they would retain their own judgement and power to act in all other areas. What they would decide to do was to hand over all calculation about what conduced to their self-preservation (in doubtful cases) to a sovereign man or institution; they would (in the words of *Leviathan*)

> ... appoint one man, or Assembly of men, to beare their Person; and every one to owne, and acknowledge himselfe to be Author of whatsoever he that so bearethe their Person, shall Act, or cause to be Acted, in those things which concerne the Common Peace and Safetie; and therein to submit their Wills, every one to his Will, and their Judgements, to his Judgement.

The sovereign was 'that great Leviathan, or rather (to speak more reverently) . . . that *Mortall God*' who has subsequently stalked the history of political thought, and who looms over a peaceful countryside in the famous frontispiece to *Leviathan*. For us, this sinister image symbolises a ruthless and all-powerful state, but it is important to stress that this was not necessarily how contemporaries read the book. Indeed, many of Hobbes's first critics were themselves committed royalists, who sensed that Hobbes's theories in some way undermined the existing structures of authority. They were right, for in many respects Hobbes's writings were highly and surprisingly libertarian. His account of the legitimate creation of a state, for example, implied that no one could renounce his right of self-defence in cases of *certainty*, where it was absolutely obvious that he was under attack: so Hobbes, to the alarm of most of his readers, proposed that even a criminal on his way to the gallows was entitled to resist and to kill his guards. Moreover, the sovereign was entitled to do only two kinds of thing – to defend himself, and to act in the cause of his subjects' preservation. Like an individual in the state of nature, his own sincere judgement as to what conduced to either of these ends was paramount, but to go beyond it would be a breach of the law of nature. His sovereign could thus be disconcertingly limited morally: he would not (for example) be justified in enforcing a policy of equalisation of income on his subjects, unless he genuinely believed that doing so preserved their lives (though his subjects, it is true, would not be justified themselves in overthrowing their sovereign for such an act).

However, the central reason why contemporary readers of *De Cive* and *Leviathan* were alarmed was that Hobbes's sovereign enjoyed absolute power over intellectual and religious matters, and that this was in a way the main object of his creation. This too might seem to us eminently good grounds for concern, but we have to remember the point of this part of Hobbes's theory. Hobbes believed profoundly that the evils of the seventeenth century were the product of strong but unjustified beliefs – beliefs fostered both by the Aristotelian dogmas of the medieval Church, and by the 'civil science' of antiquity and of humanists such as Machiavelli. None of these ideas seemed to him to have any philosophical basis, for they all asserted propositions which the sceptics had shown to be false; and men acting on them had brought the world to disaster during the sixteenth-century wars of religion and the contemporary wars and revolutions. Strong beliefs allied to powerful institutions were anathema to him: men had to be defended from the physical force of fanatics.

The power of the state to determine ideological matters was a precondition for using it to smash the ideologues, and it is not at all clear that Hobbes intended his sovereign to have any strong but mistaken beliefs of his own. The state, in the eyes of Hobbes and of many of his contemporaries, did not have an ideological axe to grind, since its function was clear and non-contentious; the institutions which would oppress men intellectually were above all Churches, since their whole *raison d'être* was to get people to believe various improbable things. *Leviathan* contains, in fact, an eloquent plea for freedom of philosophical enquiry:

> Our own Navigations make manifest, and all men learned in humane Sciences, now acknowledge there are Antipodes: and every day it appeareth more and more, that Years, and Dayes are determined by Motions of the Earth. Nevertheless, men that have in their Writings but supposed such Doctrine, as an occasion to lay open the reasons for, and against it, have been punished for it by Authority Ecclesiasticall. But what reason is there for it?

Hobbes went on to say that if there were good, *political* reasons, suppression would be legitimate; but, he implied, there were not – nor were there likely to be.

Leviathan is still in print, and has been read continuously since its first publication. What do we still get out of it? In 1984 more (probably) than at any other time since it was written. For we too are locked into political structures which have come into being as a result of radical and terrifying ideological as well as military conflict; we too cannot take seriously the beliefs so passionately held by some of our powerful contemporaries. We share with Hobbes the dilemma of the sceptic: if there is no way of establishing the truth of these kinds of belief, are we at the mercy of instability and conflict, and will our own lives (and maybe now the lives of all other men) be in danger from fanatics? If his answer is not wholly to our liking, we have at least to take it seriously, and to provide an alternative which confronts the real issues as directly as he did.

John Locke:
the politics of trust

John Dunn

John Locke was born in Wrington, Somerset, in the seventh year
of the reign of Charles I, in 1632 – before the English Civil War
had begun and before Thomas Hobbes had completed any of his
major political works. Raised in a Puritan family, he spent his
early manhood in one of the universities (Oxford) which Hobbes
despised so deeply, where he studied the standard scholastic
curriculum. Later he turned to the study of medicine and in 1667
became personal physician to, and close companion of, Lord
Ashley, the future Earl of Shaftesbury. The remainder of his life,
three decades and more, revolved around the study of philosophy
and theology, and the politics of the English court. In 1683 his
connections with Lord Ashley, who had been tried for treason,
led him to flee to Holland, where he wrote extensively. He
returned to live under William and Mary in 1689, dying in the
second year of the reign of Queen Anne, 1704. He is famous
today as the writer of three great books: the *Essay Concerning
Human Understanding*, the *Letter on Toleration* and the *Two
Treatises of Government*, all of them published for the first time in
1689.

John Locke was born in 1632 in a small Somerset village. He
came from a Puritan family of traders and petty landowners and
his father worked as a minor legal official. In the course of
Locke's childhood, however, his father also served as an officer
in the Parliamentary forces in the English Civil War, which
terminated in the execution of King Charles I. It was one of his
senior officers in this conflict who appears to have secured for
the young Locke the opportunity to continue his early education,
first at Westminster School and then at Christchurch, Oxford. If,
as a young man, Locke had been happy to follow the line of least
resistance and become a clergyman, he might well have remained at Oxford all his life or have devoted his considerable
talents to the pursuit of a prosperous ecclesiastical career in the
country at large. But from early on in his time at Oxford he

showed a pronounced aversion to this fate, devoting great energy to developing his medical knowledge (the sole readily available alternative) and keeping, meanwhile, an eye resolutely open to the main chance.

The guise in which the main chance eventually presented itself, when Locke was already in his mid-thirties, was the acutely ill person of Lord Ashley, a prominent political figure, suffering from an appalling disease of the liver. Locke presided over a drastic surgical operation which, against all the odds, Ashley survived. The two men became extremely close, and for the next decade and a half Locke served Ashley, or, as he later became, the Earl of Shaftesbury, in his turbulent and eventually disastrous political career. When he died in disgrace in 1683, Shaftesbury had been at the centre of British politics for nearly thirty years, sometimes in positions of enormous power and influence at court, at others radically at odds with his sovereign and threatening or even plotting revolution.

His patron's experience both as a leading minister of the Crown and as a revolutionary conspirator marked Locke's understanding of politics deeply. It was the sharp contrast between these two perspectives and the intensity with which he responded to each of them which rendered Locke's political thinking, especially in the *Two Treatises of Government*, so clear-sighted and profound. Almost uniquely among the great works of political theory, the *Two Treatises* faces steadily both the indispensability, in a society founded on a complex territorial division of labour, of skilful and trustworthy government and the ultimate right of every community, in the teeth of gross injustice, to resist their government by force and replace it, if they can, with a better one.

Thanks to the researches of Peter Laslett, we now know that the *Two Treatises* was written for a national movement of political opposition to King Charles II in the early 1680s. We do not know exactly how much of it was written exactly when; but we do know that it was written to justify political resistance up to and including the systematic use of force by the body of the people against the reigning monarch. The political struggle centred on the succession to the English throne, since Charles's heir, his brother James, Duke of York, was an open Catholic, and since many English Protestants were profoundly unwilling to endure the rule of an overtly Catholic king. Instead, in a nation-wide movement, carefully orchestrated from Shaftesbury's London mansion, they pressed through Parliamentary elections and through Parliament itself for the legal exclusion of James from the succession and for the recognition as heir in his stead of one of Charles II's illegitimate sons, the Duke of Monmouth. In the event, Charles defeated his enemies, forcing the more prudent and elusive, including Locke himself, into exile to Holland and executing some of the leaders amongst the remainder. In 1685 James II succeeded to the throne.

Only with the Glorious Revolution of 1688, with James's flight from England after the landing of William of Orange, could Locke safely return from his Dutch exile. In 1689, in his late fifties, Locke published for the first time three great works. Two of these, the *Two Treatises of Government* and *A Letter on Toleration*, are works of political theory. But the most important of the three, the *Essay Concerning Human Understanding*, is a general discussion of the character and limits of human knowledge which touches only very marginally on political questions.

The two political books were written for rather different audiences. *A Letter on Toleration*, composed in Holland and first published in Latin, which was still the international language of scholarship, was addressed to a European crisis, the fate of the beleaguered Protestant communities of France and the north in the face of the crusading Catholic absolutism of Louis XIV. The Revocation of the Edict of Nantes in 1685 and the full-scale religious persecution of the Huguenot population in France, accompanied by intense French military pressure on the Netherlands, fused together in the minds of the Protestant intellectuals of northern Europe the threats of foreign conquest, religious intolerance and autocratic absolutism.

Under the stress of these events, Locke set out in *A Letter on Toleration* a powerful defence of religious liberty, reversing views which he had worked out but never published in his first extended writings, as a young Oxford don a quarter of a century earlier. The *Letter* is a classic vindication of the right to freedom of religious belief and practice. It argues that since, for a Christian, sincere belief is a necessary condition for genuine worship and since genuine worship in its turn is indispensable for salvation, any human claim to dictate forms of religious expression or practice involves an impious and ludicrous attempt to take the place of the Deity; and that it must necessarily vitiate whatever measure of compliance it succeeds in securing from its victims. No man can believe or know for any other man, and the attempt to take responsibility for the beliefs of another is therefore as absurd as it is offensive. For rulers or states to make this attempt is not only ridiculous; it is, in addition, an abuse of their

John Locke (1632–1704)

legitimate powers, which may properly be exercised only for the protection of human worldly goods and interests and which neither enable them to (nor justify them in attempting to) come between any human being and God. Every man's and woman's salvation is in the last instance their own affair. In the vast majority of Christian states at the time, Protestant as much as Catholic, with their intimate ties between civil and ecclesiastical authority, this was an alarmingly radical doctrine. Today it is a moral and political commonplace, though one often more honoured in the breach than in the observance.

In the *Letter on Toleration* itself, however, it has two major provisos. The right to toleration does not obtain in the case of religious commitments which are at the same time commitments to political subversion (Locke had English Catholics in mind at this point). Nor does it obtain, more strikingly for us, in the case of atheists. The hazardousness (or indeed inadvisability) for states of conceding rights to those who freely admit to being their mortal enemies is obvious and practical enough even today; and it is worth noting that it had been one of the two principal grounds which had led the young Locke to deny a right of toleration. But it is the exclusion of atheists which should give a modern audience pause. For Locke, the right to toleration was a religious right based upon the immediacy of an individual's responsibility towards and relationship with the Deity. Atheists, to the best of their ability, enjoy no relationship to the Deity and hence can hardly claim the privileges which follow from a recognition of specifically religious duties. But crucially for Locke, they are not merely destined in due course for a disagreeable future (an experience which will be emphatically their own affair); they are also, even in this life, a source of acute hazard to their human fellows, a civil bad in themselves, because they cannot have firm, rational grounds for acting morally. For Locke, the rational basis of morality even on earth is the threats and promises of a life to come.

It is important to insist on the centrality of this theme in his thinking because it has drastic implications for the applicability in a secular world of his defence of toleration. His arguments for the absurdity of attempts to compel belief and for the categorical independence of truth from power retain some force, though the former look less reassuring than they used to do in the face of the technical resources for manipulating belief open to the more ruthless of modern power-holders. But his arguments for the right to believe for oneself against Church or state, however agreeable we may find them, have too flimsy a foundation, once their religious premise has been abandoned, to serve as a vindication of modern claims to freedom of thought or speech. It would be a fairly spectacular restriction on a modern right to think one's thoughts or speak one's mind, if this did not extend to thinking or saying that there is no God (or indeed even that there *may* be no God). What makes Locke's right of toleration hopelessly feeble in modern application is where the right comes from; what it is that is supposed to give to human beings a right to have their religious practices or thoughts tolerated by their fellows.

What gives them that right is also what establishes the framework within which Locke considers in the *Two Treatises of Government* the purposes and limits of governmental power in general:

> For Men being all the Workmanship of one Omnipotent, and infinitely wise Maker; All the Servants of one Sovereign Master, sent into the world by his order and about his business, they are his Property, whose Workmanship they are, made to last during his, not one another's Pleasure.

The source of men's duty to respect claims of right justifiably advanced by other men is called by Locke the 'Law of Nature'. The Law of Nature is God's rules for how his creation should operate. The rest of the world in which men live operates automatically in accordance with God's will.

However, human beings can and do choose whether or not to follow God's rules, the Law of Nature; and all too frequently they choose not to do so. Within the natural order all men are created equal. But as they live their individual lives, and as the societies which they form change and extend through time, many different forms of inequality appear among them. One of the most important and intractable of these is political inequality, the very distinctive form of inequality which exists between a government and its subjects. In the days of Louis XIV, as in those of Mr Reagan and Mr Chernenko (to say nothing of Pol Pot and General Pinochet), it required some steadiness of vision to see quite how this form of inequality fitted into God's conception of his workmanship.

What the *Two Treatises of Government* attempts to do is to explain what governmental power is for, how far it may legitimately extend, and who may do what to check it if it chooses to extend further. Locke certainly recognised very clearly that governmental power need not in practice exist or operate for any purpose but to serve the rapacious and exploitative desires of a tyrant. Much governmental power and activity, in the 1680s as in the 1980s, is a form of human plague visited upon its impotent and suffering victims. Such power is wholly out of place within God's workmanship, a direct violation of the Law of Nature. But governmental power can and should serve the civil interests of human beings. It can (and ought to) protect their lives, liberties and estates: their rights. What it is for, in moral theory if not always in historical experience, is to serve these interests effectively and, especially, to prevent particular human beings from interfering more or less violently with each other's worldly interests or rights.

It is important, once more, that governmental power has no capacity to serve their (in Locke's eyes) enormously more important, religious interests. The essential task of governmental power is to secure a far higher level of observance of the Law of Nature than would occur in its absence. Since in its absence all men and women in all conflicts with each other would be judges in their own case, a government has to be deeply corrupt to fail to offer its subjects some real services. The attitudes of subjects towards their government, accordingly, ought to be (and to some degree will in fact be) adjusted to the extent of these real services:

Very broadly, governments fall into two categories: legitimate and illegitimate. Illegitimate governments (those, for example, whose power rests solely on conquest) do not have any political authority over their subjects, though they may well, of course, enjoy effective coercive control over these.

The distinction between legitimate and illegitimate governments (expressed pretty vaguely in the book) rests upon differences in their origins (the conditions in which they begin) or in the basis on which they claim authority. Both differences turn on the presence or absence of the consent of the subjects. A genuinely political community (what Locke calls a civil society) is one freely founded by naturally equal human beings. It claims its authority on the basis of their past consent to be members of a single political community and on the subsequent working of political institutions which enable them to confer or withhold this consent to, among other matters, the making of laws and the levying of taxes. Because absolute monarchy denies any grounding in human consent and any responsibility to its own subjects, it cannot be a genuine political community and does not possess legitimate authority.

There are many problems with this distinction which need not concern us here. What is important for us is that it offers a clear and simple answer to the question of what governmental power is for. The point of governmental power is to combine inside a political society the advantages of impartiality with effective powers of enforcement in conflicts between its members, and to defend these members against threats from the outside world with the full force that they can collectively muster.

In so far as legitimate governments realise these purposes in practice, they are entitled to, and will in fact receive, the obedience and support of their subjects. Even governments which were illegitimate in their origins but which contrive to realise these purposes will at least deserve a measure of co-operation from their subjects; and they too are likely to receive this in practice. All governments necessarily enjoy a measure of practical discretion, what in England was known as the power of prerogative; and they need to enjoy this if they are to discharge their function effectively. Because even the most legitimate government possesses and needs to possess this discretionary power, government is irretrievably hazardous. It cannot be made wholly safe by the most complicated of legal and institutional expedients. However, it can, of course, be made notably more dangerous by the absence of any legal restraints or by ill-considered institutional design. Absolute monarchy, for example, is a condition of acute and permanent menace.

Legitimate political power, as Locke saw it, is a trust. It derives from a sort of contract between the members of a society, but it cannot itself be a matter of definite contractual rights and duties. Rather, it is exercised on behalf of subjects by rulers (or, more recently, by elected professional politicians) in accordance with their own best judgement. Men and women need govern-ment, and, if it is to serve their interests effectively, they also need to be able to trust it.

The clearest institutional division which Locke draws among contemporary states between legitimate and illegitimate forms of rule rests on the role of an elected law-making body, a legis-lature. Through such an elected assembly – in the English case, the House of Commons – each new generation can alter together the laws which it inherits and implicitly renew its assent to those which it chooses to retain.

At least as importantly, it can also decide just how much of its private economic resources the government may use for public purposes such as defence. Squabbles between government and populace over taxation, then as now, were a major point of friction between rulers and ruled. Indeed, in seventeenth-century Europe they were probably the principal cause of armed resistance to the state. Where a government's right to tax depended upon the consent of an elected legislative assembly, there could be a clear separation between individual rights to property and the entitlements of a government. Without this institutional device it was hard to see how individual rights could be reconciled with the right and duty of a government to use the resources of its people to defend them effectively against foreign enemies. Taxation without popular consent, expressed through the elected representatives of the people in Parliament, like the ship-money tax which Charles I had sought to levy before the English Civil War, was an attack on the right of property itself.

The most widely quoted phrases from the *Two Treatises* in the course of the American Revolution of the 1770s were those in which Locke denied the justification of governmental taxation which did not carry the political consent, expressed through their own legislatures, of the communities which were taxed. The dependence of governmental powers of taxation on the consent of an elected legislature had been one of the principal themes in English constitutional conflict for nearly a century by the time that Locke wrote, though it was in fact a less central issue in the Exclusion controversy of the 1680s than in the preludes to either the English Civil War or the American Revolution. Locke's own handling of it was serviceable rather than strikingly compelling or original.

What was far more novel, however, was his treatment of the nature of property right itself. It was in part an accident of ideological controversy that he should have chosen to analyse the concept of property at all. We do not know him to have shown a serious theoretical interest in the question at any point before the 1680s. At that point he chose to defend the political values and purposes of Shaftesbury's party in a very specific way. The *Two Treatises* is a work of general political theory; but it is also, and extremely explicitly, a protracted refutation of a work of royalist apologetics of the Civil War period: Sir Robert Filmer's *Patriarcha*.

Filmer was an interesting thinker, and other features of his work affected Locke's approach importantly. It was responsible, for example, for the very full and subtle account which Locke chose to offer of the moral and social character of relations between men and women, an analysis which marked his strictly political conclusions less than it might have done. But the most important and potentially troublesome aspect of Filmer's work was the damage it inflicted on the coherence of the existing non-absolutist conceptions of property right.

Filmer's own view of the status of property was less than compelling. But the question which he pressed, of how a genuine right on the part of individuals to own parts of God's workmanship could ever arise, was acutely embarrassing, as it has remained ever since. If, as the great Dutch natural law writer Hugo Grotius had assumed, God had originally given the world to mankind in common, how could any particular human being come to have a right to any bit of it against all other human beings? Grotius's own answer was simple enough in outline: that they could do so by coming to an agreement with one another. But, as Filmer pointed out, this was not at all a cogent answer. Quite apart from the historical implausibility of any single agreement of all mankind to divide up the world once and for all, it was quite unclear why any subsequent human beings who had taken no part in this putative initial agreement should be in any sense bound by it. Today our conceptions of property right, particularly internationally, still retain most of the queasy implausibility of Grotius's interpretation; and it is scarcely surprising that the more we learn about the historical sequences from which the property rights of the present day have arisen, the less we find ourselves convinced that we should in fact see these as genuinely *rights* at all.

In the fifth chapter of his *Second Treatise*, Locke attempted to provide a different and stronger answer to Filmer's needlings. This answer is important not because it is or was especially clear and cogent, but rather because it has formed the basis for the two principal and sharply opposed modern political doctrines of the nature and extent of property right: the liberal theory of free market exchange, including the sale of labour; and the socialist theory which sees the sale of labour as intrinsically a process of exploitation. Locke argues that God gave the world to men in common for their use and enjoyment, that to use or enjoy it they needed no consent from one another, and that the basis of their individual title to use or appropriate was their labour, the work of their own bodies, which certainly by nature belonged to each of them, at least against any other human being. He argued also that it was the exercise of human labour which had transformed the natural world into a far more productive and flourishing territory, creating most of the value of the material goods which were now in existence. Those who work hard and observe the Law of Nature deserve and are entitled to enjoy God's world.

It is easy to see the ambiguous relationship between this doctrine and the social order of seventeenth-century Britain (or indeed that of twentieth-century Britain or America or Russia or China). Between God's workmanship – nature – and the actual opportunities of men and women to enjoy this, there comes a tangled history of force and fraud and effort and suffering, most of the details of which have perished for ever. Who knows who should now own what? Is the notion of ownership even one to which the idea of a full moral entitlement actually applies? In Locke's own presentation, two main details – the supposedly consensual role of money and the alleged agreements to the private appropriation of land – introduce an unseemly haze into the theoretical relations between the divine order of nature and the actual property system of any particular society. If Grotius is right, the basis of claims of property right is morally sordid and intellectually incoherent. We need not be surprised that the pressure to find something more imposing has remained strong, perhaps indeed increased in strength, since the 1680s. We certainly have no superior set of resources to draw on than those which Locke cobbled uneasily together in those years, though these have naturally been worked out and formulated more elaborately, and at times more clearly, in the succeeding three centuries. However, it seems distressingly likely that, in a world in which nature is no longer conceived as God's handiwork, it was Grotius rather than Locke who was right.

The *Two Treatises* was written to justify national political resistance to a sovereign whom Locke saw as having violated his trust; and it was published to justify the removal of a second sovereign whom he saw in precisely the same terms. The book concludes with a defence of the right to revolution, the right to displace a government which no longer serves the interests of its subjects but which instead threatens these intimately and profoundly. The defence of this right is likely to seem politically commonplace to us today, though there are still and will always remain plenty of places in the world in which it would be ill advised to insist on expressing it. The right to misgovern is seldom claimed by modern states (except in practice). On this issue Locke's arguments are apt to seem unexciting because they have already swept the field so thoroughly.

However, the deepest, most equivocal and most disturbing impress which Locke left upon modern political understanding did not derive from his political writings at all. It came instead from his great *Essay Concerning Human Understanding*, the bible of the European Enlightenment. What fired the imagination of his successors, for better or worse, in that book was the picture which it gave of human malleability, of the ways in which men's beliefs, attitudes and characters are formed. It is an age-old hope of moralising intellectuals and holders of or aspirants to political power that men and women can be caused to perceive and feel as would be ideally desirable or practically convenient. Since the eighteenth century that fantasy has marched and counter-marched through the modern political imagination, shaping and reshaping the world in which we now live. Although it was not a fantasy for which Locke himself felt the least tenderness, very few single human beings have done as much by their intellectual or practical exertions to speed it on its way.

Jean-Jacques Rousseau:
moral decadence and
the pursuit of liberty
Robert Wokler

Rousseau was born in Geneva in 1712. He had little formal education and in 1728 left his homeland and thereafter led an unsettled existence in France, Italy, England and Switzerland. His writing first achieved prominence around 1750 with his *Discourse on the Arts and Sciences*, in which he contended that morality had declined with the progress of culture. That thesis, running against the current of prevailing enlightened opinion, was to form the cornerstone of many of his later writings. His second *Discourse on Inequality* of 1755 attacked the institution of private property in similar terms, while his *Social Contract* of 1762 offered instead a model of man's political redemption. In the same year appeared his most substantial work of all, *Emile*, a treatise on education. Persecuted by French and Swiss authorities for his radicalism and critique of Christianity, he spent his remaining years in dread of a conspiracy against him, dying in 1778 at Ermenonville, near Paris. By the end of the century his political ideas, widely discredited in his lifetime, had come to inspire and enflame much of French Revolutionary opinion.

Rousseau was probably the most profound and certainly the most influential political thinker of the eighteenth century. For the last thirty years of his troubled life he was scarcely ever out of the public eye, and in that time the doctrines which won him fame and notoriety throughout Europe also ensured his persecution by civil powers. No other figure of the Enlightenment was credited with more original, or more dangerous, views, and when French Revolutionary leaders of different persuasions subsequently judged that they had put Enlightenment political ideas into practice, it was to his theories above all that they professed their allegiance.

Of course, like most leading men of letters of his day, Rousseau had many interests apart from politics. He was a much admired composer and author of a distinguished dictionary of music, a subject which claimed more of his attention than any other. Although a number of his early writings may be said to deal largely with anthropology, the main passion of his later years was in fact botany, and in each case the texts he produced have won him the tribute of scholars; his anthropology in particular is sometimes alleged to have initiated the discipline in its modern form. Rousseau's *Rêveries*, moreover, comprise the first major contribution to romantic naturalism in the eighteenth century, while his *Nouvelle Héloïse* was the most widely read novel of his age. Nor should we forget that his *Confessions* form the most remarkable autobiography since that of St Augustine, or that his *Emile* is the most important work on education after Plato's *Republic*. It is, nevertheless, as a moralist and as a political thinker that he achieved his greatest distinction.

As early as 1743, when at the age of thirty-one he had been appointed Secretary to the French Ambassador in Venice, Rousseau was persuaded that in human affairs everything depends ultimately upon politics. He perceived that city's decadence in terms of its defective constitution, and when he later reflected that he had begun there to sketch the plan of a political treatise, it was inspired by the observation that the character of a people is always shaped by its government. This treatise, on which he worked for many years, was to survive in one section alone, the *Social Contract* published in 1762, while the Venetian thesis which was its point of departure formed the cornerstone of all his political thought. Throughout his career he insisted that we are only what our governments make of us and that therefore our vices stem not from human nature but rather from the ways in which we have been badly governed. So too he attributed virtue equally to a political source, and it was in the light of that conviction that several of the writings of this supreme lover of virtue of the eighteenth century were heralded with the signature, 'Jean-Jacques Rousseau, Citizen of Geneva', since Geneva was at once the country of his birth, the cradle of his political education and the focus of his patriotic zeal. In his philosophy, both evil and good were thus essentially political values, inscribed within our hearts by the constitutional principles that held sway over us.

Rousseau was certainly not the first major thinker to regard politics as the central determinant of human affairs. He may indeed have been one of the last, since nineteenth-century commentators characteristically judged the role of economic forces, or social class, or public opinion, to be of greater weight, and this shift of focus in the direction of the economy and society since about the end of the eighteenth century is sometimes said to mark the demise of political theory. The claim that man is fundamentally a political animal, moreover, can be dated at least from classical Greece, and as Rousseau frequently reminded his readers, he drew much of his inspiration from Greek sources, above all from Plato.

His concentration upon the moral effects of politics, however, differs from that of most of his ancient precursors, for perhaps two main reasons: first, because he regarded political systems as artificial and the life of man within them as a transformation of human nature; and, secondly, because he addressed himself not only or even mainly to the origins of virtue but still more to the political roots of vice. The one approach particularly underlies his conception of the social contract; the other, his philosophy of history in general.

He initially conceived the plan of his philosophy of history when in 1749 he read of a prize essay competition on the subject 'Has the progress of the arts and sciences contributed to the purification of morals?' No!, he thought, and in a flash of illumination he envisaged the whole plot of human history as a great saga of increasing misery and vice, with morality's decline due to civilisation's advance. Before our patterns of life came to be moulded by factitious needs and false values, he argued in his *Discourse on the Arts and Sciences*, our manners were simple and natural. Whereas our forebears had been robust, the excess of luxury upon which enlightenment feeds had sapped us of our original vitality and made us slaves to the trappings of culture. Sparta had formed a durable nation so long as it was unadorned by the arts and sciences; but Athens, the most civilised state of antiquity, had been unable to arrest its decay into despotism, while Rome's increasing grandeur was also accompanied by the decline of its military and political strength. Much the same fate, he concluded, has marked the progress of all other civilisations too. Everywhere 'the arts, letters, and sciences are spread like garlands of flowers round the iron chains by which men are weighed down'.

This first sketch of our moral corruption in Rousseau's *Discourse on the Arts and Sciences* forms perhaps the least original of his major writings, owing much to the influence of Montaigne, Plutarch, Seneca and Plato, among others. But the essay won the prize for which he entered it, and almost overnight the great fuss it excited transformed him from an obscure man of letters into the most celebrated scourge of the Enlightenment.

One of the main factors underlying its notoriety was its manner of reversing an almost stock-in-trade eighteenth-century perspective on the epic struggle between virtue and vice. Voltaire spoke on behalf of many men of enlightened opinion in his day when he joined virtue to knowledge and portrayed the progressive improvement of human conduct in the light of modern Europe's slow awakening from dark centuries of super-stition and ignorance. Rousseau, by contrast, appeared to extol the merits of a barbarous golden age, from which mankind had fallen and lost grace because of an idolatrous lust for learning. Not only did he thus give the impression of favouring savagery over culture; to his enlightened contemporaries he seemed also to have forgotten that the principal source of misery and despair in the contemporary world, the Christian Church, drew its power from much the same mysticism reinforced by ignorance which in the ancient world he applauded. Voltaire and his followers denounced this vision of our uncultivated innocence, and they accused Rousseau of having abandoned the causes of political and religious reform to which he should have been allied so that he might instead return to an uncouth state of nature.

This judgement of his theory of history was in many ways extremely wide of the mark, but it did place due weight upon one of the central tenets of his philosophy – avowed to be the guiding thread of all his works – that while our Creator had made everything good, all that had been forged by man was corrupt and depraved. Evil, Rousseau believed, was the characteristic outcome of human enterprise, if not always the object of human design.

In his writings of the early 1750s he developed his account of the moral impact of culture mainly with respect to the influence of music and language, subjects which then engaged his attention in other contexts as well. He took the progressive separation of music from language in the modern world – the loss of inflexion in speech, the emptiness of meaning in song – as a measure of the corruption of our morals in general, and in his *Essay on the Origin of Languages*, begun in this period of his life, he portrayed the decline of civilisation through increasingly divisive figures of speech: savage man's '*Aimez-moi*', superseded by the barbarian's '*Aidez-moi*', in turn overcome by civilised man's '*Donnez de l'argent*'. But even in this frame of reference he viewed the political consequences of cultural progress as most decisive, and claimed that languages which have come to be divorced from music – mainly French, English and German, as opposed to classical Greek and Latin – incline their native speakers to be passive in the face of authority and are inimical to freedom.

Prompted by some criticism of his first *Discourse*, he also began in these years to address himself more directly to the political and social origins of vice, and contended that as a rule our desire to excel in the arts and sciences stems from our ambition to exceed our needs and to dominate others. Rearranging his initial genealogy of vices, he now proposed that pride of place should be granted to inequality, which had given rise to wealth, which in turn made luxury and indolence possible, upon which sinister foundations our arts and sciences were formed. In his second *Discourse on the Origins of Inequality* of 1755, this revised version of his philosophy of history was elaborated in the light of what he had by then come to perceive as the most fundamental of all institutions which enshrine the principle of inequality – that is, private property.

'The first man who enclosed a piece of ground and found people simple enough to believe him', Rousseau remarked ruefully in this work, 'was the real founder of civil society.' All the crimes of humanity, he argued, were due ultimately to the appropriation of the earth by some individuals at the expense of others, with the poor forced either to become enthralled to the rich or to plunder their property. But not only was the institution of private property responsible for the emergence of war; it must also have accounted for the establishment of government, with the rich eventually traducing the poor to settle their differences. According to Rousseau, government must initially have been set up as a kind of fraudulent social compact which bound all men to maintain the peace by repudiating their claims upon one another's property. As every person was protected only in the legitimate possession of what he owned already, the poor would thus have come to be permanently subjected to the rich, running headlong into their chains in the belief that they had gained their freedom. So it is throughout the world, Rousseau reflected along the same lines in another essay on the state of war. The whole of starving humanity has been crushed by a handful of oppressors, 'with the strong, holding sway over the weak, armed with the redoubtable strength of the law'.

In his second *Discourse* Rousseau developed these propositions in the form of a conjectural history of the human race, in which he also attempted to explain the social genesis of the

Jean-Jacques Rousseau (1712–1778)

family and of agriculture, and in which he depicted the alternative types of government that must initially have been established in terms of the differing but always unequal distributions of private property which underpinned them. Rousseau contended that in his account of inequality he was obliged to 'lay the facts aside', and, although he did cite such evidence about savage and primitive man as was available to him, it is important to stress the fundamentally speculative character of his argument. The picture he drew of our primeval past was at bottom an abstraction from his account of contemporary society, and since his description of a propertyless state of nature was a fiction, there could be no point in our attempting to return to it. On the contrary, he maintained that men must make their way in this world, subject to its governments; for his part he could not live outside society, nor ever subsist on acorns.

Through his hypothetical reconstruction of the past, however, Rousseau was drawn to several notable observations in political and social theory, of which perhaps three related themes should be emphasised.

The first is that his conception of our moral decline around the institution of private property directly challenged a number of mainly seventeenth-century philosophies of natural law, and was also designed, in particular, to refute the doctrines of Hobbes and Locke. Most natural law thinkers, he claimed, ascribe to man's essential nature complex traits or institutions – such as reason, language or a sense of justice – which could not be acquired except in society. Rousseau therefore charged that such theorists had premised their unacceptable prescriptions for government upon unfounded accounts of human nature. Hobbes and Locke, above all, incurred his wrath in this matter, since the one supposed that war was natural to man, the other that this was so of private property. Neither of these institutions, he retorted, could in fact have figured in our original state of nature; both were social institutions that had developed in the course of human history, with the condition of war such as Hobbes had described indeed arising both after and from Locke's state of property.

Second, Rousseau's abstraction of natural man from social man was drawn around a fundamental dichotomy between our physical and moral attributes. Morality, he insisted, did not stem from human nature but rather from the denaturation of man in society, with the striking inequalities that shaped our lives utterly different in kind from the insignificant natural variations between us. Private property, especially, was not an expression but a deformation of human nature, artificially established, and, contrary to Locke's view, requiring the consent even of those who have none. Rousseau's account of this most fundamental economic institution thus appears to have a political foundation instead. He conceived of both the desire to own property and its recognition as a right by others in terms of human vanity and the pursuit and acknowledgement of an unequal distribution of public esteem. In his philosophy, property was deemed to express the first principle of authority.

Third, Rousseau's picture of human nature stripped away from society drew savage man closer to other animals than to civilised man. Much of the *Discourse on Inequality* is concerned with zoology, and it is noteworthy that the savage creature he fabricated, and sometimes termed an orang-utan – solitary, nomadic, frugivorous, indolent and amoral – bears an uncanny resemblance to the real orang-utan of South-east Asia. Rousseau's benign portrait of animal instincts in the second *Discourse* is almost as striking as his description of the nature of man. It led him to suppose that we differed innately from animals, firstly, by virtue less of our behaviour than of our capacities – in particular, our freedom from domination even by harmless instincts – and, secondly, by our perfectibility, a word he coined to explain how we alone in the natural world had a potential for moral improvement or corruption. Mankind, he thought, was for better or worse the only creature which could make its own history; and the history of our abused perfectibility had ensured that in society we lived more miserable lives than those naturally allotted to all other beasts.

Rousseau's *Social Contract* of 1762 was to develop some of these themes pertaining to man's denaturation in society, but almost in reverse – that is, along an uplifting path of virtue rather than the descending slope of vice. Confronted by the famous remark in chapter I that 'Man was born free and everywhere he is in chains', readers of the *Social Contract* might have expected it to be a further elaboration of the *Discourse on Inequality*. In fact, however, it provides an alternative and corrective picture of society, a prescription of how the political systems described in the *Discourse* might be changed.

'What is possible in our moral affairs', Rousseau now claimed, 'is less sharply circumscribed than we suppose', for however much we had been degraded in society we still remain capable of self-improvement. His very idea of the political determination of morals set his theory apart from any doctrine of historical inevitability according to which our miserable conduct was governed by forces independent of human will, and in the *Social Contract* he addressed himself to a reform of our political will, to a system of laws as they might be, just as in the *Discourse on Inequality* he had described the foundations of laws as they are. So whereas the compact of his earlier work was deemed to have authorised our moral decadence, the agreement of his *Social Contract*, on the other hand, was intended to inspire moral uprightness.

Promoting that end, nevertheless, required as profound a transformation of our nature as we had already undergone in the opposite direction. The alternative contract he enjoined also involved man's denaturation and 'a substitution of a partial and moral existence for our original physical independence'. To the extent that Rousseau believed that civil society was founded upon consent, he regarded both virtue and vice as artificial.

The principles of his *Social Contract* are perhaps best understood in contradiction to the terms of agreement recounted in the second *Discourse*. If in the past our ancestors must have renounced their liberty by legitimating inequality, the true social contract must realise our liberty and equality together. These were the two principles, he proclaimed, that ought to be the main objects of every system of legislation, and much of his work was devoted to explaining why that should be so. Having already differentiated the moral and political from the natural and physical spheres of our lives, Rousseau now contended that distinct forms of liberty or freedom were appropriate to each. Without governments, he argued, men can be naturally free in the sense of not being subject to the will of others, but their freedom is attached merely to the satisfaction of their organic impulses. Only in political society, whose establishment requires that our natural liberty be laid down, can we realise either civil or moral liberty, of which the first makes us dependent upon the whole community and the second obedient to laws we prescribe to ourselves.

Rousseau's conjunction of liberty with law in politics is one of the central features of his doctrine. For in portraying our moral liberty as both established and limited by laws of our own making, he attempted to show how political systems might actually enhance our freedom. According to most earlier social contract theorists, the liberty or rights men naturally enjoy must be largely forfeited when they enter into society and accept the protection of its laws. For Rousseau, by contrast, liberty would not be lost so much as gained when, in giving up our right to do as we please, we bind ourselves collectively to act as we choose. In resuscitating an ancient conception of liberty as autonomy, Rousseau thus conceived the possibility of our making ourselves truly free in properly constituted states, and it is his unswerving commitment to the political principle of liberty which marks him off most sharply from all other social contract theorists.

He maintained that the state could serve as the instrument of freedom only when all its subjects were at the same time sovereign, for then alone could the people be truly said to rule themselves. This conception of popular sovereignty, in which all citizens wield absolute authority through legislative assemblies, encapsulates the doctrine for which Rousseau is now probably best remembered, and it is difficult to underestimate its significance in the history of political thought. Before the *Social Contract*, and most conspicuously in the theories of Bodin and Hobbes, the principle of sovereignty had always referred to the supreme power of a state's ruler, generally the monarch. For Rousseau, however, the term applied equally to a nation's ruled as to its ruling element, and in embracing it within his account of the people's will he allied the principle to the moral rather than physical side of human affairs, to right rather than force or power.

He had already developed a similar thesis in the context of the arts, when in his 1758 *Letter on the Theatre* he had called for public and fraternal festivals of the people as an alternative to the professional spectacle of actors, so that in effect all the world, and not just some corners of it, might be a stage. In these respects no major political thinker before him had ever shown so much devotion to the idea of collective self-expression or popular self-rule. Although the common people could be deceived and misled, Rousseau contended, the only possible safeguard against despotism was popular sovereignty. Only when the people all took part in legislation could they check the abuse of power which some of them might seek to wield. It was in this context of compulsory participation in the sovereign assembly that Rousseau suggested, in a unique but much misconstrued passage from the *Social Contract*, that whoever refuses to obey the general will shall be 'forced to be free'.

The 'general will' was Rousseau's term for the exercise of popular sovereignty, and he ascribed it both to the public interest or common good promoted by the body politic's voting members, and to the individual will of each citizen to achieve that good, often contrary to the same person's particular interest as a man. In order that a sovereign assembly should indeed act in accordance with its own general will, at least two precautions, he added, were necessary: first, that there should be no partial associations or factions within the state; and, second, that sovereignty must never be represented. Sometimes he stressed the need for the general will to be opposed to factions rather than for it to exclude them, but in either case his conception of the place of factions in politics differs strikingly from that of other eighteenth-century European and American thinkers, such as Montesquieu and Madison, who believed that the public good could be realised only through factional and sectional conflict. It is perhaps above all because he hoped the sovereign would always ultimately speak with just one voice that Rousseau imagined that his principles might prevail best in small states with relatively few voters, such as Corsica.

On the other hand, he insisted that all voters of a community must be heard, each expressing his own opinions alone. The representation of sovereignty through any parliamentary assembly he regarded as illegitimate. Many of his contemporaries, like Montesquieu and Voltaire, had praised the liberal principles enshrined in the Constitution and Parliament of England; Rousseau, by contrast, thought the English system of political representation incompatible with the electorate's freedom. 'The people of England', he wrote in the *Social Contract*, 'regards itself as free, but it is grossly mistaken, for it is free only during the election of members of Parliament. The use it makes of the short moments of liberty it enjoys shows indeed that it deserves to lose them.'

These principles may be seen to derive from Rousseau's conception of civil and moral liberty, but they also encapsulate his commitment to equality, without which, he wrote, liberty cannot exist. All the fundamental precepts of his *Social Contract* – from that of each man's total renunciation of his natural rights, to the impartial application of the rule of law, to the full participation of every citizen in the legislative sovereign – point to his egalitarianism. So too do his statements on property, which he once again deemed to be the fount of all inequality and the source of slavery. Yet he did not suggest that the abolition of slavery required the abolition of property as well, no doubt because that might bring his principles of equality and liberty into conflict. So that liberty was not put up for auction, he contended, extremes of wealth must be prohibited, but small holdings of property, especially in agrarian republics, he regarded more as proof of self-reliance than as a danger to the state, and he nowhere advocated a socialist case for equality built around the idea of public property.

In the *Social Contract* Rousseau also put forward a conception of government, much influenced by the political thought of Montesquieu, which stipulated that there must be distinct kinds of government appropriate to countries differing in their climate, terrain and, above all, population. As a rule, he claimed, the larger the state the more concentrated the powers of government must be, although he was generally unsympathetic both to monarchy and to large states because their citizens enjoyed less freedom. But democracy was in his view equally unstable as a form of government, in part because of its susceptibility to internecine strife, in part because it could only be sustained by (what was impossible) the continuous meeting of all the people in the administration of public affairs. The form of government which he preferred, therefore, at least for states of middling size and moderate wealth, was aristocracy, though only if its officials were elected. The main point he stressed about government, however, was that it could never be sovereign and had no right to make laws; it just applied them as particular circumstances required. The legislative authority of the whole people, its moral will, was superior to any kind of government, which merely expressed the requisite form of the state's physical power.

If Rousseau's reflections on government were designed to bring his political theory down to earth, his remarks about the legislator drew it towards the sublime. The figure of the legislator in his philosophy should no more be confused with the legislative sovereign than should the idea of government. Indeed, the position of the legislator in public affairs was so extraordinary that although it alone made the foundation of a state possible, it did not form any part of a state once the social contract was agreed. Rousseau identified Lycurgus from the ancient world and Calvin in the modern world as legislators, adding the Jews' Moses and the Romans' Numa in another context and, according to some interpreters, even the fictitious Wolmar in his *Nouvelle Héloïse*. These figures were chiefly remarkable for their intelligence in framing constitutional principles and their capacity to persuade individuals to believe in them by appealing to divine powers.

The exact place of the legislator in Rousseau's argument is in fact somewhat unclear, but there can be no doubting the problem that this concept was introduced to solve. For, without the legislator, it is hard to imagine how persons could establish rules which they could really only fathom once they lived under them, and that difficulty is a familiar one in all Promethean doctrines of politics conceived around the idea of man's moral transformation since the 'philosopher-king' of Plato's *Republic*.

Much the same mixture of the sublime and the pragmatic as can be found in his accounts of the legislator and government appears in Rousseau's other political writings as well, especially his *Constitution for Corsica* and his *Government of Poland*, each detailed studies of the forms of government appropriate to fledgling regimes whose citizens had invited him to serve as their legislator. If Corsica had escaped invasion, and Poland its partitions, it might have been possible, in the late eighteenth century, to witness how the principles of the *Social Contract* were applied, directly by their author, to the constitutions of actual states. This conjunction of his own theory and real political practice, moreover, was certainly intended by Rousseau, and he was adamant, for once contrasting his philosophy with that of Plato and also More, that he had not put forward an unworldly Utopian ideal. On the contrary, he maintained, his *Social Contract* was intended to elucidate the theoretical foundations of an object close to home, in particular the constitution of Geneva, and it was just because the principles of that constitution had been betrayed, he believed, that he had incurred the wrath of the current authorities of his native state. This was one of the main arguments of his third major work devoted largely to politics, his *Letters from the Mountain* of 1764.

The feature of his *Social Contract* which in his lifetime aroused the deepest public fury, however, was its penultimate chapter on the civil religion. Rousseau there stressed the significance of a religious as well as political foundation for our civic responsibilities, according to which citizens performed and loved their duty as a matter of patriotic faith, joining them together in common devotion to an almighty, beneficient and tolerant Divinity. This aspect of his thought owed much to the influence of Machiavelli, but it did not endear him either to the religious and political establishment of his day or to many of its leading critics. To *philosophes* intent upon reforming the *ancien régime*, his religious zealotry seemed a betrayal of the Enlightenment and a dark reinvocation of blind faith in a dawning age of reason. On the other hand, his express condemnation of Christianity, which he described as favourable to tyranny because its believers were made to be slaves, outraged the Church and political authorities alike. His 'Profession of Faith of the Savoyard Vicar' in *Emile*, moreover, published in the same year as the *Social Contract*, set forth the fullest and most eloquent statement of his philosophy of natural as opposed to revealed religion, and that dismayed these authorities even more.

From their censure Rousseau was never really to recover. Both *Emile* and the *Social Contract* were banned or confiscated in Paris and burnt in Geneva. Forced to flee from the one city and subject to arrest in the other, he found himself in 1762 a fugitive from justice and thereafter remained homeless, often obliged to travel incognito, at the mercy of protectors whose true aim, he came to suspect, was to ensnare and malign him. Real persecution compounded the paranoia with which he was un-doubtedly afflicted from at least the mid-1760s, and for the rest of his life he was convinced that his former friends in the vanguard of the Enlightenment – Diderot, d'Alembert, d'Holbach and Grimm – subsequently joined by Voltaire, Hume and many others, were in league with his political enemies in a monumental network of conspiracy against him. In 1778, having found refuge just north of Paris, he died.

Yet although Rousseau had become estranged from main-stream Enlightenment thinkers, he had a great many passionate followers as well, both throughout France and among radical circles in Geneva, and above all, perhaps, in enlightened Europe's peripheries – Italy, Scotland and Germany, where Kant and Goethe were to prove the most prominent of his approximately contemporary admirers. In the course of the French Revolution, especially, when the manuscript of his *Confessions* was presented to the Convention and his remains were ceremoniously transported to the Paris Pantheon, his influence upon eighteenth-century life and thought was at its zenith. No other figure of his age had more clearly expressed the re-volutionaries' commitment to the principles of liberty, equality and fraternity. And in the political career of the Incorruptible Robespierre, in particular – his opposition to patronage and to priestly theology, his patriotic zeal and promotion of the cult of the Supreme Being – can be found the most zealous practical exposition of Rousseau's doctrines, as well as much else besides.

For his part Rousseau had claimed in *Emile* that his age was on the threshold of a century of revolutions which would bring down the monarchies of Europe, but he never himself advocated revolution, and instead observed that the liberty of the whole of humanity could not justify shedding the blood of a single man. Nevertheless, when the Revolution he had foreseen broke out, many of its leaders drew up their programmes and constitutions in the fiery light of his philosophy.

Marx, whose own theory of history and concepts of property, ideology and alienation strikingly resemble Rousseau's views, felt no close attachment to them, largely because he believed they had been realised in a merely bourgeois revolution which had still to be superseded by communism. But Marxist thinkers who regret the absence of a clear moral philosophy in scientific socialism have often turned for inspiration to Rousseau's political thought. So too have radicals of other persuasions and liberals as well; so equally have nationalists, and advocates of democratic participation, and even anarchists impressed by Rousseau's conception of autonomy if not of sovereignty. Although he believed that our morality was shaped by politics, no writer before or since ever devised a political theory more passionately informed by moral conviction.

Adam Smith:
the Enlightenment and
the philosophy of society

John Robertson

Born in 1723, *Adam Smith* was a leader of the eighteenth-century Enlightenment, and is now regarded as the founding father of Political Economy. A Scot from Kirkcaldy, Smith spent most of his life in his native country, and was for a while a professor at Glasgow University. His first book was the *Theory of Moral Sentiments* (1759), his second and greatest the *Wealth of Nations* (1776). Following as he did the bitter religious and civil wars of the seventeenth century, and preceding the revolutionary upheavals of the nineteenth century, Smith lived in a world of growing prosperity and unprecedented intellectual freedom. Like his Enlightenment contemporary, Rousseau, Smith owed a debt to the great political philosophers of the seventeenth century, Hobbes and Locke; but his distinctive achievement was to join politics to morals and economics to create a new philosophy of society. Though Smith died in 1790 just as the French and Industrial Revolutions were about to transform his world, his social philosophy survived to inspire and provoke both Mill and Marx in the next century.

Adam Smith may seem an odd choice for inclusion in a series on political thinkers. His fame, surely, is as an economic theorist, as the founder, indeed, of the modern science of economics. In the *Wealth Of Nations*, his best-known work, there is no denying that politics are given much less attention than economics. Nevertheless, it is misleading to regard Adam Smith as an economist alone. There was an important political dimension to his thought: for him both economics and politics were dimensions of a larger philosophy.

This is not to say that Smith was a political thinker to the extent of several of those considered previously in this book. He does not display the single-minded interest in political life shown by Aristotle, Machiavelli, Hobbes and Locke. In so far as Smith considers politics within a larger philosophy, he actually has more in common with the religious thinkers – Augustine,

Aquinas and Calvin. But Smith differs from these too, in a quite fundamental way: for Smith addresses himself only to the temporal world, and excludes all spiritual considerations. Neither a political thinker nor a theologian, Smith was something in between: a philosopher of society. Therein, however, lay his originality and greatness.

One of Smith's pupils later described him as the Newton of the philosophy of society. Comparison with that giant of the mind may exaggerate even Adam Smith's stature, but the resemblance between the two philosophers' historical achievements is none the less striking. Isaac Newton stood at the apex of the Scientific Movement of the seventeenth century, developing the work of notable predecessors like Francis Bacon and Galileo to construct a new 'philosophy of nature'. Adam Smith stood in a similar relation to the eighteenth-century intellectual movement of the Enlightenment, constructing his new philosophy of society out of materials contributed by a comparable range of predecessors. Before examining the themes and principles of Smith's social philosophy, therefore, we need to look a little more closely at the historical context, social and intellectual, in which the new philosophy came into being.

Adam Smith was born in 1723, in Kirkcaldy in Fife. Smith's father had died before the birth, and as Smith never married, his closest relationship appears always to have been with his mother. Thus limited in the range of his emotional commitments, Smith devoted himself to study, teaching and writing throughout his life, only towards the end accepting a post in government service which distracted him from intellectual labour. It is curious that these personal circumstances closely parallel Newton's: but it is a matter of speculation whether there was a connection between personal circumstances and intellectual achievement. At least Smith remained (unlike Newton) an amiable man in his isolation: shy and distracted, perhaps even a little jealous of his ideas, but regarded with considerable affection by his contemporaries.

In forming a philosopher of society, personal circumstances are in any case likely to be less important than the broader social context. In this respect, it is of the utmost significance that Smith was not born an Englishman, but a Scot. Even more than it is now, Scotland in the eighteenth century was a distinct society, different from England in economic and political conditions and in intellectual outlook.

Where the English economy had been set on a course of

development and growth since the sixteenth century, the Scottish economy had begun to move forward only in the late seventeenth century. Once development was under way, however, it was strikingly rapid: notorious backwardness was transformed into prosperity within the space of a century. The Scotland in which Adam Smith grew up and worked thus provided a remarkable example of the desirability of economic growth.

At the same time, Scotland had undergone a major change in its political status, losing its formal independence when its Parliament was absorbed into England's by the Union of 1707. This change reinforced the Scots' long-standing awareness of values and culture in maintaining the cohesion of society, while encouraging them to view political institutions in a wider context of relations with other societies. Above all, the change brought home to the Scots that a society's moral and political condition could not be considered apart from its economic circumstances, and that pursuit of economic development must bring changes in both values and institutions. These, as we shall see, were precisely the central problems of Adam Smith's social philosophy.

With its own distinct economic and political experience, eighteenth-century Scotland also differed from England in its intellectual outlook. Decisively, Scotland was far more open than England to the ideas of the European Enlightenment. Early in the eighteenth century there was a particular connection with Naples, like Scotland a state whose economic prospects depended on its political relations with great powers, and whose philosophers anxiously debated the links between economics and politics. But above all it was the thinkers of the French Enlightenment from whom the Scots gained inspiration. Adam Smith himself revered Voltaire and acknowledged the genius of Rousseau, though perhaps still more important was Montesquieu, whose great work, *The Spirit of the Laws*, demonstrated how politics could be seen in the broadest social context. Not for nothing was Montesquieu hailed as the Bacon of the new social philosophy.

Within Scotland Adam Smith was by no means alone in responding to the stimulus of the European Enlightenment. He was indeed one among a group of philosophers known collectively as the Scottish Enlightenment. Reflecting the challenge of Scotland's own recent economic and political experience, the thinkers of the Scottish Enlightenment were distinguished even above their European counterparts for their common interest in

Adam Smith (1723–1790)

the study of 'the progress of society'.

One in particular of Smith's Scottish contemporaries should be singled out – his closest friend, David Hume. Famous as a philosopher of the mind, Hume was equally a philosopher of society. His social philosophy was distilled into a series of brilliant essays, discussing individual topics both in economics and in politics. Through these run the central themes of the desirability of economic development and the need as a result to allow for appropriate changes in the values and political institutions of society. Unsystematic where Smith was to be systematic, Hume's insights were yet a constant intellectual inspiration. In the making of the new philosophy of society, Hume was Galileo to Smith's Newton.

Two factors help to explain Smith's adoption of a systematic approach to the philosophy of society. One is that Smith, unlike Hume, was an academic, being a professor at the University of Glasgow between 1751 and 1764. This position required Smith to give comprehensive courses of lectures in morals and jurisprudence, and it was in these that he first welded morals, economics and politics into a single framework. A second factor behind Smith's approach was his conception of philosophy itself. This was explicitly inspired by Newton, whose philosophy Smith described as 'a system whose parts are all more strictly connected together, than those of any other philosophical hypothesis'. This was a demanding conception; and it means that our understanding of Smith's philosophy of society must be based primarily on the works that he completed and published. The reports of his lectures on jurisprudence are helpful in introducing themes that are present but not developed in his published work. For the substance of Smith's philosophy of society, however, one must concentrate on his books, the *Theory of Moral Sentiments* and the *Wealth of Nations*. Although Smith projected a third book specifically on law and government, it is significant that he ordered any drafts of it burnt before his death: evidently he felt that they fell far short of the standard proper to philosophy.

Three themes discussed most fully in Smith's lectures on jurisprudence are worth mention. One is that of justice. The maintenance of justice, Smith declared at the outset of his lectures, is 'the first and chief design of every system of government'. Smith defined justice narrowly, as the abstention from doing another harm in person, property or reputation. In other words, his view of justice was 'corrective', concerned with securing to each individual what is already his own. Smith repudiated the broader idea that justice might also be 'distributive', involving the allocation or redistribution of goods to men according to their needs or merits.

A second theme on which Smith expanded in his lectures is the origin of government and the foundation of obedience. Smith expressly rejected the notion of Hobbes and Locke that obedience was founded on an 'original contract' or agreement between the members of society. (So doing, Smith also effectively denied that God, who had been indispensable to Locke's theory of obedience, and who had, at the least, given Hobbes a great deal of trouble, was relevant to the matter at all.) Instead, Smith argued that obedience arose simply from habit, as men found themselves gathered in societies for survival and reproduction. Obedience derived first of all from a simple respect for authority, especially the authority acquired by wealth; and it was then reinforced by a sense of interest, as men came to recognise the necessity of obeying a government to preserve justice and peace in society. But the formation of the habit of obedience was, Smith insisted, gradual. Its strength, and the strength of government itself, depended on the stage that society had reached in its historical development.

Historical development, or what Smith called the 'stages of society', is the third theme most fully treated in his lectures. According to Smith, the stage of a society's development could be characterised by the way its members acquired their subsistence. In turn, men's means of subsistence would shape their conception of property, and hence their ideas of justice and government. The most primitive society was one of hunters, who were virtually ignorant of property and of government. The second stage was that of shepherds, who had property in flocks and herds, and thus had rudimentary notions of justice and government. The third and fourth stages were those of agriculture and commerce, the one developing naturally into the other. In these societies property relations had become increasingly complex, requiring governments strong enough to maintain a regular system of justice. It is important to recognise, however, that this theory did not suggest that the appropriate levels of justice and government would develop automatically, in response to economic advance. On the contrary, the theory was designed to underline the problems that those in government must tackle at each stage, and at the final commercial stage in particular.

The discussion in the lectures of justice, obedience and the historical stages of society provided an indispensable preliminary to Smith's developed philosophy of society. But it was not more than a preliminary. For Smith's was not so much a philosophy of society, as a philosophy of commercial society. In the two published works in which Smith chose to present his social philosophy, he assumed that commercial society represented the highest stage of historical development, and took its existence as his starting point. Smith's object was to demonstrate the principles on which commercial society worked, in morals, economics and politics. Thus enabling his contemporaries to understand their society, Smith would then, as we shall see, encourage them to improve and even perfect it.

Smith's first book was the *Theory of Moral Sentiments*, published in 1759, while he was still at Glasgow. In it Smith sought to show how men came to form their moral sentiments or values. The foundation of his theory was the concept of sympathy. Sympathy, Smith explained, was the means by which individuals observed one another's actions, and then formed moral judgements on them. The values which, in this way, men in commercial society judged especially worthy of respect were those of justice and prudence. While underlining the importance of justice, it was of prudence that Smith appeared to write with particular eloquence, as if this was the peculiar virtue of commercial man. The prudent man was cautious and modest, sincere, industrious and frugal. But Smith's analysis was more complicated than this. Men, it emerged, did not pursue prudence for its own sake, or simply to satisfy their material needs. They pursued it for the sake of the reputation it would give them with their fellows. The wealth that prudence acquired was sought because it impressed others, not because it was necessary in itself. The needs of man – food and clothing, the comfort of a house and family – could be met by the wage of the meanest labourer: beyond that, Smith wrote, all 'the toil and bustle of this world' was but the pursuit of wealth, of power, of pre-eminence.

So saying, Smith acknowledged the force of the criticism of the morality of commercial society which had been advanced by his Enlightenment contemporary, Rousseau. Smith, however, refused to follow Rousseau in an outright condemnation of commercial values. Instead, he offered a three-fold defence of them. He argued, first, that while the pursuit of wealth and power would generate inequality in society, such inequality had a stabilising effect: in particular, it strengthened men's sentiments of justice, and without justice there could be no order and peace at all. Second, Smith pointed out that the unequal possession of wealth did not mean that the poor would go short of necessities. As Smith put it, the rich man's eye is larger than his belly: he will not be able to consume more of the necessities of life than the poor man. Moreover, the rich man must spend his surplus on goods produced by others, thus spreading wealth through society. Finally, though more tentatively, Smith suggested that as the wealth of all increased, so would their capacity to pursue the full range of moral values – not only justice and prudence, but also the more sociable value of benevolence towards others. As none of its predecessors could do, commercial society offered all its members the prospect of a civilised, moral life.

Still, however, Smith was not entirely satisfied with his own defence of commercial values. In a final revision of the *Theory of Moral Sentiments*, completed just before his death, Smith added a chapter in which he conceded that the disposition to admire and worship the rich and powerful, and to despise the poor and mean, was 'the great and most universal cause of the corruption of our moral sentiments'. Against this conviction, Smith struggled to find an adequate response. He suggested that it might be possible for a few wise and virtuous men so to exercise the great virtue of self-command as to rise above the corrupting tendency of commercial society. But Smith did not take the idea of a moral elite very far. At best, he seemed to say, commercial men could lead a life of propriety, but not of true virtue. Beyond this, a response to the moral problem of commercial society would have to be sought elsewhere, in the sphere of politics and institutions, discussed in the *Wealth of Nations*.

The *Wealth of Nations* was published in 1776, after Smith had left Glasgow, travelled abroad and spent a period in London. As the first comprehensive treatment of economics, the book is famous for its exposition of the laws of the market, laws celebrated by Smith as 'the obvious and simple system of natural liberty'. But it was not for its own sake that Smith hailed the free market economy of commercial society: the market was a means to an end. That end was economic growth, or, as Smith called it, 'the progress of opulence'. Economic growth, Smith again admitted, brought with it inequality – more inequality, indeed, than any previous stage of society had known. Yet, as Smith demonstrated with a weight of economic argument, such inequality was not incompatible with – rather it was the cause of – greater wealth for all. By the division of labour and the market, commercial society was enabled to develop towards a condition of 'universal opulence', in which even the lowest ranks would enjoy not only the necessities but many of the conveniences of life. For Smith, in short, the justification of the market economy was that it enriched not some, but all: whatever the moral consequences of commerce, Smith insisted that the happiness of society be measured first by the improving condition of its labourers.

If the system of natural liberty was justified by universal opulence, however, Smith also observed that such a system must be regarded as a Utopia. This, as we shall see, was by no means to denigrate the system of natural liberty, but it was to draw attention to the obstacles in the way of its realisation. These obstacles become evident when it is recognised that the *Wealth of Nations* was not a work of economics alone, but of 'political economy', and was consequently also concerned with government.

The government of commercial society presented Smith with a major problem. For one thing, the institutions of government were 'unproductive': those who provided society with justice, along with defence and other services, did not themselves produce wealth, but consumed the surplus produced by others. Still more problematic, the growing wealth of commercial society generated not only inequality, but also conflict between classes. In particular, Smith argued, the interest of the order of capitalists was increasingly opposed to that of society as a whole, since the rate of profit tended to decline as the wealth of society grew. Capitalists had therefore, wrote Smith, 'an interest to deceive and even to oppress the public', and would use every means possible to persuade government to interfere with the market in their favour. Meanwhile, Smith gloomily added, neither of the other two main orders of commercial society, the landowners and the labourers, was likely to be in a condition to resist the capitalists. In a commercial society landowners became indolent, while labourers were degraded by the ever more specialised division of labour.

This diagnosis of the problem of government may be seen as reinforcing the pessimistic conclusions about the moral state of commercial society reached in the *Theory of Moral Sentiments*. But if Smith found it very difficult to think of a response in moral terms, he did suggest an institutional and political solution in the *Wealth of Nations*. The first part of this solution was to insist on the limited functions of goverment. A government's prime duty was to ensure justice and the security of property; it must also defend society from aggression. But government was not, by Smith's very definition of justice, to interfere with economic liberty; still less was it to attempt to redistribute wealth. Moreover, Smith argued, those institutions which were necessary should be subjected to economic standards of performance. By applying appropriate economic principles to the organisation of defence and justice, and by ensuring that essential public works were as far as possible paid for by their users, the 'unproductive' burden of government would be kept to a minimum.

To insist on limited, economical government did not, however, sufficiently counter the problem of the capitalists' ability to subvert government in their own interests. To meet this danger, Smith urged that government be accountable to society. Taxation to pay for government should be raised by consent, and the armed forces should be officered by those who were the natural leaders of civil society. At the same time Smith urged the public provision of elementary education, to include universal military training, as a means of encouraging the labouring class to play a part in political life. By thus involving all ranks of society in public affairs, Smith apparently hoped that those in government would be enabled to resist the sectional interests of the capitalist class. Just how far such involvement was to be taken remains unclear: it seems that Smith had in mind not the direct participation of all, but a system of representation, as in the British Parliament.

That Smith was thinking in terms of representative parliamentary government is confirmed by the most remarkable idea in all the *Wealth of Nations*, the proposal of an imperial union between Great Britain and its American colonies. When the *Wealth of Nations* was first published in 1776, this idea appeared as a solution to the crisis in relations with the colonies, a crisis which led, later in the same year, to their declaration of independence. To resolve this crisis, Smith argued, Britain must not only lift all restrictions on the freedom of colonial trade; Britain must also offer the colonists representation in a united imperial parliament. Such representation should be in proportion to taxation, and when, as could be expected, the American contribution grew to be the greater, the seat of parliament should transfer from London to New York. In other words, Smith would extend to America a stake in the British parliamentary system similar to that which his own country, Scotland, had enjoyed since 1707. On a much larger scale, he would apply the lesson the Scots had then learnt: that a commercial society should be prepared to set its political institutions in the same international framework as its economic relations.

Not surprisingly, Smith admitted the proposal of imperial union to be a Utopia; and failing its implementation, he urged the British Government simply to let the colonies go. It is of the utmost significance, however, that Smith refused to heed those critics who urged him to remove the proposal from later editions of the *Wealth of Nations*. Smith's insistence on retaining the scheme even after the colonies had been lost suggests that all along it was as a Utopia that it was important. It was, in fact, the political counterpart to his other Utopia, the 'obvious and simple system of natural liberty' in economics.

Smith's commitment to these Utopias holds, I think, the key to his whole social philosophy. Smith had a strong sense of the aesthetic appeal of general systems, in politics as in philosophy: by their order and comprehensiveness, political systems aroused men to promote the happiness of society. This sense of the appeal of systems may in turn be connected with Smith's elevated idea of the office of the legislator, who by wise reforms secured the tranquillity and happiness of his fellow citizens. In associating the legislator with the application of political systems, Smith was careful to set strict limits on his actions. Smith's legislator was not to be Plato's philosopher-king, still less Rousseau's human demi-god. Smith was insistent that the legislator must not apply his political system wholesale and at once: he must reform piecemeal, accommodating his system to the circumstances of his fellow citizens. In effect, what Smith probably had in mind was less a single legislator than a parliamentary legislature: what he envisaged was not the occasional moment of grand reform, but the continuous systematic adjustment of the institutions of government to commercial society's demands.

Yet, however cautiously presented, it is the conception of the legislator and his systems or Utopias which most fully reveals the vision behind Adam Smith's philosophy of society. This philosophy was not simply about understanding commercial society: it was also about bettering it. Only if philosophers understood its problems, and if legislators then acted to ensure its security and happiness, would commercial society continue to progress towards the state of universal opulence which was its best justification.

Since his death in 1790 Smith has never long been forgotten. But, as so often with thinkers of vision, the particular concerns of subsequent generations have frequently led them to take a partial view of Smith's achievement. The immediate reception of his work in the early nineteenth century was doubly unfortunate. On the one hand there were those, the political economists and their associates, who revered Smith's name, but who sundered his philosophy by treating economics in isolation from politics and morals. On the other hand there were those, the early socialists and Marx himself, who pursued the goal of a philosophy of society, and who set their economics in a moral and political framework. But these, taking the praises of his admirers at face value, assailed Smith as the first of the bourgeois political economists. Marx indeed devoted much energy to understanding and criticising Smith's economics; but he showed no similar comprehension of Smith's larger vision.

No doubt partly because socialists had condemned him, it came to be assumed in the second half of the nineteenth century that Smith was a thinker naturally congenial to conservatives. This could not be much more than an assumption, based on Smith's obvious commitment to limited, economical government; for Smith's additional convictions of the need to counter vested interests, and to reform institutions by legislation, were not ones conservatives would care to pursue very far.

In fact it was the Liberals who most fully adapted Smith's philosophy to the times. Reluctantly seeking a secular substitute for the theological politics that had sustained him before 1850, Gladstone fashioned the new creed of Liberalism out of a blend of free-trade economics, government retrenchment and a vigorous parliamentary programme of legislation. Although Gladstone did not explicitly associate this creed as a whole with Smith, it was perhaps the closest Smith's philosophy has ever come to realisation. At the very end of the century the 'Liberal imperialists' even began to canvass ideas of an imperial free-trade union, although only the odd contemporary (including the Scottish novelist, John Buchan) recognised the connection with Smith.

By the mid-twentieth century Smith's star had been eclipsed by Keynes, whose economics of public investment underpinned a broad political consensus in Britain. The recent conservative reaction against Keynesianism has brought Smith back in favour – only for it to emerge once again that his ideas are not necessarily all that conservatives might suppose. The difficulties facing conservative thinkers, both in England and in America, are two-fold. On the one hand, Smith's system of economic liberty entailed more than limited, cheap government; it also required the constant intervention of government to check the sectional interests of capital. On the other hand, the moral implications of economic liberty, as Smith diagnosed them, are repugnant to many conservatives' preference for an organic, morally cohesive society. Though no conservative would want to disown Smith, many may have good reason to make little use of his ideas.

How much of Smith's social philosophy can still be relevant? It is certainly still possible to think in terms of applying the system of natural liberty to modern market societies. Government would then be restricted to the bare provision of justice (in its narrow sense) and defence, and would have to act to prevent the slightest distortion of the market, by capital as much as labour. But the repeated frustration encountered by advocates of such a policy in the face of societies ever more complicated than Smith's own suggests that the enterprise may be less and less worthwhile. Failing that, one must fall back, with less precision but perhaps more profit, on the essential commitments of Smith's philosophic vision.

Three commitments stand out from the account of Smith's philosophy given here. Economic growth should be pursued as the means of bettering the condition of all. To ensure economic growth, the institutions of government should be made accountable to society – which means that they may have to be as international as a society's major economic relations; and those institutions should be under constant review by the legislator. Finally, it is the task of the philosophy of society itself to provide the legislator with his guiding ideas, his Utopias.

John Stuart Mill:
the crisis of liberalism
John Gray

John Stuart Mill was born in 1806 in London and died in 1873. During his lifetime, he achieved fame as a logician, economist, political theorist and social reformer. He was described by Gladstone as 'the Saint of Rationalism' and, though he opposed many aspects of Victorian life and morality, he was widely respected for his integrity and fairness of mind, serving briefly as Member of Parliament for Westminster (1865–1868). In his essay *On Liberty*, Mill opposed the moral conformity he thought existed in Victorian England and defended the claims of individuality, but he was sympathetic to many social concerns and sought to temper the mass movements of his day, rather than to thwart them. In his optimistic belief that the use of reason is the key condition of social improvement, Mill was, and remained, an eminent Victorian, foreseeing few of the great forces that have shaped twentieth-century history.

Why should we read John Stuart Mill today? We may choose to read him as we read Plato or Locke – as a political thinker whose works capture the dominant ideas of his age in a conception of the good society which is recognisable by us, but which we cannot make our own. If we read Mill in this way, we may hope for historical enlightenment from his writings, for a better understanding of the roots in nineteenth-century thought and society of ideas and ideals which inform our political life today, but we will not expect Mill's work to assist us in resolving the major dilemmas that beset us now. Our interest in him will not be a practical interest, but the interest of an historian in unravelling Mill's contribution to the matrix of ideas that govern our present understanding of society and the state. The historical insight yielded by such an approach to Mill may help us to understand our present political predicament, and in so doing it may confer an indirect practical benefit on us, but nothing in this approach to Mill promises any real aid in our struggles with our current problems.

By contrast, many present-day students of Mill think that his writings contain much that is directly relevant to us. In grappling with issues of individual liberty and social control, in assessing the risks and prospects of democratic and socialist mass movements, and in considering questions about the limits of economic growth and the place of women in society, Mill addresses issues that not only are still with us, but which have moved to the top of the political agenda. For most Mill scholars, it is hard to accept that what he had to say about these issues has nothing to teach us today. As they see it, our dilemmas and hopes have too much in common with Mill's for any purely historical approach to his work to be satisfying. We may turn to Mill's writings, on this view, for real political wisdom as well as for historical insight.

The two contrasting approaches to Mill today that I have outlined exemplify a genuine divergence in political thought in our time – a disagreement, in the last resort, about the validity and vitality of Mill's vision of man and society. For we find in Mill, more clearly and consistently than in any other writer, all the central themes of modern liberalism. John Stuart Mill is the model liberal thinker. His thought has at its heart the moral and political claims of the individual. It rests on the belief that the use of reason can settle fundamental social conflicts, and it expresses the hope that man's future will be an improvement on his past. Individualist, rationalist, optimistic – these familiar terms characterise well enough Mill's liberal outlook, and they identify a tradition of thought about moral and political life that is still alive today. But how adequate is Mill's liberal vision to the problems which confront us today? How much of Mill's liberalism is left standing after the storms of the twentieth century have done their worst?

In order to answer these questions, we need first to understand Mill's relations with his predecessors and contemporaries in political thought. We need to grasp the nature of the intellectual tradition that he inherited, and how he reshaped it in response to the major questions of his day.

Paramount in importance here are Mill's complex connections with the English Utilitarian movement. Founded by Jeremy Bentham (1748–1832), Utilitarianism was the doctrine which adopted as the test of all moral rules and social arrangements, their contribution to the general welfare, or, as it is often summarised, 'the greatest happiness of the greatest number'. The Utilitarians sought to raise up the art of legislation on a science of human nature. Both in Bentham and in his follower, James Mill (John Stuart's father) Utilitarianism rested on a clear but narrow and limited view of man. Men were conceived as particularly complicated natural objects, as passive creatures whose mental life is governed by a law of the association of ideas and whose actions are aimed at the achievement of pleasure. This was a conception of man at once asocial and unhistorical in that it neglected the formation of personality by social life and the cultural inheritance of tradition. It was a doctrine, universal in scope and aspiration, according to which the task of the Utilitarian reformer and legislator was so to arrange social institutions that the interest each man has in the pursuit of his own pleasure meshes harmoniously with the interests of other men and thus serves the general interest. In English public life this doctrine was expressed in the movement of the Philosophical Radicals, who in the middle decades of the nineteenth century put Utilitarianism to work in the reform of public health, local government, the legal system and the civil service. The conviction of the Utilitarians was that, by employing the science of human nature in the reform of society and in the institution of a rational scheme of education, human beings could be remodelled so as best to fit them into their place in a society organised for maximum happiness.

John Stuart Mill was himself the subject of a Utilitarian experiment in the power of rational education. Brought up by his father, James, in a strict regime of daily reading and instruction, he was studying the classics in their original languages in his early childhood and reading political economy before he entered his teens. He was reared as a model Utilitarian personality, ideally equipped to promote the general happiness, but the education he received did not make him a happy man. In his early manhood he entered a period of mental crisis and nervous collapse, suffering a long depression from which he emerged only slowly and with difficulty. This mental crisis compelled him to weave all his opinions anew, to rethink the Utilitarian philosophy his father had taught him. As he himself saw it, the eventual recovery from depression was facilitated by his receptivity to influences – to poetry and natural beauty, for example – which classical Utilitarianism, the theory of Jeremy Bentham and of James Mill, had neglected. Because of their narrow and mechanical conception of man, the classical Utilitarians missed the vital importance of individuality, self-cultivation and the inner life in the promotion of happiness. All

John Stuart Mill (1806–1873)

the emphasis had been placed on changes in the external social environment, with little attention being given to the human person in his singularity and uniqueness.

Responding to his own period of despondency and inspired by the Lake Poets (Wordsworth, Coleridge and Shelley) and by German philosophy, Mill sought to reshape the classical Utilitarian conception of human nature so as to give full recognition to man's nature as an active, creative and self-transforming being, and to the distinct identity of each individual human being. This revision in his view of human nature led Mill to an altered conception of human happiness. It was not as a series of episodes of pleasure, more or less long-lasting or intense, that men pursued happiness, but rather as success in a life of activity in which their human capacities and diverse endowments were fully expressed. In this revision of the old Utilitarian view of happiness, Mill was influenced by Aristotle, for whom human happiness is a condition of well-being in which the distinctive human capacities are exercised, and by the German philosopher and educationist, Wilhelm von Humboldt, who perceived that, as the demands of each man's nature are special and peculiar, so each man's happiness has features that are unique and which distinguish it from any other man's.

Mill gave an account of these revisions of his view of human nature and happiness in his essays on *Utilitarianism* (1861), but the groundwork for this modification of the old Utilitarian view was laid in essays written in the 1830s and in his monumental *System of Logic* (1843). It was Mill's hope that the new view of human nature at which he had arrived could be given scientific support in a new science – the science of ethology, or the formation of character – which he saw as a successor of the old, bankrupt Utilitarian science of human nature. Further, Mill hoped that this new science of culture and personality, which would be better grounded in the complex realities of history and society than its predecessor, could give a foundation to the liberal outlook in moral and political life.

Mill's revisions in the Utilitarian philosophy had a major impact on the tenor of his social and political thought. Most clearly, perhaps, they enter at every stage in his argument for individual liberty. In his essay *On Liberty* (1859), Mill defends individual freedoms of thought, association and life-style on the ground that only in a context of liberty in which many competing 'experiments of living' may be tried can each of us hope to seek and find his own distinctive happiness. *On Liberty* is directed, not only or primarily against repressive laws which inhibit voluntary association and curb the growth of novel forms of social life, but also, and principally, against the tyranny of a censorious public opinion. Mill sought to protect the freedom of the individual from stunting social conventions as well as from oppressive legal controls.

Accordingly, he proposed that all legal and social interference with individual freedom be regulated by 'one very simple principle', his Principle of Liberty, which lays down that no one's liberty can be restricted unless his actions harm (or threaten to harm) the interests of others. In fact, Mill's Principle is far from being as simple as he makes out, but he intended it as a powerful barrier against invasions of liberty which thwart the development of human individuality. The Principle would not always have the effect of expanding the liberty enjoyed by people in Mill's day, since in some areas, such as the liberty to beget children, he thought the damage done to others' interests might warrant the institution of social and legal curbs. In laying down as a necessary condition of justified restriction of liberty that it apply only to actions which harm others, however, Mill's Principle sought to guarantee a sphere of self-regarding action entirely immune from social control. Within this sphere, individuals and their consenting partners could try out experiments in living even if they ran against current moral sentiment or damaged their own interests. The sphere of liberty was to be inviolable, because only in this way could human individuality be expected to flourish and the long-run well-being of man as a progressive being be assured.

Mill's new vision of human nature – a vision which he derived from sources outside the Utilitarian tradition, but which he struggled incessantly to reconcile with his Utilitarian inheritance – motivated his lifelong effort to renew liberalism and to link it with the great social movements of his day. Typical of his concern that new movements, each of them potentially liberating, might yet endanger hard-won personal freedom, are his writings on democracy and socialism. In *On Liberty*, Mill had worried lest the growth of democracy might result in a tyranny of the majority in which the claims of individuals and of small groups were stifled. Influenced by the writings of the great French aristocratic liberal, Alexis de Tocqueville, on democracy in America, Mill in his later *Considerations on Representative Government* (1861) advanced a series of proposals – for a two-chamber legislature, a complex system of proportional representation and the devolution of power to local government – all of which were designed to realise the promise of democracy while containing its dangers to liberty. In these proposals we see Mill as essentially still a classical liberal, concerned to limit the sphere of government and convinced that arbitrary power is not made less tolerable by being the offspring of a democratic majority. Mill never lost sight of the vital truth that democracy and liberty are not one and the same, but rather distinct ideals, which may or may not strengthen each other in practice. Recognising the practical irreversibility of the democratic movement in England, he sought to temper its claims and entrench those of individual liberty and minority rights.

In his relations with the socialist movements of his day Mill was no less ambivalent. He recognised clearly that the emergent capitalist system contained dangers to individuality and to justice, but he always repudiated the catastrophic or revolutionary view of socialism which he found in the writings of the French radicals. Contrary to many scholarly accounts, Mill's own socialist proposals have little in common with those of the Fabian movement, or with those that came to be realised by the Labour Government in the period after the Second World War. Mill never favoured a large extension of state ownership of industry, and he was suspicious even of the nascent welfare state of his own day.

His proposals centred on two areas: the ownership and control of firms by workers, and the redistribution of income and wealth. Mill believed that, while market competition was an essential safeguard against inefficiency and exploitation, the standard form of capitalist enterprise institutionalised a harmful separation of the interests of workers, managers and owners. In the typical capitalist firm, workers stood in an authoritarian relationship with managers and had little stake in the profitability of the enterprise. Just as in the political domain Mill favoured the extension of participation in local government, so in the economy he hoped for the growth of workers' self-management. Eventually, the major part of economic activity should be conducted by competing worker's co-operatives, with management being the hired servant of worker–owners.

On the distributive side, Mill favoured tax arrangements which would encourage the dispersion of wealth without penalising entrepreneurship or profit. Thus he suggested an accession or inheritance tax, levied on the recipient instead of the donor of gifts, which was to provide an incentive to the spreading of wealth without resulting in a transfer of resources to the state. Mill's socialism, then, was a form of market socialism with a strong commitment to the redistribution of personal wealth.

In one important respect, Mill's political economy distinguishes him from all the classical economists, including Marx, and brings him close to many contemporary concerns. In his *Principles of Political Economy* (1848), Mill envisaged a time when the growth of production and of the human population would come to a halt. All the classical economists had foreseen such a prospect, but Mill is unique among them in welcoming it as an opportunity for a large-scale transformation of social values. He sees the endless pursuit of growth in production as not only coming up against the hard constraints of finite resources, but as having social costs which diminish its benefits to all. He envisages a society in which, whereas production and population have become stationary, cultural and technological innovation proceed and bear fruit in the enhanced use of leisure. The chapter on 'The stationary state' in Mill's *Principles of Political Economy* contains the best account in his writings of the ideal society as he conceives of it: a society of men and women devoted to the higher pleasures of intellect, culture and natural beauty, without deep antagonisms of class interest but often engaged in creative conflicts of ideas and life-styles, respecting one another's freedom but never uncritical of themselves or others. Individualist, pluralist, democratic and socialist but protective of minority rights and preserving the virtues of market competition – this is Mill's liberal Utopia. What are we to make of it?

In order to assess Mill's liberal vision, and to consider its relevance to our problems today, we need to recall that Mill worked out his views partly in response to the inadequacies of Utilitarianism and partly in response to the pressing social questions of his day. He thought his time a time of transition, in which old creeds and institutions had to be reformed or replaced, and the task he set himself was that of developing the general philosophy which would guide such a social reconstruction. His own version of liberal Utilitarianism he regarded as fulfilling many of the functions once satisfied by the Christian religion, not only as a public doctrine but even as a private code of conduct. His proposals in the areas of democratic and socialist reform, and on other questions – such as the question of sexual discrimination, where his *Subjection of Women* still deserves to be read as one of the classic statements of feminism – all aimed to smooth the path of transition to the new social order. Our question, then, needs to be considered in the context of an assessment of Mill's own understanding of his age, and of his insight into the prospects of his society.

It cannot be said that Mill predicted many of the cataclysmic developments of the twentieth century. He tended to extrapolate from the trends observable in his own time, and there is no doubt that Mill expected the dominant institutions of liberal England – Parliamentary government, private enterprise and the free press – to spread across the world. It could not have occurred to him that the great bourgeois civilisation of 1815–1914 would turn out to be a century of peace sandwiched between eras of war and tyranny. With the exception of Nietzsche, all of Mill's contemporaries shared Mill's lack of prophetic insight: none of them glimpsed the apocalyptic twentieth century realities of the Holocaust and the Gulag, of the inexorable proliferation of weapons of mass destruction and the rise of totalitarian political movements.

In Mill's case, part of the fault lies in his conception of human nature. In spite of his efforts to free his view of man from the crude errors of classical Utilitarianism, his account still seems to us at once narrowly rationalistic and unrealistically optimistic. Modern depth psychology has uncovered dark forces in the human mind which are deaf to the voice of liberal reason. Much of the history of our century has been dominated by movements which Mill's theory of human nature not only failed to predict but cannot explain. The steady trajectory of progress which he expected depended in the end on the realism of his account of human nature. Now that we know man to be more fixed and intractable than Mill's theory allowed, we have less reason to expect the human future to be an improvement on the past.

History has not been kind to Mill's attempt to forge a new liberalism in response to the dilemmas of his age. His suspicion of democracy, and his proposals for the avoidance of a democratic tyranny of the majority, remain relevant, even if democratic institutions have not had the permanence and irreversibility that Mill expected of them.

Mill's vision of a decentralised market socialism, for all its appeal to current opinion, seems utterly at odds with contemporary economic developments. Like his proposals for redistribution, Mill's conception of a worker–co-operator economy projects a halfway house between the socialist command economy and market capitalism which has some of the defects of each and seems less viable than either. Where a form of market socialism has been attempted, as in Yugoslavia, it has involved great sacrifices in efficiency and in equity, and, in general, the idea of an economy of self-managed worker co-operatives presupposes a break-up of large-scale industrial units, with consequent losses in economies of scale, which no modern population is willing to risk.

Again, Mill's welcome to the stationary state seems utterly inapposite at a point in history when the masses of mankind need continued economic growth to carry on with their long haul from immemorial poverty. Though Mill was not himself a Utopian thinker, his vision of a society of individualists organised in worker co-operatives producing for a stationary state economy seems thoroughly Utopian in that it defies all the dominant trends of our age.

Among Mill's attempts to revise classical liberalism by addressing it to the questions of his day, the libertarian proposals of *On Liberty* seem best to have stood the test of time. With most advanced societies containing a pluralism of cultures and many styles of life, something like Mill's Principle of Liberty seems clearly appropriate if only as framing the minimum conditions of peaceful coexistence among rival traditions. His criticisms of legal moralism and of state paternalism have been accepted by public opinion and have informed legal reforms in the fields of homosexuality, divorce and censorship. In his adamant opposition to legal coercion aimed at preserving moral uniformity in society and at protecting men from themselves, Mill actually surpasses contemporary progressive opinion and suggests a line of further libertarian advance which is worth our attention. In many other areas, Mill's adherence to a libertarian approach, which is the direct descendant of the classical liberalism of Adam Smith and David Hume, goes against the current of progressive opinion, but it is none the worse for that. His belief that a state education might be used to promote general mediocrity seems less alarmist now than in the middle of the nineteenth century, and his proposal that the state should fund schooling by defraying the family costs of education rather than run a school system of its own seems not without merit in a multi-cultural and multi-racial society such as ours.

It is where Mill stays closest to his classical liberal forebears, rather than in his efforts at a radical revision of liberalism, that he still has something to say to us. Where Mill's works contain the political wisdom we need, it derives from the tradition of classical liberalism which was mediated to him by such writers as Alexis de Tocqueville. His own project of a revisionist interpretation of liberalism has as little to offer us as it had to his contemporaries.

In the last analysis, then, our assessment of Mill's thought turns on our appraisal of the prospects of his liberalism. I have argued that not much of Mill's hopeful and rationalistic creed has survived the rigours of our time. Where he has a voice that we can still hear, Mill recalls to us the sceptical and pessimistic classical liberals of the Scottish Enlightenment, whose hopes of progress were always mixed with forebodings of social decay and of a renewal of barbarism. Because his work can still reach us in this way, we would be wrong to read it only as historians of ideas. At the same time, the practical irrelevance of Mill's liberalism should lead us back to an older liberalism which was less hopeful and, beyond that, to the works of the founder of modern individualism, Thomas Hobbes, who wrote for men in an age much like ours, full of the clamour of barbarous religions and possessed by a longing for peace.

Karl Marx:
gravedigger of the capitalist class

Terrell Carver

Karl Marx was born in 1818 in Trier, Germany (then part of Prussia) to Jewish parents who later converted to Lutheranism. He studied at Bonn, Berlin and Jena, where he gained his doctorate, and then embarked on a career of radical journalism and political writing, often in collaboration with Friedrich Engels. He eventually settled in London where he wrote *Das Kapital*, and this and the *Communist Manifesto* are now among the most widely published, translated and distributed works the world has ever known. He died in London in 1883.

Marx's lifetime coincided with those decades of the nineteenth century in which the new technology of modern industry re-shaped the physical and social world in Europe and North America, and made inroads elsewhere. In his work Marx drew on the rationalism of the Enlightenment and the socialism just developing in France and England. His political outlook was revolutionary, as befitted a radical of the 1840s and participant in the stirring events of 1848. Twentieth-century politics bears the unmistakable imprint of Marx's critical scorn for capitalist society and his advocacy of a communist alternative.

Karl Marx was the political theorist of capitalism. His dedication to this subject over the forty years 1843–1883 was truly astonishing. No one has come remotely near Marx's achievements: a general theory of society and social change, and a special theory of capitalist society. An examination of those theories does not lead us away from politics towards economics, but to a new conception of the economy as highly political and of politics as crucially structured by economic activity. Marx was as unmoved by the tradition of academic territoriality in studying man and society as he was by the political territoriality of the nation-state when he took part in the international workers' movement.

For Marx, what happens in the workplace is quintessentially political for the individual and, in 'hitherto existing society', for his rulers. For the individual and society alike the very business of getting a living – production, consumption, exchange and distribution – is the structure within which personal and national politics are played out, and the way in which these economic activities are organised is itself political, malleable and contentious.

Marx's mid-nineteenth-century world was in the first throes of the technological development and social change so vividly described in the classic *Communist Manifesto* (published in 1848):

> Subjection of Nature's forces to man, machinery, application of chemistry to industry and agriculture, steam-navigation, railways, electric telegraphs, clearing of whole continents for cultivation, canalisation of rivers, whole populations conjured out of the ground – what earlier century had even a pre-sentiment that such productive forces slumbered in the lap of social labour?

Marx was pre-eminently the political theorist of capitalist development: the introduction of new technologies, new forms of social organisation, and new values and expectations into societies all around the world that were quite unprepared for the shock. The stress of economic and social change in these societies was enormous, as it still is in comparable societies today. When national economies are restructured, so political strain increases; leaders and led appeal for guidance. It is no accident that Marx is most influential in countries where modern technology in production and western patterns of consumption have been recently introduced, or are still developing, because it was this process of rapid economic expansion and social reorganisation that interested him and absorbed his intellectual energies.

Marx openly identified himself with the cause of industrial workers in the new industries and with the oppressed in society generally, yet his own work, so he said, was to be scrupulously scientific; interesting to academic specialists, employing their standards of rigour and surpassing them in political awareness. Marx's social science developed from his political orientation, and he himself popularised his analysis of capitalism for working-class audiences in the lectures *Wage Labour and Capital* (published in 1849) and *Value, Price, and Profit* (written in 1865). This combination of political commitment and scientific analysis lacks the detachment and neutrality that we have, since Marx's time, come to associate with scientific work; scientists, whether social or natural, are properly concerned, in the modern

Karl Marx (1818–1883)

view, with the facts, not values. For Marx, a value-free consideration of society or of any of its aspects would be no consideration at all, as values are themselves intrinsic to the subject matter and to the scientist. At the very least his work has the merit of leaving us in no doubt why he undertook it and what precisely it was for. Even for a reader who does not share his political sentiments, Marx's work on society, social change and capitalism can be illuminating precisely because his commitment led him deeper and deeper into the mechanics, even (as he claimed) the fundamental logic of our society. Marx's scientific work, on his own terms, was never intended to stifle further inquiry.

Practically nothing in Marx's background and early life would presage for us his career and achievements. He was born in 1818 in Trier in the German Rhineland. While his family was Jewish, his father converted to Lutheranism in order to preserve his career as a lawyer. The Rhineland and Marx's family were both politically liberal by the standards of the time, and Karl had formal academic training leading to university as well as informal education in literature, philosophy and politics from, among others, his future father-in-law, who lived close by.

It is worth remembering, however, that adolescent liberalism does not lead inevitably to the radicalism and communism that Marx espoused by the time he was twenty-five; many liberals become conservative as they grow older and take a self-interested view of their prospects and careers. Conversely, revolutionaries and communists have sprung just as readily from strictly conservative backgrounds; Friedrich Engels (1820–1895), Marx's friend and occasional co-author, is a prime example.

During Marx's university years, 1835–1841, he became associated with liberal intellectuals dissatisfied with the conservatism of the Prussian monarchy. To the hierarchy, censorship, Christianity, and inherited wealth stressed by the regime, they opposed the egalitarian doctrines of the rights of man and the citizen, representative and responsible government, toleration of religious practice and scepticism, and freedom of the press. This was a revolutionary programme in conservative eyes, and steps were taken by the state to make sure that academic careers were closed to such free-thinking radicals and that the universities were purged of their teachings. The liberals themselves drew a philosophical validation for their views from an imaginative reading of G W F Hegel (1770–1831), whose abstruse and highly ambiguous philosophy, originally published from 1807 and then collected in a major edition begun in the 1830s, had come to dominate German intellectual life. Hegel dedicated himself to revealing how rationality manifests itself in every aspect of the world, including politics. Those who saw in Hegel's work an implicit criticism of the existing order and a critical method that transcended his conservative views were known as Young Hegelians, and Marx's formative intellectual experience took place in this political context.

In his own autobiographical sketch (published in 1859 in the Preface to *A Contribution to the Critique of Political Economy*) Marx introduced the reader to his life and work with only a passing reference to his university career (and none to the Young Hegelian milieu) by giving pride of place to his first important job: the editorship of the liberal newspaper *Rheinische Zeitung* published in Cologne. That the twenty-four-year-old Marx was made editor is in itself an indication of the troubles the paper endured in promoting the cautious liberalism favoured by its commercial backers but steering clear of the conservative censorship imposed by provincial authorities. During the six months before the paper finally closed (in March 1843), Marx experienced for the first time the 'embarrassment' of having to take part in discussions on 'so-called material interests' – issues related to the reorganisation of German society along modern capitalist lines and the policy of the state in promoting this for the good of some at the expense of others. He planned to resolve this embarrassment by making himself as knowledgeable as possible about modern economic activities in theory and in practice, making sure that any spurious justification of the effects of capitalism on individuals and classes was thoroughly unmasked, and any Utopianism in socialist and communist alternatives to capitalism similarly exposed.

He began this project straightaway in 1844 with the *Economic and Philosophical Manuscripts*, written in Paris but unpublished in his lifetime. Over the next few years Young Hegelians were castigated by Marx in works such as *The Holy Family* (published in 1845), *The German Ideology* (written between 1845 and 1847) and *The Poverty of Philosophy* (published in 1847). He attacked them for their ignorance of the facts of contemporary economic life and for merely interpreting the world, when 'the point', as he stated in his *Theses on Feuerbach* (written in 1845), was 'to change it'.

Marx's lifelong project, the critique of political economy, was the sort of political work that would, in his view, get to the root of the evils for which capitalism was undoubtedly responsible and thus highlight the unworkable character of the system as a whole. No piecemeal reform, he argued, could ever eradicate from the capitalist system a tendency to worsening cyclical depressions and increasing mass unemployment. Only part of this massive study of the capitalist economy was completed in Marx's lifetime; this appeared as *Capital*, volume one, in 1867, in German; and an English translation, to which he particularly looked forward, was published in 1887, four years after his death.

The communist alternative to capitalism, where 'society [will] inscribe on its banners: From each according to his ability, to each according to his needs!', was recommended in principle by Marx (as in this quotation from his *Critique of the Gotha Programme*, written in 1875), but the institutions of the new society were never drafted in detail. This was in keeping with his distaste for Utopian schemes and his respect for the exigencies of national and international politics as the 'workers of the world' came, one way or another, to 'unite' (the slogan of the *Communist Manifesto*) for the replacement of capitalism with a planned system of production and (in time) a moneyless system of distribution.

Although Marx argued that those who did well out of capitalism would not surrender their power and property without a fight, he did not advocate violence as a good in itself, nor did he pronounce on the political role of a communist party within the 'dictatorship of the proletariat' that he occasionally mentioned. In *The Civil War in France* (published in 1871) he commented on the recently defeated Paris Commune, in which revolutionaries had seized control of the city. This article contains an endorsement of representative democracy, organised from the village or workplace through successive delegation of representatives to regional and national assemblies. These representatives were to have no more privileges than the other working people in society, to be strictly mandated by their constituents' instructions, and to be revocable from their offices when their constituents determined that their wishes had not been carried out. Marx expressed few doubts about the desirability and practicality of a communist system of production and distribution, a democratic, representative and responsible organisation of society, and the superiority of economic planning over the capitalist market in the means of production, in goods for individual consumption and in labour itself.

Moreover, his vision of the world's workers uniting in an

international opposition to capitalism was based on an optimistic view that the evident irrationalities of national competition and the absurdities of cyclical depression would lead workers (and open-minded intellectuals) pretty directly to the conclusions he had reached in his critique.

Marx's own experience of revolution in the events of 1848–1849 sustained his inspiration. As liberal insurrection swept across Europe, he edited the *Neue Rheinische Zeitung* from Cologne and wrote scores of articles advocating liberalism and outlining the interests of the newly emergent working-class where it existed. But as liberals were crushed or compromised, political reaction set in and Marx spent his life from 1849 onwards in exile in England, on the merest periphery of German and continental politics.

During the hard years of the 1850s he scraped a living as best he could by writing political journalism while attending, as much as possible, to his critique of political economy (unpaid). Though he was among the founders of the International Working Men's Association in 1864, he was not much involved in politics in the trade unions or in the mass socialist party as it began to emerge in Germany. Yet his own work on political economy, because it was theoretical, abstract and general in its presumed validity, was for Marx of the utmost political relevance wherever capitalism had been generated or introduced, in Europe or elsewhere.

In his general theory of society he argued that 'the mode of production of material life conditions the social, political and intellectual life process in general', contrary to views that our ideas alone, whether religious, philosophical, traditional or merely political, set the basic structure within which we must live our lives and make critical decisions. Technological change and the reorganisation of production are thus for Marx the most important structural features of modern society limiting the ways in which the law, political institutions, religion, and even aesthetics and philosophy are altered: 'With the change of the economic foundation the entire immense superstructure is more or less rapidly transformed.'

Marx referred to these insights (recorded in the 1859 Preface to *A Contribution to the Critique of Political Economy*) as the guiding thread or principle for his studies, most notably of capitalist society, where his theories of the commodity, money and capital delineated the fundamental laws that determine the functioning of capitalism. Thus, in what appears to be an abstruse work on political economy we find the kernel of Marx's political theory: from the dynamics of capitalist economic relationships emerge modern social classes – pre-eminently workers (or 'proletarians') and capitalists (or 'the bourgeoisie') – and with the class structure arises the whole web of conflicting interests within which modern political life takes place. No account of political phenomena, in Marx's view, could pretend to accuracy unless a thorough explication of the economic interests of the participants were included.

We can see Marx's insight at work in his own studies of contemporary politics: *The Class Struggles in France* (published in 1850) and *The Eighteenth Brumaire of Louis Bonaparte* (published in 1852). The first was an account of the revolutionary events of 1848–1849 and the latter a sequel covering the period 1850–1851, when the Second Republic succumbed to a *coup d'état*, military dictatorship, and (eventually) to the Second Empire of Napoleon III. In these lively works Marx analysed the startling events of contemporary French politics by exploring the complicated interaction between individual and class interests within the drama of violent revolution, political intrigue, party manoeuvre and personal caprice. Marx himself commented in a Preface to *The Eighteenth Brumaire* that he had demonstrated 'how the *class struggle* in France created circumstances and relationships that made it possible for a grotesque mediocrity to play a hero's part'. In the opening passages of the work itself he announced more generally: 'Men make their own history, but they do not make it just as they please; they do not make it under circumstances chosen by themselves, but under circumstances directly encountered, given, and transmitted from the past.' Thus his approach to politics was not determinist in the sense that every event could only have been as it was; rather, Marx led the reader from individuals and parties to the economic interests according to which they were bound to trim their courses.

The work was, in any case, as much about the future as the past. Marx's intention in exposing Louis Bonaparte and the contradictions inherent in his policies and political position was to rally support for the recently defeated liberals and proletarians, to convince them that the regime could not last, and to demonstrate that Bonaparte's 'confused groping' would 'humiliate first one class and then another', making 'some tolerant of revolution, others desirous of revolution'.

Marx's research on non-capitalist societies was undertaken in support of his view that capitalism was in its very definition quite different from previous forms of society in the west and elsewhere, whether extinct or continuing into the present: 'In broad outlines Asiatic, ancient, feudal, and modern bourgeois modes of production can be designated as progressive epochs in the economic formation of society' (1859 Preface). More specifically he was interested in the Roman empire, the transition to feudalism, a further transition to capitalism, the Russian commune and the Indian village community. Much of his work on non-capitalist society was undertaken with scrupulous regard for deficiencies in his sources, so there is no wholly coherent theory in Marx of non-capitalist societies in general or in specific instances, nor is there a completely developed theoretical account of the origins of capitalism itself.

Just as capitalism was essentially different from other types of society that had already developed, so was it different, according to Marx, from the communist society that would succeed it. In his view, capitalism drew its strength from the way that it, for a time, fostered technological change and economic growth. But that era, so he predicted, would pass as ever-worsening economic crises inhibit the use of the new technologies that human ingenuity produces. Only a classless society would make the best use of modern technology, and ensure its further development.

In Marx's view, capitalist society was bound to collapse because profits must decline as a proportion of total capital invested in industry. He deduced this 'law of the tendency of the rate of profit to decline' as a consequence of his theory that it is human labour alone that creates the value in commodities which we exchange on the market. As industry makes increasing use of machinery to raise the productivity of labour, so the number of workers tends to fall in relation to the capital invested in industrial plants. Marx argued that new investment would be increasingly difficult to finance because it would be ever more expensive compared with the profit that a decreasing labour force could generate. Thus production for profit brings about its own demise as investment dwindles, unemployment rises and crises of confidence shake the system. Marx's 'rational' organisation of production in accordance with a plan was the socialist alternative he proposed, arguing that its advantages were clear compared with the self-contradictory, self-destructive and egregiously wasteful character of the capitalism portrayed in his analysis.

The socialism Marx so confidently expected to arise from capitalism was to be built on its technological achievements.

Capitalists, who were for Marx the owners of the means of production, would have their assets expropriated by the socialist community, which would itself control the means of production. How and why contemporary workers and their sympathisers were to achieve this change was a problem on which Marx made few pronouncements beyond editorial encouragement. Theories of political consciousness, action and organisation are barely sketched in his work.

Marx's political theory is not of the conventional kind – a theory of human requirements or human nature, a theory of the state and citizenship, a theory of justice, the law and rights. His was rather a theory of the structure within which political ideas, behaviour and institutions themselves arise, a structure which, as he said, 'conditions' these phenomena and to which they 'correspond' (1859 Preface). In a letter of 5 March 1852 he summed up his own achievements:

> What I did that was new was to prove:
> 1) that the existence of classes is only bound up with particular historical phases in the development of production;
> 2) that the class struggle necessarily leads to the dictatorship of the proletariat;
> 3) that this dictatorship itself only constitutes the transition to the abolition of all classes and to a classless society.

Marx's guiding thread or principle has been taken as a deterministic law of human behaviour, and then criticised as false, since there are many instances of individual and collective behaviour running contrary to economic interest. But if Marx's generalisations are taken in a more elastic sense – for instance, that economic interest has only a limiting or conditioning effect on behaviour as a rule or in general – then the propositions, so critics say, are merely vague at best and banal at worst. It is worth noting, however, that Marx described his generalisations as merely a guide, and that in the intellectual context of his day they found genuine targets in those who believed otherwise about the nature of society and social change, or were unclear about exactly what they believed on the subject. Marx's guiding principle, in his hands, had a diagnostic role in analysis, exposing conflicts of interest that lie beneath the smooth surface of temporary political agreement and alerting participants in politics to the likelihood of disagreement or even more violent consequences in future. Thus Marx's political theory was angled towards political action – indeed, interaction between scientist and subject-matter – since the theorist expected to learn from an examination of events and then to use that knowledge to influence further developments.

Marx's detailed work on the dynamics of capitalist society exposed the logic of the system as he extracted it from the works of contemporary political economists. Whereas it is evident that a considerable part of his analysis has stood the test of time (the material on exploitation, the working day and machinery in modern industry), it is also apparent that some of his most basic definitions and laws (the theories of value, surplus value and rate of profit) are difficult to defend even in the abstract. It is still unclear whether capitalism survives because the ineluctable logic of collapse specified by Marx has not yet worked itself past the countervailing tendencies that he also identified, or whether the Marxian analysis of the system is simply flawed in attributing to it a set of properties that will cause its downfall. In any case, he seems to have undervalued the economic and political factors in capitalist society that draw mass support, and overestimated the revolutionary enthusiasm of workers for an alternative system of a communist character.

Marx's ideas became influential chiefly through the medium of works written by his friend Engels, who began a lifelong association with Marx in 1844 (when Engels was nearly twenty-four). Engels outlived Marx (who died in 1883) by twelve years, and during that time he wrote more than twenty introductions and prefaces to various editions of Marx's works. Engels also compiled the second and third volumes of *Capital* from manuscripts left by Marx. During Marx's lifetime, however, the two worked jointly on only three substantial projects (*The Holy Family, The German Ideology* and the *Communist Manifesto*), and both published their own writings during those years under their own names (with the exception of a few anonymous works and works written by Engels in English and published as Marx's, such as *Revolution and Counter-revolution in Germany*, published in 1851–1852). The correspondence between Marx and Engels does not support the view that they considered their individual works to be collaborations, though they did, of course, exchange information and material from time to time.

The extent to which Engels's works say exactly the same things as Marx's, whether or not he spoke for Marx on some issues which Marx did not address directly, and the possibility that Marx came to agree late in life with views espoused by Engels that contradict his own writings are now very vexed questions.

From Engels's works and from his view of his relationship with Marx came much of traditional Marxism, and, indeed, the traditional interpretation of Marx's life and works, whether pro-Marxist, anti-Marxist or non-partisan. Blanket assumptions, such as the view that what Engels said may stand in every case for Marx's own words, are quite out of place in any serious consideration of their careers, not least because such an assumption begs the question whether or not Engels's version of things is correct.

In presenting Marx's life and works to the public Engels attributed particular importance to method (arguably much more so than Marx) and an especially important methodological debt to Hegel (again, more so than Marx in his very few comments on the subject). Engels situated Marx's work in a philosophical context, explaining Marx's relation to traditional concepts such as materialism and idealism and to specifically Hegelian ones such as contradiction and dialectic. Moreover, Engels attributed to Marx the 'discovery' that laws of dialectics underlie nature, history and thought, though these laws were nowhere formulated by Marx himself. Engels was thus the originator of an overall approach to Marx's work, and he became the authority on the 'scientific' system which Marx's writings supposedly supported.

Engels coined the phrases 'materialist conception of history', 'historical materialism' and 'false consciousness'; these and many other phrases and views of Engels are commonly attributed to Marx. Engels's struggle to make Marx systematic and 'scientific' contributed, in turn, to the abiding characterisation of him as doctrinaire and dogmatic. Although he was never diffident about the results of his investigations and never slow to criticise views that he considered erroneous, it is now evident that this authoritarian view of the man and his work is overdrawn. In any event, it gives a poor impression of the tentative, investigative and self-critical character of much of his writing.

Marx's work stands very well on its own without the materialist 'dialectics' of Engels, not to mention the hagiography or demonology supplied by commentators working in the shadows cast by the 'Marxisms' constructed since Marx's own time. Marx himself has profoundly altered our view of political theory and, more importantly, of politics itself.

The Moderns:
liberalism revived
Alan Ryan

Bertrand Russell, born in 1872 in Ravenscroft, Monmouthshire, was born into the liberal aristocracy, the grandson of Lord John Russell, and son of Viscount Amberley, a radical, feminist and internationalist. Russell's intellectual achievements in logic and mathematics led to a Fellowship of the Royal Society in his thirties and an Order of Merit in his seventies, but he never had an academic post of any permanence, and is remembered for his polemical essays and his work for nuclear disarmament as much as for his 'pure' philosophical work. He died in 1970, still the centre of controversy over his opposition to the American campaign in Vietnam.

R H Tawney, born in 1880, came from the upper middle class ranks of the Indian Civil Service (his father ran the Indian Education Service) and spent his life in the service of three passions. These were the economic history of the seventeenth century, from which his marvellous *Religion and the Rise of Capitalism* came, the cause of adult education – he was one of the founders of the Workers' Educational Association – and the Labour Party, whose conscience he was for thirty years before his death in 1962.

John Rawls, born in 1921 in Baltimore, USA is notable precisely because in many ways he ought not to be so: he has for thirty years taught philosophy at Harvard, has not taken a visible public part in the controversies which have rocked America in those years, and has, while preserving his privacy, had an astonishing impact on political argument outside the academy simply through the quality of a string of essays in philosophical journals which culminated in his masterpiece, *A Theory of Justice*.

It is often said that the twentieth century has been devoid of political thinkers who can stand comparison with Locke or Mill or Marx, let alone with Hobbes, Aristotle or Plato. It is almost equally often said that this strange vacuum exists only in what might be called 'Anglo-Saxon political thinking' – in the United States and Britain – the suggestion being that Europe has been in continual intellectual ferment. This view was famously put forward by Perry Anderson in his essays, *The Peculiarities of the English* in the *New Left Review* some twenty years ago. The tranquillity of British politics has meant that there has been no great pressure to rethink the intellectual foundations of social and political life. More importantly, the absence of class conflict and of revolutionary challenges to the existing order has meant that there have been no ideologists thinking on behalf of a major social class – no George Lukacs trying to work out the relationship between Marxist philosophy, the Communist Party and the proletariat of which it is the vanguard; no Antonio Gramsci applying the Marxist theory of class conflict in a society where the Catholic Church might be a bastion of reaction or a revolutionary force.

There are two or three things to be said about these contrasts. One is that the most compelling twentieth-century philosophy has been anti-political or unpolitical. Jean-Paul Sartre, for instance, was never very persuasive as a political analyst, but painted a marvellous picture of the agonies and anxieties of the intellectual who desperately wanted to make an impact in the political sphere. Martin Heidegger's brief flirtation with the Nazis was not a considered attempt to derive political conclusions from his analysis of human loneliness in the face of death. Albert Camus remains vastly more impressive as a novelist than as a political thinker. Private anguish rather than political organisation was the existentialist forte.

A second is that the pupils of Marx were impressive as political technicians and tacticians rather than as political thinkers. Lenin and Trotsky obviously stand out among political actors for the way in which they decisively imposed their will on the political chaos which had overwhelmed Russia in 1917, but it is harder to take them seriously as social and political thinkers. Lenin's gift to the world was his theory of the revolutionary party and his thoughts about the techniques of the seizure of power. His views on social organisation and economic administration are absurdly simple, and the crudeness of his outlook on everything for which one might fight a revolution is quite alarming. Lenin and Trotsky were vastly important political actors: to my mind, they are not very impressive political thinkers.

The third point is perhaps more important. The twentieth century has been a century of doubts about reason. The success of the Nazis who were avowedly contemptuous of rationality brought home both to their supporters and to their victims the limited success of appeals to reason in political affairs. The rise of analytical, anti-metaphysical philosophy gave intellectuals, at least, rather strong grounds for doubting whether there was such a thing as rational moral commitment. Books like A J Ayer's *Language, Truth and Logic* popularised the notion that moral expressions were a sort of emotional bludgeon rather than candidates for truth or falsehood. This was often called the 'boohooray' theory of ethics because of the way in which it analysed statements like 'democracy is better than fascism' as 'democracy hooray, fascism boo'. Even before this philosophical movement got under way, turn-of-the-century sociologists and psychologists had already made the move which H. Stuart Hughes chronicled in his *Consciousness and Society* towards exploring the irrational and unconscious springs of our behaviour. Freud, of course, stands out among these explorers of the unconscious, but among sociologists, too, writers like Georges Sorel wrote of the role of irrational 'myths' in rousing men to action, and dourly reasonable thinkers like Max Weber struggled to explain the paradoxical ways in which reason and unreason interacted.

I want to suggest that the Anglo-Saxon tradition has not been boring, vacuous or devoid of resources to deal with the challenges of Marxism and irrationalism. Indeed, I think that three thinkers – Bertrand Russell, R. H. Tawney and John Rawls – between them show that the liberal tradition has not fared so badly as its critics think. Of course, in saying this I ought also to say that Russell was a sort of socialist, Tawney a lifelong member of the Labour Party and one of the most important influences on its development between the wars, and Rawls a decidedly radical liberal by American standards. But, Russell's response to the horrors of war, to the ugliness and boredom of much industrial life, and to the sense of futility which many serious and sensitive people feel amid even affluent surroundings, was essentially a reworking of the values and ideals of his 'secular godfather', John Stuart Mill, in the light of twentieth-century sociological and psychological insights. Tawney's concern to appeal to a sense of community, his attacks on greed and self-seeking, and his invocation of the seventeenth-century radicals who first insisted that the 'poorest he that is in England hath a life to lead as doth the richest he' all added up to reminding the twentieth-century reader that the liberalism of Locke rested on an ethic of service to society, which we needed even more than Locke's contemporaries had done. And Rawls' *A Theory of Justice*, a book which was hailed as a classic on its appearance in 1971 and which looks even more impressive with the passing years, defends what amounts to the liberal welfare state against doctrinaire enthusiasts for the rights of private property on the one hand and doctrinaire enthusiasts for the revolutionary millennium on the other. Rawls' theory does not rule out a socialist solution to the problem of achieving social justice, just as it does not rule out all alternatives to socialism either. What it does is to take the central ideals of the liberal tradition and render them more credible in a twentieth-century context.

If I begin with Russell, this partly reflects chronology. Although he was active in the anti-nuclear movement almost until his death in 1970 at the age of ninety-eight, his most interesting work on politics was written in 1915. *The Principles of Social Reconstruction* was the title he gave to a set of lectures which he hoped to deliver to audiences in the main industrial cities of Britain as part of his campaign against the First World War and against the British Government's programme of conscription. The Defence of the Realm Act was invoked to stop him lecturing in Liverpool and Glasgow, but his lectures were read for him by others and, anyway, they were freely and cheaply available in print shortly afterwards.

In the *Principles* Russell addressed himself to the problem of why people did not behave in what he and they would usually have called a 'reasonable' fashion: why did men fight one another on the Somme when they had no real quarrel with one another, and when such real economic disputes as divided the competing colonial powers could have been settled by straight-forward bargaining? The answer seemed to Russell to lie in two directions. First, men are moved by passion rather than by calculation, propelled by instincts which demand satisfaction at all costs, not guided by a calculation of what would do themselves good or make them happy. Certainly, men get some pleasure out of satisfying their impulses – the painter is glad to see his canvas finished, the mountaineer is glad to see his peak conquered – but they do not work out which things will give them most pleasure and then adjust their desire to those things. The mathematician striving to prove a theorem will willingly, if not happily, starve to death for its sake. It is not pleasure that lures him but the instinct of intellectual mastery which drives him forward. When men fight, they don't enjoy it, but they hurl themselves into it willingly. Russell always feared that industrial civilisation was chronically vulnerable to warfare because it stifled so many impulses, thwarted the instinct to grapple with and master the world, and left many men in a state where almost any old fight was more attractive than the stifling boredom of everyday life.

The second part of Russell's case is that men are motivated by two sorts of instinct – possessive instincts and creative instincts. Possessive instincts drive us in pursuit of things that simply cannot be shared, whose possession therefore sets us at odds with other men. The creative instincts, on the other hand, lead us to seek what can be shared. The painting I create is not something I can or wish to keep to myself; your enjoyment of it does not and cannot lessen mine. What has gone wrong with western civilisation is that we have organised ourselves to satisfy our possessive impulses and not our creative ones. Russell did not mean by this that we had simply become greedy and money-grabbing; one of his consistent claims was that most writers grossly overestimated the role of materialistic impulses in people's behaviour. Russell, I think rightly, saw that what drove the Rockefellers and the Pierpoint Morgans could not be the desire for more money – they had more of that than they could spend. The impulse had to be the impulse for power; having more money than anyone else was both a source of power over them and proof that you had that power. The 'robber barons' of American capitalism really were robber barons as far as their motivation went – and, indeed, as far as the rationality of their behaviour went.

Russell was never one for guaranteeing solutions to the problems he saw, nor was he one for sticking to the same solutions for very long at a time. The most notorious example of this was the way in which he advocated a preventive nuclear war against the USSR in 1948; by 1953 he was ready to sue others for saying that he had done so – though he had done so in print several times over the course of three years. In 1959, he willingly agreed that he *had* once done so, but had rightly changed his mind when the policy ceased to make sense. In fact, a good case can be made for supposing that the Americans ought to have used their superior power when they had it, and ought to have thought of something quite different once the Russians had a rough equality of weaponry; what is much odder is that Russell was able to forget his old views so completely that he could think it a communist fabrication to suggest that he had held them.

The Principles of Social Reconstruction is more sober than that. Russell defends policies which the Social Democratic Party would mostly find congenial now. Industry should be reorganised on the basis of workers' co-operatives, save where it is impracticable (as on the railways) where something more like elected managers would meet the case. This is not to envisage wholesale expropriation of the owners of capital in the Marxian fashion, but rather to pension them off and deny them the right to appoint managers and share in capital gains. The extent of Russell's allegiance to the traditional liberal and radical causes comes out even more clearly when he discusses the limits of state authority in general. Characteristically, there is no thought that the state might 'wither away' as in Marxist theory, and no suggestion – another of Marx's optimistic anticipations – that under socialism there would be no such thing as power and politics, only socialist self-administration.

What Russell aims at is more or less what radicals of his vintage always aimed at: to use the power of the state to tax away the unearned increment of landlords and the like who made huge capital gains from the productive efforts of others. This would then be used to provide a welfare floor so that those who had toiled all their lives should not end up in the workhouse, to provide education for all and to encourage the growth of scientific research and other forms of intellectual curiosity – without at the same time allowing the state to encroach on our private lives, our consciences and our moral allegiances generally. The package is one which is sometimes criticised as inconsistent by opponents both to left and right – the right taking the view that the state ought to provide defence and law and order and otherwise leave people alone to fend for themselves; the left holding that the state can be used for any purpose that seems good to the people at large, or their representatives.

What provides the consistency in Russell's account is the underlying picture of human psychology. His critics have always complained that he moves too swiftly from elation to despair about the prospect for humanity. One kindly version was offered by Keynes when he observed that 'Bertie thinks politics is terribly simple; at present everything goes badly because people are mad and wicked, but they have only to behave well, and then everything will be marvellous'.

However, Russell is not quite as vulnerable as that; he thinks that mankind does lurch from displaying marvellous qualities to displaying appalling ones, but it is not a pure effort of will that causes the lurch – different conditions bring out different sides of our natures, which is why it is worth thinking about political arrangements at all. Human nature as the constant puts the appropriate limits on what states ought to do, how they ought to do it, and so on. People are corrupted by power, but not always, and not if the citizenry at large is vigorous in defence of its rights. So the active welfare state is combined with decentralisation, with a whole-hearted attempt to secure genuine equality of the sexes, with institutions which will make work engaging and interesting rather than drudgery, and with a system of education which encourages children to be intellectually adventurous, sexually unafraid and emotionally alive without being unduly sentimental. In total, this amounts to a liberalism which takes on board the new consciousness of our irrationality and struggles to turn it to creative purposes.

Russell was always an individualist; his autobiography constantly dwells on the sense of loneliness he felt all through his life: he could envisage us feeling momentary ecstatic unity with one another, but social and political life always involved a sort of compromise between the demands of our individuality and the needs of others. Just as he always thought he was a terrible performer on committees when he worked for the No Conscription Fellowship in the First World War, so he always thought that the ideal of a society of entirely spontaneous co-operation which the anarchists professed was mere wishful thinking. The best we could achieve would be a balance of goods and evils.

It was this, as much as anything, which made Russell the target of some suspicion to socialist contemporaries. It is instructive to see what the differences are between Russell and Tawney in this light. Both, after all, were non-Marxist socialists; both looked forward to large measures of decentralisation; both looked forward to the disappearance of the functionless shareholder; both looked forward to the extension of a decent education to everyone, regardless of the depth of their parents' purses. Both thought socialism impossible to achieve by revolutionary means; the destruction it would involve would force a meaner and more authoritarian existence on the very workers it was meant to liberate, and the hatred it would stir up would poison political life for many years to come. Tawney was no doubt less radical – or more practically minded – than Russell; he, after all, helped to set up wages councils to improve the lot of the low paid, and he had much more experience of the work of trade unions in getting decent material conditions for their members. All the same, it is true enough that Russell and Tawney were part of the movement from which the Labour Party has benefited so much, which saw the Labour Party as the means by which the programme of radical liberalism could be carried out.

Anyone who has read both of them will flinch at this – and

rightly. I have deliberately left out what really does separate them, and what in the end makes Russell far more of a liberal than a socialist, and what makes Tawney a much more straightforward socialist than Russell. Russell's individualism, and his interest in the irrational springs of human conduct made him an elitist, not about people but about their experiences. Nothing compared with the discovery of an important abstract truth: in 1914 Russell wrote an essay on the ethics of war in which he denied that we had a general right to self-defence which would justify our killing the highwayman who accosted us with drawn pistol, but went on to say that if, for instance, we had just discovered a mathematical theorem of the first importance, we were certainly entitled to kill our assailant for the sake of preserving our theorem.

It is inconceivable that Tawney would ever have thought like that. His view of the decent society was one in which anyone could tell anyone else to go to hell but nobody felt inclined to do so. *The Acquisitive Society* and the more famous *Equality* are built round the assumption that the ordinary, hard-working, decent Englishman is as important in the eyes of God, and ought to be as important in the eyes of society as the ecstatically truth-seeking mathematician – let alone the idle landlord. Tawney did not have Russell's anxieties about the lonely intellectual's sense of the meaninglessness of existence, and did not have his obsession with the intermittent moments of soul-to-soul communication. Rather, he thought that most people would feel happier and more satisfied with life if they felt – and were right to feel – that they were contributing something useful to society. So, when they discuss education, for instance, Russell is always looking out for the moment when we ought to turn our attention to the brightest and the best, while Tawney is always insisting on the absurd loss of talent which an inegalitarian educational system involves and looking for ways in which a comprehensive secondary education system would create feelings of neighbour-liness and fraternity. Again, Russell knew nothing of the world of the Workers' Educational Association in which Tawney worked for so long, and had no conception of the way in which the ordinary man might bring to complicated subjects a good sense and shrewdness which intellectuals might quite fail to possess.

To my mind, Tawney's is the more attractive character, but the sceptic might retort that Tawney was ready to believe in the good sense of the ordinary man only because he never wholly came to terms with the way in which 'ordinary men' have in the twentieth century run concentration camps, dropped high explosives and, twice already, atomic bombs on their fellows. The domestic qualities of Tawney's thinking, and his reliance on old English habits of civility and forbearance, are very nice, and, indeed, they have so far proved to be perfectly sensible guides to action. But do they address as many of our anxieties as they should?

Perhaps the feeling that somehow political thinking had got trapped between extravagant jeremiads about the horrors of the twentieth century on the one hand and decent reformism on the other is one of the factors that accounted for the barrenness of political thinking in English and American universities until very recently. The idea expressed in Daniel Bell's famous essay on *The End of Ideology* in 1954 seemed to sum up the consensus – Marxist Utopianism was simply incredible, and one could hardly imagine trade unions and political parties searching for Valhalla or the Elysian Fields with any degree of conviction. All that seemed left was the management of the affluent society where it existed, and the attempt to emulate it where it did not. Political theorists were hardly needed in such a universe; social scientists were some use – they could advise on how to maintain full employment and keep down the crime rate and so on – but political theorists were not needed because there were no real political disagreements to think about.

What put an end to the world described in *The End of Ideology* is hard to say; the discovery of Black discontent in America, the Vietnam War, an increasing sense of unease over the nuclear stalemate all played their part. At all events, while Marxist Utopianism was being revived by Herbert Marcuse and brought on to the Paris streets by students who wanted *l'imagination au pouvoir*, the latest attempt to reconstruct liberalism's defences against blind reaction and wild Utopianism was being made by John Rawls, a Professor of Philosophy at Harvard University, who had been patiently working away at the fundamental principles of liberalism from the mid-1950s.

A Theory of Justice appeared in 1971; unlike most philosophy books it did not drop stillborn from the press, but became compulsory reading for almost every American intellectual. Its aim was to give an account of the basic principles to which any rational person would have to assent if he were to imagine himself charged with the task of drawing up the principles governing a society in which he would have to live and in which he might occupy any position from the top to the bottom. Rawls argued that, faced with such a thought experiment, we would want to institutionalise two principles. The first is that everybody should have as much freedom as is compatible with a like freedom for everybody else. The second is that where there were gains from social co-operation, these should be shared out in such a way that the worst-off person did as well as possible. (The intuitive thought behind this second principle is simple enough; suppose you know that the result of offering incentives to people to develop their talents in various ways will be to make them better off than you. What you should work out is what incentives to them will give you as big a pay-off as possible. If £40,000 paid for your managerial skills makes my income £20,000, and £20,000 paid for your skills only yields me £10,000 I ought to vote for you having £40,000.) Moreover, these two principles stand in a determinate order to each other; the first takes absolute priority over the second – no rational person would risk his liberty for the sake of prosperity.

None of us has ever been asked to design the principles by which the societies we live are governed, and almost all of us have a pretty clear idea what social position we shall occupy in the society in which we live. This, however, is the point which Rawls relies on. Our knowledge of our own talents and tastes, and our knowledge of our own probable social place, stand in the way of fairness all round. Either we are guilty of simple egotism – we just hold out for as much as we can get as the price of our co-operation with the rest of our fellows; or we are guilty of complicated and self-deceiving egotism – our social position deludes us about the real values of ourselves (teachers think education is madly undervalued, doctors think the medical profession is madly overworked, and so on). Reflecting on these familiar facts, we can see that one way of clearing our minds about what a just society would be like is to ask ourselves what rules we could all agree to, supposing that we lacked the information which either tempts us to selfishness or deludes us about fairness.

The thought is that we would, in this state of ignorance, think about what might happen to us if we turned out to come at the bottom of the social heap; and the only sensible thing to do would be to design rules which required that the people at the bottom did as well as they could possibly do. Where it is a matter of one's civil liberties, the right to a fair trial and other fundamental rights, the basic requirement that we should not be used as means to other people's ends simply means that we want to be as free as possible, and cannot accept being at the mercy of other people any more than they would agree to be at ours. In essence, justice, and the liberal panoply of rights, are reflections in social institutions of a desire to take advantage of the benefits of social co-operation, but to do so with a caution that reflects our awareness of human beings' limited altruism and their disposition to self-preference.

Rawls insists that none of this begs the question whether socialism or a 'social market economy' is the more desirable. There is no 'natural right' to private property, just as there is no natural, prior ownership of our talents or abilities. What there are, are those rights which rational contractors would establish as the framework of their society. All the same, the theory places pretty tight restrictions on what sort of socialism one could implement consistently with the dictates of justice. Freedom of choice in education and occupation, for instance, which are part of our basic liberties, would knock on the head any idea of implementing a command economy on the Soviet model, except as an emergency measure in time of war or civil war, when the whole system of civil liberties was at risk. It certainly looks easier to implement the theory in something like welfare-state capitalist surroundings.

But they are certainly welfare state surroundings, if they are capitalist at all; the worst-off people have a right to be as well off as possible – they are not to be dependent on the good will or the charity of the rich. Or, to put it differently, the better off only have a right to those advantages which also benefit their less well-off fellows. And the theory is certainly a radically liberal theory. Take, for instance, the theory of civil disobedience to which Rawls commits himself. Where Russell defended his campaigns of civil disobedience on the general ground that anything which might stop the slide to the holocaust was worth trying, Rawls sees a place for civil disobedience as part of normal politics. The state can claim our allegiance only if it is a just state. If it is generally just, we shall only expect others to obey it out of a sense of its general justness; if it departs from the paths of justice, we positively ought to refuse to obey it in order to call attention to its failings, and to ask for 'reconsideration' by those who have taken the decisions objected to. To object to the Vietnam War, for instance, and to refuse to aid the state in conscripting young men to fight in an unjust cause, Rawls would argue, is part of good citizenship, not a halfway house to revolution.

In terms of my initial claim that what modern liberal theorists have had to do is come to terms with the twin pressures of

Marxist attacks on liberalism, and irrationalist accounts of political motivation, Rawls' theory is both more old-fashioned than Russell's or Tawney's and yet in some ways more successful. It is more old-fashioned in simply assuming that if we think hard about our moral obligations and put our minds to meeting them, we shall on the whole act rightly. Rawls does have a bit to say about political psychology and the way in which an egalitarian society will generate fraternity and tolerance, but he does not confront head-on the doubts about our motives which Freud, or Sorel, or Marcuse confronted. On the other hand, it is less vulnerable than Russell's theory to the objection that it is simply the outpourings of a romantic individualism, and less vulnerable than Tawney's to the charge that it is parochial and relies much too heavily on a particular society's traditions. And compared with both of them, it sticks to one crucial task – clearing liberalism of the charge that its conception of justice and its notions of human rights are simply a screen for the operations of the capitalist economy.

Neither individually nor collectively do these liberal and reformist socialist theories have the dramatic quality of, say, the Utopianism of Marcuse or the nostalgic republicanism of Hannah Arendt. They are perhaps less emotionally satisfying than some sorts of conservative theory – whether the discreet, rather Hegelian conservatism of an Englishman like Michael Oakeshott or the 'blood and soil' conservatism of a Frenchman like Charles Maurras. However, if politics is amenable to serious thought at all, rather than to expressions of elation, world-weariness and despair, it is in this middle ground that serious thinking is generally done; and in that realm Russell, Tawney and Rawls are by no means an embarrassment to the reputation of the twentieth century.

The Moderns:
Herbert Marcuse and
Hannah Arendt –
'critics of the present'
Liam O'Sullivan

Herbert Marcuse was born in Berlin in 1898 and educated at Berlin and Freiburg. Before emigrating to America in 1938 he became a member of the Frankfurt School of Social Research, with which he continued to be associated. He was employed by the American State Department during the war and after a long period of research in major American universities he became Professor of Political Thought at the University of California. His name is indissolubly linked with the surge of activity and expression which characterised the political tumult of the late 1960s, the student revolt, the New Left, and the politics of imagination. He died in 1980.

Hannah Arendt was born in Hanover in 1906 and educated at Marburg, Freiburg and Heidelberg. In her student days she formed close links with the philosophers Martin Heidegger and Karl Jaspers. Fleeing Germany, she lived in France until 1941 when she emigrated to the United States. Both in France and the USA she worked with various Jewish organisations and in that way was politically active during the Hitler period. After some years as a publisher's editor she had teaching posts at several major American universities and achieved eminence as an essayist and controversialist as well as writing ambitious works in political theory and in philosophy. Since her death in 1975 her reputation as a unique and distinctive figure has continued to grow.

The idea that serious thinking about politics on a grand scale has ceased in the twentieth century as a consequence of catastrophic events and disabling insights regarding the nature of mind itself is an Anglo-American idea, a mid-Atlantic – one might almost say Nato-politan – thought. In the epoch of the camp, the bomb and the bureaucrat, it came to seem that to write, to teach with urgency and ambition regarding the human condition or politics was to be part of the problem rather than a contributor to possible solutions. For a while the crucial challenges of the twentieth century seemed to have stunned political philosophy into silence; and this was particularly true of Britain and America, where a certain distance from the central dramas and ideological conflicts had added strength to the belief that Belsen and the Gulag, Freud and Marx were evidence of the fact that the promise of politics is a lie. Often it has been emigrés, exiles and intellectually displaced persons who have responded most directly to these dramas and conflicts, and in attempting to make them intelligible have generated fresh ways of thinking about our present situation.

Two such figures are Herbert Marcuse and Hannah Arendt. They have much in common, yet there is much that separates them. Both were exiles to the United States who were born and educated in Germany and settled into the academic community in middle life after long periods of relative independence. Both gained a certain fame and public attention, by no means always favourable, in their maturity. They were each shaped in response to Nazism and the emergence of totalitarian rule and were pre-occupied with the problems of mass civilisation. Marcuse and Arendt are comparable figures in terms of their indebtedness to a European intellectual tradition, in terms of the large issues which they address and in the thoroughness of their responses to the crises of our time. They are at opposite poles with regard to their commitments, their diagnosis, and in the sense which they may give of possible solutions to the modern predicament.

Not without surprise, the slogan 'Marx, Mao, Marcuse' brought to prominence a writer whose reputation had rested on Hegelian scholarship, critical discussion of Russia, and elaborate essays on psychoanalysis and cultural criticism. Until his death in 1980 he was identified with political radicalism.

A common feature of radical views of politics from earliest times until the present is that they counterpose to the obvious world of politics a vision of human possibilities, possibly discernible in the present order but in sharp contrast to common experience. A Golden Age, a fully human world, varied and full, can be imagined, where the neglected potentialities of life may be realised. The radical, in this sense, is one who is permanently alerted to a gap between what is and what should be, between the suffering, waste, untruth and peril of the present, and the joy, plenitude, significance and security of a possible future. If the conservative understands the present, which he is inclined to cherish, in terms of a past whose achievements should be preserved for those to come, the radical is inclined to see the present as a time of tension and difficulty which may give rise to a new movement or stifle its birth, and to see the past as both evidence of possibility and catalogue of defeat. The conservative and the radical have a different relationship with the dimension of time, a different understanding of the character of history.

Marcuse's radicalism is distinctive, and problematic, in that without relinquishing hope he casts a cold eye over the possibilities of its fulfilment. His view of the present is marked by outrage, bleakness and pessimism, his sense of a future Golden Age by a sharp emphasis upon the powers and obstacles that lie in the way of its realisation. The circumstances of the modern world are, for Marcuse, overwhelmingly concentrated in favour of power structures which deaden, misuse and abort the life – affirming energies of humanity which they exploit to sustain their own dominance. The present industrial civilisation with its 'warfare' states, its consumerism, its ecological crisis, its growing violence and cynicism, the banality and emptiness of its culture and its administration of mass consciousness is threatened by the growing and ever-present threat of catastrophe, resurgent fascism and totalitarian closure.

For Marcuse the rise of totalitarianism in the twentieth century is not a single phenomenon which has a general character. Distinction must be made between the great dictatorships, between Nazism and Stalinism. Nazism is an outcrop, a sort of tumour of monopoly capitalism, a barbarism produced by capitalism at the end of its tether. Soviet rule is a species of tyranny, the dominance of populations by unassailable elites, a kind of perversion of Marxism conditioned in part by a global struggle with the capitalist powers. Both represent a blighting of traditional left-wing hopes for revolution through the agency of a politicised working class.

It is against such an account that Marcuse undertakes the critique of modern civilisation for which he is mainly remembered – notably, in two polemical and speculative works, *Eros and Civilisation* (1953) and *One Dimensional Man* (1964), which enjoyed an underground reputation before they emerged in the late 1960s as perhaps largely unexamined emblems of liberation.

Eros and Civilisation is a work of great ambition which seeks to retrieve the promise of liberation by an examination of the theories and circumstances which most strongly suggest that it is an impossibility and an illusion. Part of its purpose is to engage with the diagnosis of Sigmund Freud (whose claims and insights generally are a stumbling block for political theory) that the progress of civilisation is necessarily purchased at the cost of common unhappiness and must carry with it an unavoidable burden of discontent. The title of the book is a play upon that of Freud's essay *Civilisation and its Discontents*, in which Freud postulated (contentiously) the existence of an aggressive or death instinct whose release waits upon those who try too ambitiously to cure the ills of society through revolutionary urgency. Freud argues that the hopes of a Golden Age are illusory, representing the attempt to engage fully with the repressed energies and desires, the secret wishes for gratification, unwelcome to social mores and disruptive of them, which must remain relatively unconscious to individuals as they engage in the tasks which their lives assign to them. To the degree that unconscious needs and wishes are repressed and occluded, they are points of vulnerability which may always express themselves in perverse and regressive forms, as disabling neuroses. Through psychoanalysis the mature individual may gain sufficient self-mastery to suppress those urges which have become visible to him, and through work and sublimation to deploy those energies for necessary and exalted tasks. 'Liberation' is a possibility which Freud views with extreme caution and sobriety.

For those who accept (as Marcuse does) the essential argument of the later Freud, it would seem that radical hopes are blighted. And it is for this reason, among others, that many attempts to politicise psychoanalysis by thinkers as diverse as Erich Fromm and Wilhelm Reich have found it necessary to revise or undermine the central tenets of psychoanalysis. Marcuse tries to remain within the Freudian orthodoxy and yet retain a radical vision. In order to do so he seeks to demonstrate that civilisation itself has become pathogenic, that progress has become a form of barbarism. In this sense, the modern world, with its damage to people and its hideous dangers, speaks of an excessive dominance of society over human needs even though its vast and indeed greatly superfluous accumulation of wealth provides the possibility of a material abundance. It should be possible that suffering humanity might at last relax and engage in the many-sided gratification of life energies which are overdue for expression and release. Combining a Marxian idea with the Freudian claim, Marcuse contends that industrial society extracts an unnecessary payment, a 'surplus repression' of individual yearnings such that the life processes of individuals are diverted into the accumulation of material rewards of a doubtful or damaging character. The life tasks of individuals are now, according to Marcuse, redundant to worthwhile purposes, and the 'reality' which we are forced to engage with is organised and controlled by dominating powers that have lost their progressive character. In this sense the juggernauting trajectory of capitalism has over-reached itself and has become overwhelmingly destructive of human potentialities and of nature.

In Marcuse's version of psychoanalysis, the liberation of Eros (the life instinct) is both possible and necessary. But it can only be achieved through the coming into existence of a higher order of civilisation than that which Freud seemed capable of imagining. With the acceleration of commodity production, the demands of work and the imperatives of an historically conditioned society have, according to Marcuse, shaped the lives of human beings so that effort and sacrifice of gratification have become the principle of their existence, the so-called 'performance principle', an ingrained discipline and striving, which, in the circumstances described above, become obsolete. But they cannot merely be set aside, for to do so would be to dissolve the achievements of culture, to destroy the human world as such. Liberation, without the replacement of the principle of performance by some other, more fittingly human foundation of life would entail a regressive collapse back into the natural world.

Where can we look for an alternative basis for life other than in a technical industrial reality which has outlived itself? How can freedom be deployed humanly, significantly? Marcuse believes that the intimation of such a new direction is to be discerned in the world of artistic creativity and achievement, in the aesthetic dimension. In art we can see the possibility for a grounding of life in which 'order is beauty and work is play'. A new shape of consciousness can emerge in which the aesthetic principle becomes, so to speak, generalised. Human activity will take on a play-like character so that the kind of freedom experienced by the artist as a bohemian and peripheral figure in bourgeois society whose product is destined for the museum will inform all the relations between human beings. Our work will cease to be alienated, and our conflict with nature will take on a harmonious character.

This transcription of leisurely Californian values onto humanity as a whole is not derived simply from Marcuse's self-confessed 'romantic sentimentalism'. It is, he believes, a real material possibility, consistent with tolerable prosperity. As work in the old sense becomes redundant, strivings for achievement can be replaced by playful and artistic values. In such a way the aesthetic dimension – given a central place within the human faculties in the philosophy of Kant and erected into a principle of education and personal development by Schiller – can be seen as an emergent alternative to the harsh drives of work and the ingrained principle of performance. The eternal struggle between Eros and Thanatos (the death instinct), those 'ancient adversaries', can be shifted in favour of life and against death. Whether or not the kind of Utopia that Marcuse projects, in which there is a deep return to a long-repressed narcissism where persons may embrace the world and see it as their own, confers an adequate dignity and significance on human existence, is indeed 'fully human', it is clear that he foresees nearly insuperable obstacles to its realisation.

Modern society, as portrayed in *One Dimensional Man*, is not simply aggressive, exploitative and dominated by an overwhelmingly powerful ruling class; it has also acquired the capacity to absorb into itself the forces which might seek to oppose it. This is true not only of the supposed revolutionary subject, the industrial working class, whom Marcuse believes to have entered into a collusive relationship with a capitalism which 'administers its needs'. It is true of ideas, of science and indeed of art also. The flatness and mediocrity of modern existence is for Marcuse a consequence of this absorption. Modern reality is oppressive because it denies the power of the 'negative'. Only the given facts have reality, and ideas, claims or fantasies which cannot be accommodated to the pragmatic needs of the status quo are either swept aside or given a positive function within prevailing society.

The arts, the sciences and philosophy are confined, become instruments for inculcating greed, developing the technique of war or are limited to a commonplace agenda. And modern society, in its permissiveness, offers 'a repressive desublimation', a shallow liberation removing the tensions of conflict and reducing critical energies. There is, he claims, a growing ability to accommodate all refusal, all challenge to the available means of thought and expression. With the administration of consciousness, the imagination has no play of movement such that we may discriminate between what is and what should be. It is possible to discern in the activities of those at the edges of society – students, blacks, various minorities and in Third World liberation struggles – the basis of a refusal to accommodate to the demands and thought-ways of capitalism. Nevertheless, it seems, for Marcuse, that the techniques of control have grown so that the prevailing order is unchallengeable, and perhaps can be dislodged only by catastrophe. Modern toleration admits cynicism and aggression in increasing quantities. If the societies of the east are held down by main force, for Marcuse, the west is in some ways in a worse condition, such that refusal to be absorbed begins to disappear even at the level of imagination.

It is not yet possible to assess the significance or value of Marcuse's ideals, or to give full sense to the alternative for which they reach. Within his work he brings together a variety of competing traditions which might be thought to be grossly at odds with one another. His analysis combines Marxism and Utopianism, the pessimism of Freud and its transcendence, the attempt to combine the spirit of Romanticism with that of the Enlightenment. At the close of the second millennium, it is an argument which has a millennial, an apocalyptic flavour, and is sometimes expressed obliquely and obscurely, and sometimes with clarity and passion. Sometimes he writes unfairly and crudely and is, in a bad way, journalistic; sometimes he is scholarly, judicious and perhaps profound. But always there is the sense, as he puts it, 'as at the close of a Shakespearian tragedy of the hope that henceforth things can be other than this'.

Hannah Arendt is preoccupied with precisely the same themes as left-wing radicals such as Marcuse. She isolates a virtually identical set of symptoms with regard to the present problems of the world, but she disagrees about the nature of the disease. For her, the central issue of politics is the struggle of life against death – not, as for Marcuse, of biologically understood life against mechanistic death, but rather of human, meaningful life against the attritions of biological decay which may seem to reduce all human strivings to pointlessness and futility.

For Arendt a central thought which influences everything that she writes is the wonderful sense of newness, openness of possibility, that arises within us at the birth of a child. The most signal of all events, that of '*natality*', of new beginning, of the unpredictable possibilities enshrined within the unique and irreplaceable person at the outset of their lives, preoccupied her from her earliest studies (a student thesis on St Augustine). The realisation of the promise of freedom, the development of our humanity in the active life, is the route through which the individual – who, as the Greeks insisted, 'lives only for a day' – may gain immortality. Politics takes on an existential meaning in that, for Arendt, in the public life freedom can become an actuality. The darkness of our times occurs because the spaces in which our humanity may come into existence are closed off, and the conditions for freedom are no longer understood.

Her argument is complex but self-consistent. As for so many theorists in the western tradition, a permanent point of reference for Hannah Arendt is the ancient world, and in particular the Greek *polis*. In the *polis*, she claimed, where public life is developed to a high degree, the conditions existed whereby citizens could come together to deliberate about common purposes. In the exchange of unique points of view upon topics of common concern, opinion is formed and individuality developed. People are both united and separated. Politics, deliberation and presentation of the self in public space, marked by the desire to excel rather than to dominate, is seen as a vital component of the active life. Through an undetermined talking out of ourselves in public spaces, along with our fellows, action (which includes speech) flourishes. In the Greek view, according to Arendt, it is through immortal words and deeds, deathless acts celebrated in the endless talk of others, that human life attains significance.

How does any of this affect our understanding of the present? Arendt develops her central idea into a theory of human nature in the major work of her middle period, *The Human Condition* (1958). The search for meaning and significance in the sphere of action is seen by Arendt as inscribed in the essential character of mankind. We are by nature earth-bound creatures, destined to labour in order to satisfy our biological needs. The very essence of labour, shown in the language we use to describe birth and parturition, is that it is biological. Here, mankind is bound by the rhythms of the seasons, struggling to survive as a human animal, and passes from the earth unnoticed, tied into metabolic functions. The celebration of these functions, the view of man as *animal laborans*, consigns us to the world of nature and of anonymity. It also conceals the distinctive character of work. Work, as distinct from labour, produces objects and artefacts which endure. In its essential character, as developed by the craftsman, work both expresses personality and provides us with tools, instruments, dwellings, a framework for activity, a 'world'. Finally, action, which is self-determined and free, and through which our human character makes itself manifest, requires circumstances in which our bodily needs have been attended to by labour, and the fabric of our common life constructed by work. Arendt here continues to draw upon the ancient distinction between the world of the household which requires biological and economic functions and gives us privacy, and the world of the *polis* which gives us a sphere for action, 'publicness'. It is a central mistake to believe that we can be liberated from necessity, from work, according to Arendt, through political means. Such has been the programme of revolutionaries who mistake their task.

With modernity, she argues, the three realms of labour, work and action have been collapsed into one another. Work, through mass manufacture, has become mere labour, producing objects made not to endure but to be consumed. Art tends to merge into entertainment and becomes disposable, again fulfilling only a biological necessity, for rest and recreation. And the sphere of politics, has, she claims, lost its distinctiveness through obsessive concentration upon the administration of needs, rather than with deliberation on common purposes within the space of freedom. Bureaucracy, which is the rule of the office (or 'no one') swells, and preoccupation with economics and with social problems comes to fill the political agenda, as matter for the development of expertise rather than the formation of opinion and the genuine interchange of distinctive points of view. Examples and intimations of real politics in Arendt's sense occur periodically, in the town meetings which still persist in the United States, in councils of workers and soldiers – which appeared in Russia and Europe in times of revolution and again in Hungary in 1956 – in the Paris Commune, and possibly in the student movement of the 1960s. We see, she thinks, instances of spontaneity, serious-ness and self-governance, which reach for the possibilities lost in mass society. It has also been exhibited in the politics of the labour movement in consequence of its exclusion from normal channels of influence.

As publicness, in her particular sense, is diminished, so too is privacy. Society (in her view a recent development) expands to fill all our lives, human beings become superfluous, replaceable and interchangeable, and the individual a kind of fiction. Great actions which issue from unique individuals and are the sub-stance of 'genuine' history lose significance, and the quest for immortality is vested in the progress of society, which takes on a life of its own. Such processes are carried to the limit with totalitarianism, which she sees as the distinctively modern form of domination.

In *The Origins of Totalitarianism* (1951) on which her early reputation was based, she sets out to identify those forces which made it a possibility and to analyse the meaning of its character-istic intention, namely, the destruction of individuality. In an elaborate analysis she tries to show that totalitarianism, including Nazism and Stalinism, is a nightmare extension of widely prevalent modern tendencies. Pre-conditions for its emergence had been nurtured within mass society. And through imperialism, colonial administration and the growth of nationalism, there had developed shapes of consciousness in which humanity was seen as indefinitely malleable, changeable through domination and effort of will, and in which meaning and significance in life could be gained through the sacrifice of the individual to the larger social whole.

The short-lived history of totalitarian states – with their arbitrariness and violence designed further to detach individuals from one another, to pulverise them into a mass; with propaganda intended less to indoctrinate than to make it impossible for people to think; with gigantic emphasis on world-changing projects made to show that anything is possible – is a story of a concentrated attempt to destroy the basis for independent action. Genocide, bureaucratically administered – the concentration camp – should not be seen simply as evidence of vast cruelty and excessive power, nor as instrumental to any particular interests. Genocide is a feature of human history; cruelty and brutality are recurrent in our lives. Totalitarian genocide and horror are not, she thinks, gratuitous. They are designed to destroy the possibility of human meaning. In that sense the concentration camp, she thinks, is an experiment for the administration of states. To see it as an exercise of power is mistaken, for power is a political phenomenon which grows from the concerted action of individuals. It is, rather, the logical extension of the trajectory of mass society where meaning is provided by ideology, and in which rootless and isolated human beings are vulnerable to total manipulation through the collapse of both publicness and privacy.

Arendt is pessimistic. Politics, for her, has always been a struggle between freedom and tyranny. But the new forms of domination are worse than tyranny in that they seek to eliminate in a clinically conceived fashion the very grounds of human action. But she writes to warn rather than to prophesy. In her view of modernity, the decline of the public realm has opened the possibility of systematic lying as the basis of politics, and the lie is endemic in totalitarian systems which seek to create a fictional world where anything is possible. Herein lies a sharp contrast with the view of Marcuse. For Arendt, one major problem of modernity is that people come *too easily* to value imagination over reality. 'Reality' is itself a product of the public realm, for only where we act in concert so that others can see and hear what we also witness is truth promulgated. In the absence of publicness and the light of common experience, fantasy may reign untrammelled and populations become the playthings of demagogic illusionists. Realism and its attendant value of common sense are our only defence against the wilful imposition of false worlds.

It would be misleading to counterpose Herbert Marcuse and Hannah Arendt as if their ideas were in systematic opposition – he an out-of-the-ordinary radical, she an unusual kind of conservative, and so on. For what they both demonstrate is that openness and sensitivity to important issues may generate creative reflection upon the questions which we must all face, and this, in its way, unites them.

The Contributors

Chapter 1 Plato
Dr *Christopher Rowe*, born in Cambridgeshire in 1944, read Classics at Trinity College, Cambridge from 1962–65. After three years' research on Aristotle for his PhD, also at Trinity, he joined Bristol University, where he is now a Senior Lecturer in the Department of Classics and Archaeology, working mainly on Greek philosophy and literature. He is author of *The Eudemian and Nicomachean Ethics: A Study in the Development of Aristotle's Thought*, Cambridge University Press, 1971; *An Introduction to Greek Ethics*, Hutchinson, 1976 and *Essential Hesiod*, Bristol Classical Press, 1978. (See also 'Book List', p 199.)

Chapter 2 Aristotle
Peter Nicholson was born in Guildford, Surrey in 1940. He studied Government at the University of Exeter where he gained a BA (Soc sts) in 1961. He lectured in the Department of Political Theory and Government at the University College of Swansea (University of Wales) from 1963–79 and then moved to the University of York where he is now a Senior Lecturer in the Department of Politics, teaching mainly on the history of political thought. He is Treasurer of the Society for the Study of Greek Political Thought, which promotes the study of Aristotle and other Greek thinkers, and of the times in which they lived, and would be glad to answer any queries about membership. Please address enquiries to him c/o the following address: Department of Politics, University of York, Heslington, York, YO1 5DD.

Chapter 3 St Augustine
Dr *Janet Coleman*, born in New York in 1945, was educated at Yale University where she gained an MPhil and PhD in Medieval Studies in 1970. From 1970–71 she was a post-doctoral Fulbright Fellow at L'Ecole des Hautes Etudes at the University of Paris. She then became college supervisor in History at

Cambridge for various colleges and was a member of Clare Hall and St Edmund's House; she also lectured in Medieval History at Cambridge from 1972–78 for the History Faculty. She was a Senior Research Fellow at the Warburg Institute, University of London, from 1974–75 and now lectures in Politics at Exeter University where she has been since 1978. She is co-founder and co-editor of the journal, *History of Political Thought*. She is author of *English Literature in History, 1350–1400: Medieval Readers and Writers*, Hutchinson, 1981 and *Piers Plowman and the Moderni*, Edizioni di Storia e Letteratura, Rome, 1981 (in English).

Chapter 4   St Thomas Aquinas

Dr Antony Black was born in Leeds in 1936. He studied History at King's College, Cambridge from 1957–60 and then went on to study for a PhD from 1960–63, which he obtained in 1967. In 1963 he became a Lecturer in the Department of Political Science at the University of Dundee (which was then Queen's College, Dundee, University of St Andrews) where he has been ever since, with the exception of 1975–76 when he was Visiting Associate Professor at the American University in Washington DC. He is now Senior Lecturer at the University of Dundee. He is author of *Monarchy and Community: Political Ideas in the Later Conciliar Controversy 1430–50*, Cambridge University Press, 1970; *Council and Commune: the Conciliar Movement and the Fifteenth Century Heritage*, Search Press, 1979 and *Guilds and Civil Society in European Political Thought from the Twelfth Century to the Present*, Methuen, 1984.

Chapter 5   Machiavelli

Professor Sydney Anglo, born in London in 1934, studied History at London University and, in 1959, completed his PhD under the supervision of Frances Yates at the Warburg Institute. In 1961 he was appointed Lecturer in the History of Ideas at the University College of Swansea, where he is now Professor in that subject. In 1965 he was elected Fellow of the Society of Antiquaries; in 1971–72 he was a Senior Fellow at the Warburg Institute, and a Leverhulme Research Fellow from 1979–80. He has published several books, including *Spectacle, Pageantry and Early Tudor Policy*, Clarendon Press, 1969, and has contributed numerous articles to learned journals. He is currently completing two books – one on the history of the tournament and duel, and the other on the reception of Machiavelli. (See also 'Book List', p 199.)

Chapter 6   Calvin

Harro Höpfl was born in Berlin in 1943. He was educated at Wimbledon College and the London School of Economics where from 1962–66 he studied politics and political thought, and took a BSc (Econ) and MSc. He has been a Lecturer in Political Thought at the University of Lancaster since 1967 and has written on Calvin and on early modern political thought. Currently he is engaged in research into the political doctrines of the Jesuits to 1630. (See also 'Book List', p 199.)

Chapter 7   Hobbes

Dr Richard Tuck was born in 1949 at Newcastle upon Tyne. He read History at Jesus College, Cambridge, where he has been a Fellow since 1971. He is Director of Studies in History at the college and is a University Lecturer in History. He is the author of *Natural Rights Theories*, Cambridge University Press, 1979.

Chapter 8   Locke

John Dunn, born in Fulmer in 1940, took his BA in History at King's College, Cambridge in 1962 and was a graduate student in the Faculty of History at Cambridge from 1962–64; from 1964–65 he held a Harkness Fellowship at Harvard University and since 1966 has been a Fellow of King's College, Cambridge. He became Lecturer in Political Science at Cambridge University in 1972 and has been Reader in Politics there from 1977. From 1968–69 he was a Visiting Lecturer at the University of Ghana and later at the Universities of British Columbia and Bombay, and at Tokyo Metropolitan University. He is author of numerous books, including *Modern Revolutions*, Cambridge University Press, 1972; *Western Political Theory in the Face of the Future*, Cambridge University Press, 1979 and *The Politics of Socialism*, Cambridge University Press, 1984.

Chapter 9   Rousseau

Dr Robert Wokler was born in France and educated at the University of Chicago, from which he received his BA in Social Studies in 1964, and at Oxford where he took his DPhil. He also studied the History of Political Thought at the London School of Economics and was a Senior Research Fellow at Sidney Sussex College, Cambridge. He works mainly in the history of eighteenth and early nineteenth century social thought, on Rousseau and on anthropology in the Enlightenment. He is currently Senior Lecturer in Government at the University of

Manchester. His writings include *Rousseau's 'Discours sur l'inégalité' and its Sources* and monographs on Rousseau, Diderot and Rameau.

Chapter 10   Smith
Dr John Robertson was born in 1951 in Dundee. He read Modern History at Wadham College, Oxford (1969–1972) for his MA; subsequently he did research under Professor Hugh Trevor-Roper for his DPhil. A Research Lecturer of Christ Church 1975–1980, since then he has been a University Lecturer and Fellow and Tutor in Modern History at St Hugh's College, Oxford. He is author of *The Militia Issue and the Scottish Enlightenment*, John Donald, in press, and has published articles on David Hume and Adam Smith.

Chapter 11   Mill
Dr John Gray was born in South Shields in 1948. He studied Philosophy, Politics and Economics at Oxford from 1968–71, where he now teaches as a Fellow of Jesus College. He gained his doctorate on John Stuart Mill and has published a book entitled *Mill on Liberty: a Defence* (see 'Book List', p 199). He is also author of *Hayek on Liberty*, Blackwell, 1984 and is currently working on a book entitled *Liberalism* for the Open University Press.

Chapter 12   Marx
Dr Terrell Carver, born in Idaho, USA, in 1946, studied for his BA in Government at Columbia University, New York where he graduated in 1968. He took a BPhil and DPhil at Balliol College, Oxford (both in Politics) and then became a Lecturer in Politics at the University of Liverpool. He now lectures in Politics at the University of Bristol where he has been since 1980. He has written and translated books on Marx and Engels (see 'Book List', p 199) and is currently working on a life of Engels and a book on the political relationship of Marx and Engels to follow up his work *Marx and Engels: the Intellectual Relationship*, Wheatsheaf Books, 1983.

Chapter 13   The Moderns (I)
Alan Ryan was born in London in 1940. Reader in Politics at the University of Oxford since 1978, he read Philosophy, Politics and Economics at Balliol College, Oxford and then taught at Cambridge, Keele, Essex and New York. He has written on John

Stuart Mill (see 'Book List', p 199) and topics in the social sciences. He has just published a book called *Property and Political Theory* and is writing a book on Russell's politics for Penguin.

Chapter 14   The Moderns (II)

Liam O'Sullivan, born in 1937, was educated at London and Southampton Universities. He held a research fellowship at Southampton in 1964 and has taught Political Theory there since 1965. In 1969 he was a Visiting Professor at the State University of New York and has also been Visiting Professor on two occasions at the University of Frankfurt, in 1975 and 1983. His present research interests are concerned with relations between politics and the creative imagination, and with the implications for political philosophy of theories of the emotions. He has recently completed a book entitled *A Politus of Acknowledgement.*

Series consultant

Iain Hampsher-Monk was born in London in 1946. He was educated at St Marylebone Grammar School and the Universities of Keele and Sheffield. He is author of articles on seventeenth and eighteenth century English political thought and on contemporary political theory. He is co-founder and editor (with Dr Janet Coleman) of the journal *History of Political Thought*. He has taught at the University of Exeter for twelve years and is currently Visiting Associate Professor at the University of Missouri, St Louis, USA.

Series presenter

Brian Redhead is a journalist and broadcaster. He was Northern Editor of The Guardian from 1965 to 1969, and Editor of the Manchester Evening News from 1969 to 1975. He is now a presenter of the Radio 4 *Today* programme and a director of World Wide Pictures Limited, a film and television production company.

Book List

Each section has been compiled by the author of the chapter concerned.

Chapter 1 Plato

Works by Plato

Laws Penguin, 1970.
Republic (n.e.) Penguin, 1974.
Republic Pan Books, 1981.
SKEMP, J.B. *Plato's 'Statesman'* Routledge and Kegan Paul, 1952. o.p.

Works on Plato

ANNAS, J. *An introduction to Plato's 'Republic'* Clarendon Press, 1981.
BAMBROUGH, J. R. Ed. *Plato, Popper and politics* W. Heffer and Sons, 1967. o.p.
ROWE, C.J. *Plato* Harvester Press, 1984.
STALLEY, R.F. *An introduction to Plato's 'Laws'* Blackwell, 1983.

Chapter 2 Aristotle

Works by Aristotle

BAMBROUGH, J. R. Ed. *The philosophy of Aristotle* Mentor Books, 1963.
The Nicomachean ethics (Books I, V and X) Penguin, 1969.
The politics Penguin, 1980.

Works on Aristotle

BARNES, J. *Aristotle* (Past Master Series) Oxford University Press, 1982.
LLOYD, G.E.R. *Aristotle: the growth and structure of his thought* Cambridge University Press, 1968.
MULGAN, R.G. *Aristotle's political theory: an introduction for students of political theory* Oxford University Press, 1977. o.p.

Chapter 3 St Augustine
Works by St Augustine

The city of God Penguin, 1972.
The confessions Penguin, 1970.
The confessions of St Augustine (trans. F. J. Sheed) Sheed and Ward, 1944.

Works on St Augustine

BROWN, P. *Augustine of Hippo, a biography* (n.e.) Faber and Faber, 1967. o.p.
CAMPENHAUSEN, von, H. *The fathers of the Latin church* Black, 1964. o.p.
DEANE, H. *The political and social ideas of St Augustine* New York: Columbia University, 1963. o.p.
MARROU, H.I. *St Augustine and his influence through the ages* New York: Harper Torch Books; London: Longman, 1957. o.p.
MOMIGLIANO, A. Ed. *The conflict between paganism and Christianity in the 4th century* Clarendon Press, 1963. o.p.

Chapter 4 St Thomas Aquinas
Works by St Thomas Aquinas

BIGONGIARI, D. Ed. *The political ideas of St Thomas Aquinas* Hafner, 1966.
D'ENTRÈVES, A.P. Ed. *Aquinas: selected political writings* Blackwell, 1948; 1981.
GILBY T. Ed. *Summa Theologiae vol. 28: Law and political theory* Eyre and Spottiswoode, 1966.
SIGMUND, P. Ed. *Aquinas on politics and ethics* New York: Norton, 1984.

Works on St Thomas Aquinas

GILBY, T. *Principality and polity: Aquinas and the rise of state theory in the West* Longman, 1958. o.p.
McINERNY, R. *St Thomas Aquinas* Notre Dame, Indiana: Notre Dame Press, 1982.
WEISHEIPL, J.A. *Friar Thomas d'Aquino; his life, thought and works* Blackwell, 1974.

Chapter 5 Machiavelli
Works by Machiavelli

Machiavelli: the chief works and others (3 vols) North Carolina: Duke University Press, 1965, o.p.

Works on Machiavelli

ANGLO, S. *Machiavelli: a dissection* Victor Gollancz, 1969; Paladin, 1971. o.p.

BERTELLI, S. and INNOCENTI, P. *Bibliografia machiavelliana* Verona: Edizioni Valdonega, 1979.

HALE, J.R. *Machiavelli and renaissance Italy* The English Universities Press, 1961. o.p.

SKINNER, Q. *The foundations of modern political thought* (2 vols) Cambridge University Press, 1978.

WHITFIELD, J.H. *Discourses on Machiavelli* Heffer and Sons, 1969. o.p.

WHITFIELD, J.H. *Machiavelli* Blackwell, 1947. o.p.

Chapter 6 Calvin

Works by Calvin

DILLENBERGER, J. Ed. *John Calvin: selections from his writings* New York: Anchor Books, 1971. o.p.

Institutes of the Christian religion (2 vols – Library of Christian Classics) Westminster, 1960; USA: T. and T. Clark, 1980.

Works on Calvin

HOPFL, H. *The Christian polity of John Calvin* Cambridge University Press, 1982.

McNEILL, J.T. *The history and character of Calvinism* Oxford University Press, 1954. o.p.

PARKER, T.H.L. *John Calvin* Dent, 1975; (2nd r.e.) Lion Publishing, 1982.

WENDEL, F. *Calvin* Fontana, 1965.

WOLIN, S.S. *Politics and vision* Boston: Little, Brown and Co; Allen and Unwin, 1961. o.p.

Chapter 7 Hobbes

Works by Hobbes

MACPHERSON, C.B. Ed. *Leviathan* Penguin, 1968; (n.e.) 1981.

Works on Hobbes

AUBREY, J. *Brief lives* Penguin, 1972.

OAKESHOTT, M. Ed. *Leviathan* (Introduction) Blackwell, 1946. o.p.

RAPHAEL, D.D. *Hobbes: morals and politics* Allen and Unwin, 1977. o.p.

WATKINS, J.W.N. *Hobbes's system of ideas* (2nd ed.) Hutchinson, 1973. o.p.

Chapter 8 Locke

Works by Locke

GOUGH, J.W. and KLIBANSKY, R. Eds *Epistola de tolerantia/A letter on toleration* Clarendon Press, 1968.
LASLETT, P. Ed. *Two treatises of government* Cambridge University Press, 1967.
NIDDITCH, P. Ed. *Essay concerning human understanding* Oxford University Press, 1979.

Works on Locke

DUNN, J. *Locke* (Past Master Series) Oxford University Press, 1984.
DUNN, J. *The political thought of John Locke* (n.e.) Cambridge University Press, 1982.
PARRY, G. *John Locke* Allen and Unwin, 1978.
TULLY, J. *A discourse on property* Cambridge University Press, 1980; (n.e.) 1982.

Chapter 9 Rousseau

Works by Rousseau

Emile Dent, 1974.
MASON, J.H. Ed. *The indispensable Rousseau* Quartet Books, 1979.
The social contract and discourses (2nd r.e.) Dent, 1973.

Works on Rousseau

CRANSTON, M. *Jean-Jacques* Allen Lane, 1983.
CROCKER, L. *Jean-Jacques Rousseau* (2 vols) Collier Macmillan, 1968, 1973. o.p.
HENDEL, C.W. *Jean-Jacques Rousseau: moralist* New York: Bobbs-Merrill Company, 1962. o.p.
MASTERS, R.D. *The political philosophy of Rousseau* Princeton University Press, 1968.
SHKLAR, J.N. *Men and citizens* Cambridge University Press, 1969. o.p.

Chapter 10 Smith

Works by Smith

Lectures on jurisprudence (The Glasgow Edition) Oxford University Press, 1978.
The wealth of nations (The Glasgow Edition) Oxford University Press, 1976. (Also available in editions by Dent, Chicago University Press and Penguin.)
Theory of moral sentiments (The Glasgow Edition) Oxford University Press, 1976.

Works on Smith

CAMPBELL, R.H. and SKINNER, A.S. *Adam Smith* Croom Helm, 1982.

HONT, I. and IGNATIEFF, M. Eds *Wealth and virtue. The shaping of political economy in the Scottish enlightenment* Cambridge University Press, 1983.

LINDGREN, J.R. *The social philosophy of Adam Smith* The Hague: Nijhoff, 1973.

SKINNER, A.S. and WILSON, T. Eds *Essays on Adam Smith* Oxford University Press, 1976.

WINCH, D. *Adam Smith's politics* Cambridge University Press, 1978.

Chapter 11 Mill

Works by Mill

A system of logic Longman, 1930. o.p.

ROSSI, A. Ed. *The subjection of women* In *Essays on sex equality* Chicago University Press, 1970.

Utilitarianism with *On liberty* and *Considerations on representative government* (Everyman University Library) Dent, 1972. o.p.

WINCH, D. Ed. *Principles of political economy* Penguin, 1970. o.p.

Works on Mill

GRAY, J. *Mill on liberty: a defence* Routledge and Kegan Paul, 1983.

HALLIDAY, R.J. *John Stuart Mill* George Allen and Unwin, 1976.

RYAN, A. *John Stuart Mill* Routledge and Kegan Paul, 1975.

TEN, C.L. *Mill on liberty* Oxford University Press, 1980

Chapter 12 Marx

Works by Marx

Capital (3 vols) Lawrence and Wishart, 1976; 1978.

Selected correspondence (3rd r.e.) Lawrence and Wishart, 1975.

Selected works (3 vols) Lawrence and Wishart, 1973; (1 vol.) 1982.

Works on Marx

BERLIN, I. *Karl Marx* (4th ed.) Oxford University Press, 1982. (Guide to further reading on pp.209–223.)

CARVER, T. *Marx's social theory* Oxford University Press, 1982.

McLELLAN, D. *The thought of Karl Marx* (2nd r.e.) Macmillan, 1980.

SUCHTING, W.A. *Introduction to Marxism* Wheatsheaf Books, 1983.

Chapter 13 The Moderns (I)

Works by the Moderns

RAWLS, J. *A theory of justice* Oxford University Press, 1975.

RUSSELL, B. *The practice and theory of Bolshevism* (2nd ed.) Allen and Unwin, 1963.

RUSSELL, B. *Roads to freedom* (11th ed.) Allen and Unwin, 1966.

RUSSELL, B. *Power* (n.e.) Allen and Unwin, 1975.

RUSSELL, B. *The principles of social reconstruction* (n.e.) Allen and Unwin, 1980.

TAWNEY, R.H. *Equality* (5th r.e.) Allen and Unwin, 1965.

TAWNEY, R.H. *The acquisitive society* (n.e.) Harvester Press, 1982.

Works on the Moderns

BELL, D. *The end of ideology* Collier, 1962. o.p.

BERLIN, I. *Political ideas in the twentieth century* in *Four essays on liberty* (n.e.) Oxford University Press, 1975.

CLARK, R. *Bertrand Russell and his world* Thames and Hudson, 1981. o.p.

DANIELS, N. Ed. *Reading Rawls* Blackwell, 1975.

TERRILL, R. *R. H. Tawney and his times: socialism as fellowship* Deutsch, 1974. o.p.

Chapter 14 The Moderns (II)

Works by the Moderns

ARENDT, H. *The human condition* University of Chicago Press, n.d.

ARENDT, H. *The origins of totalitarianism* Cambridge University Press, 1958. o.p.

ARENDT, H. *On revolution* (n.e.) Greenwood Press, 1982; Penguin, 1973.

MARCUSE, H. *Eros and civilisation* Routledge and Kegan Paul, 1956. o.p.

MARCUSE, H. *One dimensional man* Routledge and Kegan Paul, 1964.

Works on the Moderns

CANOVAN, M. *The political thought of Hannah Arendt* Dent, 1974.

KATZ, B. *Marcuse and the art of liberation* Verso, 1982.

PAREKH, B. *Hannah Arendt and the search for a new political theory* Macmillan, 1981.

ROBINSON, P. *The Freudian left: William Reich, Geza Roheim, Herbert Marcuse* New York: Harper and Row, 1969. o.p.

Chronological table of major
political thinkers

The following list is not, of course, complete. As well as all the thinkers mentioned in the essays, it contains most thinkers who have written systematic treatises on politics with some serious claim to originality; it contains authors of important tracts and polemical essays dealing with major politico-historical issues; and it contains some thinkers whose work, although not a conventional theory of politics, was nevertheless directed *at* politics in some way. Examples are as divergent as Tolstoy, or Lorenzo Valla, whose scholarship exposed the fraudulent *Donation of Constantine*, the chief ideological prop of the concept of Papal Supremacy in the Middle Ages. The list also tries to be representative, consequently a better known thinker will sometimes be sacrificed for a lesser in order that a particular tradition of political viewpoint is included.

Iain Hampsher-Monk
(Series Consultant)

d 559 BC	**Solon**	Athenian Constitution (594 BC) Political Elegies	
d 399 BC	**Socrates**	No writings	
d 347 BC	**Plato**	Republic Laws (unfinished)	(c380 BC)
d 338 BC	**Isocrates**	On the Areopagus	(354 BC)
d 322 BC	**Aristotle**	Ethics Politics Rhetoric	
d c264 BC	**Zeno**	No writings	

d c210 BC	**Chrysippus**	No writings	
d 129 BC	**Carneades**	No writings	
d c125? BC	**Polybius**	The Histories	(c146 BC)
d 109 BC	**Paneatius**	On Duties	
d 43 BC	**Cicero**	De Oratore De Republica De Legibus De Officiis	(c88-1 BC) (45 BC)
d 65 AD	**Seneca**	Moral Letters/Essays (c64 AD)	
d c117	**Tacitus, C.**	A Dialogue on Eloquence Histories	(c90) (c110)
d c135	**Epictetus**	Discourses Encheiridion	
d 180	**Aurelius, Marcus**	Meditations	
d 270	**Plotinus**	Enneads	
d 304	**Porphyry**	Against the Christians	
d 397	**Ambrose**	De Officiis Ministrorum	(386)
d 430	**St Augustine of Hippo**	On Christian Doctrine The City of God	(397) (413/27)
d 496	**Gelasius I**	Address	(494)
d 565	**Justinian I**	Digest (Pandects) Institutes Codex	(533) (533) (528/9)
d 882	**Hincmar of Rheims**	Opisculum LV Capitulorum	(c863)
d 1085	**Gregory VII Hildebrand**	Decree Against Lay Investitures Dictatus Papae	(1075) (1075)

d c1159	**Gratian**	Decretum	(c1148)
d 1180	**John of Salisbury**	Polycraticus	(1159)
d 1268	**Bracton, Henry**	Of the Laws and Customs of England	(1268)
d 1274	**Aquinas, St Thomas**	The Rule of Princes (1265/67) Summa Theologiae (c1266/73)	
d 1306	**John of Paris**	De Potestate Regia et Papali	(1302)
d 1316	**Giles of Rome (Agidius Romanus)**	De Ecclesiastica Potestate	(1302)
d c1320	**Dubois, Pierre**	De Recuperatione Terrae Sancte	(c1306)
d 1321	**Alighieri, Dante**	De Monarchia	(1310)
d 1342	**Marsilius of Padua**	Defender of the Peace	(1324)
d 1349	**William of Ockham**	The Dialogue (1343) The Powers of Emperors and Popes	(1346)
d 1357	**Bartolus of Sassoferrato**	Commentary on the Code of Justinian (1389) Tract on City Government	
d 1384	**Wycliffe, William**	On Civil Lordship (1376) De Officio Regis	(1379)
d 1406	**Salutati, Coluccio**	Letters A Treatise on Tyrants	(1400)
d 1415	**Huss, John**	De Ecclesia	(1413)
d 1420	**d'Ailly, Pierre**	On the Authority of the Church	(1416)

d 1429	**Gerson, Jean**	On Ecclesiastical Power (1417)
d 1444	**Bruni, Leonardo**	Dialogues A Eulogy of the City of Florence (1403/4) A History of the Florentine People (1414/20)
d 1444	**Vergerio, Pier Paulo**	On Good Manners (1402) Letter to Petrarch (1394) On Monarchy or the Best Form of Rule (1394/1405) Fragment on the Republic of Venice
d 1457	**Valla, Lorenzo**	A Declamation on the False Donation of Constantine (1445) On the Elegance of the Latin Language (1471)
d 1464	**Nicholas of Cusa**	On Universal Concord (1433) Dialogue (c1440) On the Peace of Faith (1453)
d 1476	**Fortescue, Sir John**	In Praise of the Laws of England (c1490)
d 1498	**Savonarola, Girolamo**	On Political and Kingly Government (?1494) A Tract of the Constitution and Government of the City of Florence (1498)
d 1520	**de Seyssel, Claude**	The Monarchy of France (1519)
d 1527	**Machiavelli, Niccolò**	The Prince (1513) The Discourses (1513/19) The Art of War (1520) Florentine History (1520/27)
d 1529	**Castiglione, B.**	The Courtier (1528)
d 1531	**Zwingli, Huldreich**	On True and False Religion (1525)

d 1535	**More, Thomas**	Utopia	(1516)
d 1536	**Erasmus, D.**	Praise of Folly New Testament (Greek Text)	(1509) (1516)
d 1536	**Tyndale, William**	The Obedience of a Christian Man	 (1528)
d 1540	**St Germain, Christopher**	A Dialogue in English betwixt a Doctor of Divinity and a Student of the Laws of England	 (1523)
d 1540	**Guicciardini, F.**	Considerations on the Discourses of Machiavelli Dialogue on Florentine Government Maxims and Reflections	 (c1530) (1523) (1528/30)
d 1546	**Luther, Martin**	Open Letter to Christian Nobility Temporal Authority Against the Murderous Thieving Hordes of Peasants	 (1520) (1523) (1525)
d 1550	**Mair, John Major**	The Power of the Pope in Temporal Affairs	
d 1560	**Melanchthon, Philipp**	Philosophiae Moralis Epitome Augsburg Confession	 (1550) (1530)
d 1564	**Calvin, John**	Institution of Christian Religion	 (1559)
d 1572	**Knox, John**	A First Blast of the Trumpet against the Monstrous Regiment of Women Letter to the Commonalty, and Appelation	 (1558) (1558)

d 1573	**Giannotti, Donato**	The Florentine Republic (1522) Dialogue on the Republic of the Venetians (1540)
d 1577	**Smith, Sir Thomas**	De Republica Anglorum (1583)
d 1582	**Buchanan, G.**	De Jure Regni apud Scotos (1579)
d 1590	**Hotman, F.**	Franco-Gallia (1573)
d 1592	**de Montaigne, Michael**	Essays (1571–1588)
d 1596	**Bodin, Jean**	Method for Easy Comprehension of History (1560) Six Books of the Commonwealth (1576)
d 1600	**de Molina, Luis**	Six Books on Justice and Law (c1595)
d 1600	**Hooker, Richard**	Lawes of Ecclesiastical Polity (1593–7)
d 1605	**Beza, T.**	On the Right of Magistrates over their Subjects (1574) On the Punishment of Heretics by the Civil Magistrates (1554)
d (1608)	**Gentile, Alberico**	De Jure belli Libri tres (1598)
d 1617	**Botero, Giovanni**	Della Ragion di Stato (1589)
d 1617	**Suàrez, Francisco**	Tractatus de Legibus ac Deo Legislatore (1611)
d 1621	**Bellarmine, Cardinal Robert**	On The Power of the Supreme Pontiff in Temporal Matters (1610)
d 1623	**du Plessis-Mornay, Philippe**	Vindiciae Contra Tyrannos (1579)

d 1625	**James I of England**	Trewe Law of Free Monarchies	(1598)
d 1626	**Bacon, Francis**	Essays New Atlantis	(1597 f.f.) (1626)
d 1638	**Althusius, J.**	Politica	(1614)
d 1639	**Campanella, Thomaso**	City of the Sun	(1623)
d 1682	**Hunton, Philip**	A Treatise of Monarchy	(1643)
d 1645	**Grotius, Hugo**	De Jure Belli et Pacis	(1625)
d 1652	**Winstanley, Gerard**	The Law of Freedom on a Platform	(1652)
d 1653	**Filmer, Sir Robert**	Patriarchia (written 1636–42, pub. 1680)	
d 1654	**Selden, J.**	Titles of Honor A History of Tythes The Law of Nature and Nations	(1614) (1618) (1640)
d 1657	**Lilburne, John**	England's Birthright Agreement of the People	(1645) (1647)
d 1669	**Prynne, W.**	The Soveraigne Power of Parliaments and Kingdoms	(1643)
d 1674	**Milton, John**	Areopagatica Tenure of Kings and Magistrates Eikonoclastes Defence of the English People	(1644) (1649) (1649) (1651)
d 1674	**Pufendorf, S.**	The Law of Nature and of Nations	(1672)

d 1677	**Harrington, James**	Oceana	(1656)
d 1677	**Spinoza, B.**	Tractatus Theologico-politicus Tractatus Politicus	(1670) (1677)
d 1679	**Hobbes, Thomas**	Leviathan	(1651)
d 1683	**Williams, Roger**	The Bloudy Tenet of Persecution for Cause of Conscience Discussed	(1644)
d 1687	**Petty, Sir William**	Treatises of Taxes and Contributions	(1662)
d 1695	**Halifax, George Saville, Marquis of**	The Character of a Trimmer	(1688)
d 1704	**Bossuet, Jaques**	La Politique tirée de L'Ecriture Sainte	(1709)
d 1704	**Locke, John**	Two Treatises of Civil Government	(1689)
d 1706	**Bayle, P.**	Critical Dictionary Commentaire philosophique	(1696–7) (1681)
d 1713	**Cooper, Antony Ashley (Lord Shaftesbury)**	Characteristics	(1711)
d 1733	**Mandeville, Bernard**	The Fable of the Bees	(1714)
d 1744	**Vico, Giambattista**	Principles of a New Science	(1752)
d 1751	**Bolingbroke, Henry St John Viscount**	Dissertation on Parties The Idea of a Patriot King Study and Use of History	(1734) (1738) (1735)

d 1755	Baron Montesquieu, Charles	L'Esprit des Lois (1748) Greatness of the Romans and their Decline (1734) Persian Letters (1721)
d 1771	Helvetius, Claude	De l' Esprit (1758)
d 1774	Quesnay, François	Tableau Oeconomique (1758)
d 1776	Hume, David	Treatise of Human Nature (1739) Essays Moral and Political (1741 & 2) Political Discourses (1752)
d 1778	Rousseau, Jean-Jacques	Discourses (1749–1755) Emile (1762) Social Contract (1762)
d 1778	Voltaire	Lettres anglaises ou philosophiques (1734) Essay on Custom (1756) Discours sur l'Homme (1738)
d 1780	Blackstone, William	Commentaries on the Laws of England (1785–69)
d 1781	Turgot, A. R. J.	Letters on Tolerance (1753–4) Reflections on the Formation and Distribution of Wealth (1766)
d 1783	d' Alembert, Jean	The Encyclopaedia (with others) (1751–65)
d 1784	Diderot, Denis	The Encyclopaedia (with others) (1776)
d 1785	Mably, Gabriel	Rights and Duties of Citizens (1758)
d 1789	d' Holbach, Baron	Système de la Nature (1770) Système Social (1773)

d 1790	**Smith, Adam**	The Theory of Moral Sentiments	(1759)
		Wealth of Nations	(1776)
d 1791	**Price R.**	Observations on Civil Liberty	(1776)
d 1794	**Beccaria, C.**	Tratto Dei Delitti e delle Pene	(1764)
d 1796	**Burke, Edmund**	Reflections on the Revolution in France	(1791)
		Appeal from the New to the Old Whigs	(1792)
		Speech on American Taxation	(1774)
		On Conciliation with America	(1775)
d 1797	**Babeuf, Francois**	Tribune of the People	(1795)
d 1797	**Wollstonecraft, Mary**	A Vindication of the Rights of Men	(1791)
		A Vindication of the Rights of Women	(1792)
d 1799	**Tucker, Josiah**	A Treatise Concerning Civil Government	(1781)
d 1803	**von Herder, Johanne**	Outlines of a Philosophy of the History of Man	(1791)
d 1804	**Hamilton, Alexander**	The Federalist (with Jay and Madison)	(1787/8)
d 1804	**Kant, I.**	Perpetual Peace	(1795)
		Metaphysics of Morals	(1797)
d 1804	**Priestley, J.**	First Principles of Government	(1768)
d 1805	**von Schiller, Johann F.**	Letters on the Aesthetic Education of Mankind	(1794–5)
d 1809	**Paine, Thomas**	Common Sense	(1776)
		Rights of Man	(1791)

d 1814	**Fichte, Johann Gottlieb**	The Closed Commercial State (1800) Addresses to the German Nation (1808)
d 1816	**Ferguson, Adam**	Essay on History of Civil Society (1767) Institutes of Moral Philosophy (1772)
d 1823	**Ricardo, David**	Principles of Political Economy and Taxation (1817)
d 1825	**Saint-Simon, Henri**	System of Industry (1820–3)
d 1826	**Jefferson, Thomas**	A Summary View of the Rights of British America (1774) Declaration of Independence (1776)
d 1831	**Hegel, G. W. F.**	The Philosophy of Right (1821) The Philosophy of History (1831)
d 1832	**Bentham, Jeremy**	Introduction to the Principles of Morals and Legislation (1789)
d 1832	**Godwin, William**	Political Justice (1793)
d 1832	**von Humboldt, Wilhelm**	Limits of State Action (written 1792, pub. 1852)
d 1836	**Madison, James**	The Federalist (1787/8)
d 1836	**Mill, James**	Essay on Government (1820)
d 1836	**Sièyes, Abbé**	What is the Third Estate? (1789)

d 1837	**Fourier, Charles**	Social Destiny of Man or, the Theory of the four Movements (1808)
		Treatise on Domestic and Agricultural Organisation (1822)
		The New Industrial World (1830)
d 1840	**de Bonald, Louis**	Theory of Political and Religious Power (1796)
		The Natural Laws of Social Order (1800)
d 1847	**de Maistre, J.**	Considérations sur La France (1796)
		On the Generative Principles of Political Constitutions (1814)
d 1850	**Calhoun, John C.**	Disquisition on Government (c1840)
		Discourse on the Constitution (c1850)
d 1854	**Schelling, Freidrich**	The Ages of the World (1811)
		Of Human Freedom (1809)
d 1858	**Owen, Robert**	A New View of Society (1813)
d 1859	**Austin, John**	Province of Jurisprudence Determined (1832)
		Lectures on Jurisprudence (1863)
d 1859	**De Tocqueville, Alexis**	Democracy in America (1835)
		Ancient Régime (1856)
d 1860	**Schopenhauer, A.**	The World as Will and Idea (1819)
d 1862	**Thoreau, H.**	Walden, or Life in the Woods (1854)

d 1864	**Lassalle, Ferdinand**	The System of Acquired Rights	(1861)
d 1865	**Proudhon, J. P.**	What is Property? Philosophy of Poverty	(1840) (1846)
d 1872	**Feuerbach, Ludwig**	The Essence of Christianity	(1841)
d 1872	**Mazzini, Joseph**	Duties of Man	(1840–3)
d 1873	**Mill, John Stuart**	On Liberty Considerations on Representative Government On the Subjection of Women	(1859) (1861) (1869)
d 1876	**Bakunin, Mikhail**	God and the State	(1882)
d 1877	**Bagehot, W.**	The English Constitution Physics and Politics	(1867) (1869)
d 1881	**Blanqui, Louis**	Instructions For Taking Up Arms Critique sociale	(1868) (1881)
d 1881	**Carlyle, Thomas**	Heroes Chartism	(1840) (1839)
d 1882	**Gobineau, Count Arthur**	Essay on the Inequality of Human Races	(1853–5)
d 1882	**Green, T. H.**	Lectures on the principles of Political Obligation	(1882)
d 1883	**Marx, Karl**	The German Ideology The Communist Manifesto (with Engels) Capital	(1845/7) (1848) (1867)
d 1888	**Arnold, Matthew**	Culture and Anarchy	(1869)
d 1888	**Maine, Henry**	Ancient Law Early Law and Custom	(1861) (1883)

d 1895	**Engels, Friedrich**	Origins of the Family Private Property and the State	(1885)
		Socialism, Utopian and Scientific	(1882)
d 1896	**Morris, William**	News From Nowhere	(1890)
d 1896	**von Treitschke, H.**	Freedom	(1861)
d 1900	**Nietzsche, Friedrich**	Birth of Tragedy and the Genealogy of Morals	(1871)
		Thus Spake Zarathustra	(1883)
d 1900	**Sidgwick, H.**	Methods of Ethics	(1874)
		Principles of Political Economy	(1883)
d 1903	**Spencer, Herbert**	Man Versus the State	(1884)
d 1910	**Tolstoy, Count Leo**	A Confession	(1879–82)
		What I Believe	(1882–4)
d 1917	**Durkheim, E.**	On the Social Division of Labour	(1893)
		Rules of Sociological Method	(1894)
d 1918	**Plekhanov, Geo.**	Fundamental Problems of Marxism	(1908)
d 1919	**Luxemburg, R.**	Social Reform or Revolution	(1900)
		The Accumulation of Capital	(1913)
d 1920	**Weber, Max**	Theory of Social and Economic Organisation	(1925)
d 1938	**Boukharin, N.**	ed. *Novy Mir*	(1916)
		ABC of Communism (with Preobrazhensky)	(1921)
		Theory of Historical Materialism	(1921)
d 1938	**Kautsky, K.**	The Materialist Interpretation of History	(1927)

d 1939	**Freud, Sigmund**	Civilization and its Discontents (1930)
d 1940	**Trotsky, Leon**	The Defence of Terrorism (1921) Literature and Revolution (1925)
d 1941	**Bergson, Henri**	Two Sources of Morality and Religion (1932)
d 1941	**Mosca, G.**	Elements of Political Science (1896)
d 1943	**Weil, Simone**	Oppression and Liberty (1955)
d 1944	**Gentile, Giovanne**	Theory of Mind as Pure Act (1922)
d 1921	**Kropotkin, Prince Peter**	Mutual Aid (1902) Fields, Factories and Workshops (1898) The Conquest of Bread (1888)
d 1922	**Sorel, G.**	Reflections on Violence (1908)
d 1923	**Pareto, V.**	Mind and Society (tr. 1935)
d 1924	**Lenin, V. I.**	What is To Be Done? (1902) State and Revolution (1917) Imperialism, the Highest Stage of Capitalism (1917) Left Wing Communism, an Infantile Disorder (1920)
d 1929	**Hobhouse, L. T.**	Metaphysical Theory of the State (1918)
d 1932	**Bernstein, Edouard**	Evolutionary Socialism (1899)
d 1937	**Gramsci, A.**	Letters from Prison (1947)

d 1946	**Keynes, J. M.**	The End of Laissez Faire (1926)
		General Theory of Employment, Interest and Money (1936)
d 1947/43	**Webb, S. & B.**	Industrial Democracy (1897)
		Decay of Capitalist Civilisation (1921)
		Soviet Communism: A New Civilisation? (1935)
d 1948	**Gandhi, M.**	Nonviolent Resistance (1935)
		Nonviolence in Peace and War (1942–9)
d 1951	**Lindsay, A. D.**	The Modern Democratic State (1943)
d 1952	**Croce, Benedetto**	History as Thought and as Action (1936)
d 1952	**Dewey, J.**	Democracy and Education (1916)
		Liberalism and Social Action (1935)
d 1952	**Maurras, C.**	ed. *L'Action française*
		Enquiry into the Monarchy (1900)
d 1961	**Fanon, Frantz**	The Wretched of the Earth (1961)
d 1962	**Tawney, R. H.**	Equality (1931)
		The Acquisitive Society (1924)
d 1969	**Jaspers, K.**	Man in the Modern Age (1933)
		The Future of Mankind (1961)
d 1970	**Russell, Bertrand**	The Principles of Social Reconstruction (1915)
		The Prospects of Industrial Civilisation (1923)
		Power: A New Social Analysis (1938)

d 1971	**Lukacs, C.**	History and Class-consciousness	(1923)
d 1971	**Niebuhr, R.**	Moral Man and Immoral Society	(1932)
d 1973	**Kelsen, H.**	Legal Technique in International Law	(1937)
		General Theory of Law and the State	(1945)
d 1973	**Maritain, Jacques**	Man and the State	(1951)
d 1975	**Arendt, Hannah**	The Origins of Totalitarianism	(1951)
		The Human Condition	(1958)
		On Revolution	(1963)
d 1976	**Heidegger, M.**	Being and Time	(1962)
d 1976	**Mao Tse-tung**	Mao Tse-Tung unrehearsed (ed. Schram, 1974)	
d 1980	**Marcuse, H.**	Eros and Civilisation	(1953)
		One Dimensional Man	(1964)
d 1980	**Sartre, J. P.**	No Exit	(1945)
		Critique of Dialectical Reason	(1964)
	de Jouvenal, Betrand	Sovereignty	(1957)
	Djilas, M.	The New Class	(1957)
	Hayek, F. A.	The Road to Serfdom	(1944)
		The Constitution of Liberty	(1960)
	Popper, K.	The Open Society and its Enemies	(1945)
		The Poverty of Historicism	(1957)
	Oakeshott, M.	Rationalism in Politics	(1962)
		On Human Conduct	(1975)

Habermas, Jurgen	Toward a Rational Society	(1970)
Rawls, J.	A Theory of Justice	(1971)
Nozick, R.	Anarchy, State and Utopia	(1974)
Millet, K.	Sexual Politics	(1970)